Slandering the Jew

DIVINATIONS: REREADING LATE ANCIENT RELIGION

Series Editors: Daniel Boyarin, Virginia Burrus, Derek Krueger

A complete list of books in the series is available from the publisher.

Slandering the Jew

Sexuality and Difference in Early Christian Texts

Susanna Drake

PENN

UNIVERSITY OF PENNSYLVANIA PRESS

PHILADELPHIA

Published by
University of Pennsylvania Press
Philadelphia, Pennsylvania 19104-4112
www.upenn.edu/pennpress

Printed in the United States of America on acid-free paper
10 9 8 7 6 5 4 3 2 1

Library of Congress Cataloging-in-Publication Data
Drake, Susanna.
    Slandering the Jew : sexuality and difference in early Christian
texts / Susanna Drake. — 1st ed.
        p. cm. — (Divinations : rereading late ancient religion)
    Includes bibliographical references and index.
    ISBN 978-0-8122-4520-2 (hardcover : alk. paper)
    1. Sex—Religious aspects—Christianity—History of doctrines—
Early church, ca. 30–600. 2. Christianity and other religions—
Judaism—History—Early church, ca. 30–600. 3. Judaism—
Relations—Christianity—History—Talmudic period, 10–425.
4. Church history—Primitive and early church, ca. 30–600. I. Title.
II. Series: Divinations.
BR195.S48D73 2013
261.2'609015—dc23
                                                        2012047257

To Richard Drake

and to the memory of
Julia Angevine Drake
Thomas Strickler
and Mildred Martin Strickler

Contents

Introduction   1

1. The Making of Carnal Israel: Paul, *Barnabas*, Justin   19

2. Origen Reads Jewishness   38

3. Sexual/Textual Corruption: Early Christian Interpretations of Susanna and the Elders   59

4. "A Synagogue of *Malakoi* and *Pornai*": John Chrysostom's *Sermons against the Jews*   78

Conclusion   99

List of Abbreviations   107

Notes   111

Bibliography   141

Index   165

Acknowledgments   175

Introduction

Antioch, 386 CE

In his first sermon against the Jews, delivered in Antioch in the autumn of 386 CE, John Chrysostom told a story of an abduction in which a "defiling and unfeeling man" forced a Christian woman, "elegant and free, well-behaved and faithful," to enter a synagogue. The woman resisted her attacker. She pleaded with Chrysostom to help her. Heroically, the newly ordained priest came to her rescue: "I was fired with jealousy," Chrysostom said, "and burning with anger, I rose up, I refused to let her be dragged into that transgression, I snatched her from the hands of her abductor! I asked him if he was a Christian, and he said he was. . . . I told him he was no better than an ass if he, who said that he worshiped Christ, would drag someone off to the dens of the Jews who had crucified him."[1] This licentious abductor claimed to be a Christian, but, in Chrysostom's eyes, he was tainted with the stain of Jewishness. The abductor believed that an oath sworn in the synagogue was more powerful than one sworn in the church. It was precisely this sort of dangerous religious hybrid—this impure "half Christian"[2]—that Chrysostom railed against in his sermons *Adversus Iudaeos*. The sexualized depiction of the heretical Christian-Jew as a male predator who preyed upon pure Christian women was not lost on Chrysostom's audience.[3]

In *Adversus Iudaeos*, John Chrysostom frequently depicted Jews and so-called Judaizers as lascivious wolves in pursuit of innocent Christian sheep, and he asserted that he himself was the good shepherd who protected the sheep from their Jewish predators.[4] His self-presentation as a stalwart guardian of Christian women went hand in hand with the gendered and sexualized portrayal of his religious opponents. Delivered at a time when the church in Antioch was more imperial than imperiled, his first sermon against the Jews made use of this narrative of violent abduction and aggression to map differences between "true" Christians and their heretical Others, Jews and Judaizers especially. Chrysostom's portrait of a heretical Judaizer luring a pure(ly)

Christian woman into the synagogue was just one example of how he denigrated his opponents by constructing them as sexual aggressors.

By the fourth century, the depiction of Jews and Judaizers as carnal, sexual deviants had become a topos in early Christian texts. Writing several decades before Chrysostom in 344, Aphrahat, the Christian sage of Persian Mesopotamia, claimed that Jewish interpreters of his day "stumbled" in their interpretation of scripture because of their "lasciviousness and the immodesty of their bodies."[5] Jews had it backward, he asserted. Rather than associating purity and holiness with virginity, as Aphrahat would have it, Jews thought that purity and holiness were achieved through marriage and sexual reproduction.[6] Eighty years later in Roman North Africa, Augustine, like Aphrahat before him, insisted that Jewish carnality was rooted in Jewish hermeneutical error: "Behold Israel according to the flesh," Augustine wrote, quoting Paul's phrase in 1 Cor 10:18. "This we know to be the carnal Israel; but the Jews do not grasp this meaning and as a result they prove themselves indisputably carnal."[7]

How did the figure of the "carnal Jew" come to function as a topos of early Christian literature?[8] When did this topos first appear, and what purposes did it serve? How did the stereotype of the "carnal Jew" serve Christian leaders as they forged boundaries between orthodoxy and heresy, Christianity and Judaism? And what can the development of this topos tell us about ancient understandings of gender and sexuality?

This book explores these questions by examining the sexualized representation of Jews in writings by Greek church fathers from the first through fifth centuries CE. The construction of the Jew as a subject of perverse and excessive sexual desire was implicated in several major developments of the early Christian era. As Christian theologians developed methods for interpreting the Bible, the carnal, literal-minded Jewish reader served as a convenient foil for the spiritual Christian exegete. Moreover, as Christian leaders embraced practices of asceticism and sexual renunciation, the carnal, hypersexualized Jew served as a warning against indulging the appetites of the flesh. Christian theologians also used the stereotype of the fleshly Jew as a way to classify heresies. They figured the Judaizing heresy (the fall into Jewishness) as a degeneration from spirit to flesh, purity to impurity, health to sickness. And as the interests of Christian leaders began to dovetail with the interests of the empire, the figure of the carnal Jew served to dehumanize Jews and justify violent acts against them.

Situating Anti-Jewish Sexual Slander

The portrayal of cultural difference as sexual(ized) difference was nothing new in the ancient Mediterranean world, nor has it disappeared in modern times. Today, as then, visual and textual depictions of the Other as sexually deviant or abject serve as a rationale for state violence.[9] In recent times, for instance, various representations of Muslim men as overly domineering, sexist, hyper-sexualized, homophobic, or effeminate have served as ways to justify the wars in Iraq and Afghanistan.[10] In late antiquity, Christian preachers created disparaging sexual stereotypes of those whom they opposed. Heretics, "pagans," and Jews, in particular, came under attack as Christian writers sought to define an orthodox Christian identity that was distinguished, significantly, by practices of bodily self-control and sexual purity. Christian writers portrayed these Others, alternately, as sexually aggressive or vulnerable. Their men were too feminine, their women too masculine, their bodies too wild, their morals too loose. The creation of an orthodox Christian attitude toward the body thus coincided with the construction of an abject "heretical" sexuality. Once Christianity became the religion of the state in the late fourth century, the construction of the heretical, Jewish, or Judaizing subject as perversely sexual functioned as a way for the church to justify the use of force against these groups.

As Christian writers began to define the boundaries of orthodoxy, they often encountered difficulties in tracing the border line between Christianity and Judaism, in particular. Christian writers framed their battles with heretics in this way: on the one hand were heretics who refused to use the Hebrew Bible altogether (such as Marcion); on the other hand were heretics who insisted on following Jewish law and practices according to biblical precepts (so-called Judaizers). Faced with such a diversity of attitudes toward Judaism, the writers of Christian orthodoxy defined a middle way: they appropriated the Hebrew Bible for Christian use while simultaneously distinguishing between Christian and Jewish practices, interpretations, and identities. Heresiology, or the representation of heresy, was thus largely caught up with the project of defining Christianness in relation to Jewishness.[11] The Christian use of sexual stereotypes to construct a carnal Jewish subject was part of this larger heresiological project to produce Jewish-Christian difference and identify practices that stood in opposition to orthodox Christian practice.

Early Christians and Jews shared not only a common scripture (the

Hebrew Bible or Christian Old Testament) but also common practices of piety. In some communities, Christians celebrated Easter at the same time as the Jewish Passover, and in other communities (such as Chrysostom's Antioch), it is reported that Christians worshiped, fasted, and feasted with Jews. The creators of Christian orthodoxy reacted to these situations of proximity by expressing their *desire* for the Jews—their sacred scriptures, their God—and, simultaneously, their *disavowal* of this desire. Some of the fiercest anti-Jewish rhetoric occurred within the context of Christian interpretations of the Hebrew Bible, where the dynamics of desire and disavowal were in full view. As Christians sought to claim the Bible as their own, they slandered their Jewish contemporaries, depicting them as overly licentious, immoral, and misguided interpreters of their own texts and traditions. Christian preachers turned the biblical prophets against Jews, accusing their Jewish and Judaizing contemporaries of the same crimes of adultery, prostitution, and impiety that the prophets claimed biblical Israel committed. Although sexual slander was a particularly useful tool for any ancient writer who wished to malign an individual, group, or culture, Christian sexual slander against Jews was particularly virulent because it occurred within this volatile context of cultural hybridity, in which the lines between Christian and Jew, orthodox and heretic, were in a constant state of negotiation and contestation.[12] Indeed, the church fathers' continual enforcement of the boundaries between Christian and Jew exposed the instability of these categories of identity.

Daniel Boyarin and Virginia Burrus have observed that "hybridity inflects Jewish and Christian identity in precisely the places where 'purity' is most forcefully inscribed."[13] Faced with borrowed and overlapping cultures, practices, and texts, early Christian preachers inscribed and, later, enforced the "purity" of Christianity by attending to the boundaries of their communities with the same strict vigilance with which they attended to the boundaries of the Christian body. The discourse of asceticism—which served to construct an ideal Christian subject of bodily and sexual purity—was accompanied by a rhetoric of dehumanization that characterized the Jew as sexually impure, promiscuous, immoral, diseased, and animalistic. The Jewish reprobate served as the *negation* of the Christian ascetic. This rhetoric of dehumanization, in turn, produced the conditions for the anti-heretical and anti-Jewish violence that would secure Christian dominance in the late ancient Mediterranean world.

Sexuality is "an especially dense transfer point for relations of power," argues Michel Foucault in *The History of Sexuality*.[14] Foucault understands the category of sexuality as a specifically modern construction. Yet his insight into the relation between power and cultural understandings of sex applies not only to Western modernity (Foucault's concern in the first volume of his aforementioned work) but also to the late ancient Mediterranean world, where discourses of sex and gender functioned as a "dense transfer point" for Christian assertions of power over Jews, Judaizers, and other heretics.[15] The portrayal of relations of power between Christians and Jews shifted according to the changing contexts and needs of specific Christian communities and writers, from Paul to Origen to John Chrysostom. Chrysostom, in particular, used representations of Jewish and Christian sexualities to construct, amplify, and reiterate Christian power in a time that witnessed not only the rise of Christian asceticism but also the alignment of Christian identity with that of the empire. It is in this imperial context that late ancient Christian writers crafted discourses of sexuality not only to distinguish "spiritual" Christians from their "carnal" religious Others but also to justify the use of power and coercion against these "enemies" of Christ. The use of sexual stereotypes as justification for violence is a topic that serves as a touchstone throughout this study.

Early Christian authors (such as Origen and John Chrysostom) often found it useful to portray Jews and Judaizers as (male) aggressors who preyed upon innocent Christians (imagined here as victimized women). At other times, Christian writers maligned their Jewish and Judaizing counterparts by depicting them as "soft," feminized men (*malakoi*) who were incapable of enforcing proper gender hierarchies within their households.[16] Christians themselves were alternately cast as besieged women or courageous men. Such identifications across genders attest not only to the destabilization of gendered categories in late ancient Christianity but also to the ways in which church fathers utilized sexual slander to construct, reinforce, and contest traditional understandings of gender performance. Early Christian authors thus invoked sexuality, gender, and the body to produce Jewish-Christian difference and assert Christian dominance in an era that also witnessed the formation and (attempted) stabilization of Christian identity, the development of Christian asceticism, and the eventual triumph of Christianity as the religion of empire.

Theoretical Provocations

Categories such as "Christian" and "Jew," far from being metaphysical givens, emerge over time in discourse and practice. Jewish and Christian subjects are historically constituted and constructed in relation to each other. Foucault's insight into the formation of the subject proves useful here. In his earlier work, Foucault, following Nietzsche, argued that the constitution of the subject unfolds within the constraints of institutional and regulating power.[17] In later work, Foucault subtly shifted his position to explore the "techniques of power" that the self used in relation to itself. Instead of focusing solely on how the modern subject is produced through regulatory powers outside itself, Foucault turned to antiquity to demonstrate how the self styles itself according to a certain *ascesis*. He writes that "there is no sovereign, founding subject, a universal form of subject to be found everywhere. . . . I believe, on the contrary, that the subject is constituted through practices of subjection, or, in a more autonomous way, through practices of liberation, of liberty, as in Antiquity, on the basis, of course, of a number of rules, styles, inventions to be found in the cultural environment."[18] Foucault thus insists on two meanings of the word "subject": "subject to someone else by control and dependence, and tied to his own identity by a conscience or self-knowledge. Both meanings suggest a form of power which subjugates and makes subject to."[19] *Assujettissement* (Foucault's term for the making of the subject) signals the way that the subject is produced not only in relations of power that are beyond its control but also in the disciplinary practices to which the self subjects itself.[20] These practices of the self, Foucault observes, need not always be conceived as forms of coercion and control but, sometimes, as practices of freedom.

As Foucault and Judith Butler, among others, have insisted, the fact of the subject's formation as *subject to* power does not mean that the subject lacks agency. Rather, *assujettissement* acts on a subject in a regulatory way and simultaneously enables the subject to intervene productively in its own formation.[21] *Assujettissement* signals not only the formation of the self through subjection to external structures of power but also the opportunities for resistance, subversion, parody, and creative reappropriation of that very formation.

My interest in subjectivation and subject-defining rhetorics shapes the way that I approach the sermons, biblical commentaries, and treatises written by Christians about Jews in late antiquity. Although the Christian construction of the carnal Jewish subject went hand in hand with the subjection of Jews to Christian power, this construction—indeed, this subjection—was neither complete nor successful. The fact that Christian preachers in the fourth, fifth, and sixth centuries, for instance, could endorse such violent acts as the burning of synagogues and the forced conversion of Jews did not mean that late ancient Jews were without power.[22] Indeed, the very centuries in which

Christian preachers and bishops authorized anti-Jewish violence also witnessed the flourishing of several Jewish communities, the formation of rabbinic identities, the development of rabbinic exegetical practices, and the construction of several major synagogues throughout Palestine (this despite imperial legislation that restricted the building of new synagogues).[23]

Theorists of modern colonialism can help us to understand how discourses of power shape and are shaped by the material situation of historical subjects. In separate works that investigate different colonial encounters, Homi Bhabha, Robert J. C. Young, and Ann Laura Stoler explore the various ways that discourses of sexuality functioned within literary representations of colonial subjects.[24] Colonized people, they argue, were often represented as subjects of excessive, dangerous, or deviant sexual desires, and the threat of social and racial contamination was often depicted as a sexual threat. Asymmetrical power relations, dynamics of domination and resistance, and simultaneous constructions of ethnicity, religion, gender, and sexuality were some of the key features that characterized the late ancient Roman world. These are some of the cultural dynamics that postcolonial theory helps illuminate.[25] Postcolonial discourse analysis is also helpful for understanding late ancient texts insofar as it calls attention not only to the complex intersections of discourses (sexual, cultural, religious, and otherwise) but also to the material effects of such discourses.[26]

In his analysis of Victorian race theory, Robert Young argues that sexuality "stands in" as a metaphor for cultural interaction and racial mixing in colonial discourse. Hybridity, conceived in this context as the "mongrel" product of illicit sexual encounters, threatens the "purity" of categories. This dangerous intermixture jeopardizes the clear boundaries between self and other, colonizer and colonized. As Young suggests, one effect of the sexual underpinnings of hybridity lies in the discursive association of the colonized Other with dangerous fecundity or deviant sexuality.[27] In European colonialist texts, he observes, racial degeneracy was often described as sexual degeneracy. Young's insight about the mutual construction of race and sex helps to illuminate the church fathers' simultaneous constructions of Jewishness and sex, where Jewishness was conceived as a marker of religious, ethnic, and cultural identity.[28] Early Christian accusations of Jewish sexual deviance and immorality occurred in a context of late ancient cultural hybridity—a context in which church fathers, faced with messy "border lines" between Christians and Jews, nevertheless sought to define Christianity and Judaism as pure, bounded, and distinct categories.

Homi Bhabha's work on the stereotype in colonial discourse also provides a fruitful lens through which to examine Christian stereotypes of Jews. Bhabha argues: "The objective of colonial discourse is to construe the colonized as a population of degenerate types on the basis of racial origin, in order to justify conquest and to establish systems of administration and instruction."[29] The stereotype functions as "the major discursive strategy" by which this objective is accomplished.[30] Bhabha's analysis of the stereotype, moreover, exposes the *ambivalence* that underlies the colonialist desire to "fix" the identity of the Other.[31] "The colonial presence," writes Bhabha, "is always ambivalent, split between its appearance as original and authoritative and its articulation as repetition and difference. . . . Its discriminatory effects are visible in those split subjects of the racist stereotype—the simian Negro, the effeminate Asiatic male—which ambivalently fix identity as the fantasy of difference."[32] Bhabha's conception of cultural difference as that which is both *desired* and *disavowed* provides a helpful framework for understanding the formation of Christian identity in relation to Jewishness. Likewise, his understanding of the stereotype as one of the major strategies of colonial discourse informs an exploration into early Christian stereotypes of Jews.

Christian writers such as Origen and John Chrysostom relied upon the stereotype to "fix" the identities of their opponents; yet the contexts of their writings suggest that religious identity was anything but fixed in third-century Alexandria and Caesarea and fourth-century Antioch. Bhabha's work helps to illuminate the "processes of subjectification" made possible through stereotypical discourse, especially with regard to Chrysostom's sermons. Bhabha's theory sheds light on the ways in which the church fathers interpellated Jews as colonial subjects, worthy of domination and violence.

Such theories of colonialism help to elucidate the variety of ways that sexuality functioned as a "dense transfer point for relations of power" among late ancient Christians and Jews. Sexual slander operated as a rhetorical weapon that early Christians utilized to assert Christian dominance and to justify violence against Jews. Before examining Christian sexual slander against Jews, however, it is important to place these early Christian representations of Jewish sexuality in context by analyzing not only Jewish accusations of Gentile immorality but also other non-Christian portrayals of Jewish sexuality in antiquity.

Sexual Slander in the Ancient World

Accusations of carnality and *porneia*—the ancient Greek term for sexual immorality—were part of a wider repertoire of ancient rhetorical invective. Greek writers portrayed their cultural Others—"barbarians," in particular— as bestial, sexually and emotionally unrestrained, and prone to violence and anger—traits that stood in stark opposition to that "great Platonic virtue," *sōphrosynē* (bodily self-control).[33] At other times, barbarians were cast as soft, luxurious, and effeminate in an effort to construct Greeks as manly and courageous (*andreios*).[34] Ancient Roman moralists often charged their opponents with a variety of vices, including economic vices such as excess, indulgence, and luxury, and sexual vices such as adultery, licentiousness, and effeminacy (*mollitia*). These charges of immorality functioned "in defining what it meant to be a member of the Roman elite, in excluding outsiders and in controlling insiders."[35] Ancient moralists thus used sexual slander as a way to police social and cultural boundaries.

In a similar way, early Christian accusations of Jewish *porneia* contributed to the formation of emergent Christian identity. As Christian writers forged an orthodox identity amid pagans, Jews, Judaizers, and other heretics, they fashioned the border line between Christianity and Judaism, in particular, as a line that separated the pure from the impure, the chaste from the licentious. The Judaizing heresy, which these Christians constructed, thus signaled a cultural degeneration into promiscuity, carnality, and immorality.

According to the Christian apologist Minucius Felix, early Christians themselves suffered charges of sexual impropriety, most notably at the hands of M. Cornelius Fronto, who called Christianity a "religion of lust" and accused Christians of debauchery, incest, cannibalism, and worshiping their priests' genitalia.[36] Early Christians retaliated against their accusers by drawing on the same set of charges. For example, one second-century Christian convert, Justin Martyr, took aim at Greeks and Romans who created false gods and worshiped them. In his *First Apology*, Justin argued that the material of which these idols were fashioned was recycled from "vessels of dishonor."[37] Then he contended that the "artificers" of these idols were "practiced in every vice," including the corruption of young girls.[38] Whereas Christians were recognized by their bodily self-control, Justin asserted, pagans, idolaters, and heretics were defined by practices of *porneia*.

Since sexual invective was a favored means of slandering an opponent in antiquity, early Christians (like Justin) put these charges to use in denouncing pagans and heretics. As Jennifer Wright Knust notes: "Sexualized invective serves several purposes at once: outsiders are pushed further away, insiders are policed, and morality is both constituted and defined as 'Christian.'"[39] By portraying their opponents as sexually licentious, early Christian writers not only accentuated the difference and distance between "us" and "them" but also promoted the ideal of *sōphrosynē* as orthopraxis within their own communities.

Jewish Portrayals of Gentile Lust

> The idea of making idols was the beginning of fornication, and the invention of them was the corruption of life.
> —*The Wisdom of Solomon* (14:12)

Not only was the accusation of sexual immorality a topos in early Christian literature; it was also a topos in ancient Jewish texts. In Jewish texts, however, Gentiles were the primary culprits. As early as the Torah, sexual immorality was associated with "outsiders"—Canaanites and Egyptians especially. For example, in Leviticus 18, the Lord commands Moses: "You shall not do as they do in the land of Egypt, where you lived, and you shall not do as they do in the land of Canaan, to which I am bringing you" (Lev 18:2–3). Following this commandment is a lengthy list of prohibitions against sexual intercourse with various relatives, menstruating women, and animals. The text declares that these forms of sexual relations are "perversions" (Lev 18:23), and, as such, they defile people as well as places: "Do not defile yourselves in any of these ways, for by all these practices the nations I am casting out before you have defiled themselves. Thus the land became defiled and I punished it for its iniquity, and the land vomited out its inhabitants. But you shall keep my statutes and my ordinances and commit none of these abominations" (Lev 18:24–26). In this passage, the Lord commands Moses to avoid the defiling sexual practices that characterize non-Israelite cultures.[40] One implication of this command is that Israelite culture is defined, ideally and in part, by adherence to a strict sexual code.[41] Gentile culture, by contrast, is associated with sexual immorality and moral impurity.[42]

In the *Letter of Aristeas*, a pseudonymous Jewish text composed in Greek in the second century BCE, sexual morality characterizes Jewish "insiders," while Gentile "outsiders" are depicted as licentious and deviant. The letter describes non-Jewish men as those who "defile themselves by intercourse, working great unrighteousness. . . . Not only do they have intercourse with men, but they even defile mothers and daughters." By contrast, Jews "have kept apart from such things."[43] Here male same-sex relations and incest are singled out as particularly defiling acts perpetrated by Gentiles. The third Sibylline Oracle, a Hellenistic Jewish composition from the second century BCE, also distinguishes Jews from other *ethnoi* on the basis of sexual purity: "More than any men they are mindful of the purity of marriage. Nor do they hold unholy intercourse with boys, as do the Phoenician, Egyptians, and Latins, and *spacious* Hellas, and many nations of other men, Persians and Galatians and all Asia, transgressing the holy law of the immortal God."[44] These texts produced Jewish-Gentile difference, in part, by drawing on the criterion of sexual practice. Whereas these texts formulated Jewish identity according to separation from sexual vices, they marked Gentile identity by a willingness to participate in defiling intercourse.

In several biblical texts, sexual immorality is linked more explicitly to Gentile idolatry. In the story of the renewal of the covenant in Exodus, for example, the Lord commands Moses and the Israelites to avoid making a covenant with the inhabitants of other (Gentile) lands, "for when they prostitute themselves to their gods and sacrifice to their gods, someone among them will invite you, and you will eat of the sacrifice . . . and their daughters who prostitute themselves to their gods will make your sons also prostitute themselves to their gods" (Exod 34:15–16). Deuteronomy contains a similar linkage of prostitution and idolatry: "The Lord said to Moses, 'Soon you will lie down with your ancestors. Then this people will begin to prostitute themselves to the foreign gods in their midst, the gods of the land into which they are going'" (Deut 31:16). In these passages, the worship of foreign gods is figured as a type of prostitution. Not only does idolatry of this sort lead to *porneia*; it is itself an act of *porneia*.[45]

This association of sexual immorality and idolatry continued in other Jewish writings of the Second Temple period. For example, the Wisdom of Solomon, composed in Greek in the late first century BCE, states that "the idea of making idols was the beginning of fornication, and the invention of them was the corruption of life" (14:12). According to this text, worship of idols leads to a litany of sins: "a raging riot of blood and murder, theft and deceit, corruption, faithlessness, tumult, perjury, confusion over what is good, forgetfulness of favors, pollution of souls, sex perversion, disorder in marriage, adultery, and debauchery" (14:25–26). Several decades later, another

Hellenistic Jew, Paul of Tarsus, reiterated this polemic against Gentile idolatry when he argued that lust, impurity, and "passions of dishonor" originated in—and were punishment for—the exchange "of the glory of the immortal God for images resembling a mortal human being or birds or four-footed animals or reptiles" (Rom 1:23–26). For Paul and the author of the Wisdom of Solomon, idolatry bred *porneia*.

In his treatise *On the Contemplative Life*, written in the first half of the first century CE, Philo of Alexandria contrasts the idolatry and immoderation of various Greek, Roman, and Egyptian cultures to the piety and self-mastery of the Therapeutae, a Jewish ascetic community of philosophers reported to live outside Alexandria.[46] Philo luridly depicts Greeks as lovers of luxury and wealth, fine food and drink, who indiscriminately sate their desires on "baked meats and savory dishes" and "full-grown lads fresh from the bath and smooth shaven."[47] Philo describes a Greek symposium: "The chief part is taken up by the common vulgar love which robs men of the courage which is the virtue most valuable for the life both of peace and war, sets up the disease of effeminacy in their souls and turns into a hybrid of man and woman those who should have been disciplined in all the practices which make for valor."[48] The Therapeutae, by contrast, are skilled in healing arts that provide "therapy" for souls "oppressed" by diseases of passion and pleasure (hence the name, Therapeutae).[49]

In another treatise, *On the Special Laws*, Philo employs categories of gender and sexuality to trace differences between Jews and the "many people" who inhabit other lands. Philo argues that, in contrast to Jews, men from other lands derive pride and reward from practices of immoderation (ἀκρασία) and "softness" or "effeminacy" (μαλακία).[50] Philo provides details about these "soft" men from other lands, taking particular aim at the worshipers of Demeter:

> [N]ow it is a matter of boasting not only to the active but to the passive partners, who become accustomed to enduring the feminizing disease [νόσον θήλειαν], let body and soul waste away, and leave no ember of their maleness to smolder. Mark how conspicuously they braid and adorn the hair of their heads, how they scrub and paint their faces with cosmetics and pigments and the like, and smother themselves with fragrant perfumes. . . . In fact, without blushing, they practice the transformation of the male nature to the female as an art. These persons are rightly judged worthy of death by those

who obey the law, which ordains that the man-woman [ἀνδρόγυνον] who debases the custom of nature should perish.⁵¹

Here Philo argues that non-Jewish "outsiders" are prone to engaging in sexual practices that jeopardize their masculinity. As hybrid "men-women," they "debase" themselves and threaten the order of nature. By contrast, Philo implies that those who "obey the law" (that is, follow the rules about sex laid out in the Torah) are assured of their masculinity. In Philo's text, gender is co-constructed alongside ethnic and religious identities.

Josephus, a Roman Jewish historian who wrote in the second half of the first century, insisted upon the unique sexual virtue of Jews. In *Against Apion*, Josephus defends the "Jewish race" against Gentile detractions by arguing for its antiquity, merit, and virtue. In the course of his defense, he contends that Jews, unlike their Gentile counterparts, adhere to a strict sexual code. The Jewish law, he writes, "recognizes no sexual connections, except the natural union of man and wife, and that only for the procreation of children. It abhors and punishes any guilty of such assault with death." Furthermore, the law encourages the proper treatment of women: "It commands us, in taking a wife, not to be influenced by dowry, not to carry off a woman by force, nor yet to win her by guile and deceit."⁵² For Josephus, Jews are distinguished by their stringent sexual ethics and their proper treatment of women.

From Leviticus to Josephus, these authors endeavored to define Israelite or Jewish identity in and through its relation to proper sexual practices. Sexuality functioned here as one of the predominant mechanisms by which Jewish identity was distinguished as superior to Gentile identity. Paul's polemic against Gentile idolatry and *porneia* was rooted in this Jewish tradition (a point I take up in Chapter 1). Subsequent Christian authors reformulated Paul's arguments to contend that it was Jews themselves who were guilty of sexual immorality and Christians who upheld the mantle of sexual purity. Early Christians, however, were not the first to level charges of sexual licentiousness against the Jews. Greek, Roman, and even Jewish writers themselves at times accused Jews of sexually immoral practices.

Ancient Portrayals of Jewish Lust

Perhaps the most famous non-Christian caricature of Jewish lust occurs in the fifth book of Tacitus's *Histories*, where he writes that "although as a race, [Jews] are prone to lust, they abstain from intercourse with foreign women; yet among themselves nothing is unlawful."[53] The Jews, he contends, "regard as profane all that we hold sacred; on the other hand, they permit all that we abhor."[54] Their customs, he continues, are "base and abominable, and owe their persistence to their depravity."[55] With these depictions, Tacitus constructs the figure of the hypersexualized Jew and uses this figure as a foil against which to extol the sexual virtue and self-control of Romans. As Judith Lieu argues in regard to Tacitus's sexualized portrayal of Jews: "That for such authors 'otherness' of customs should be most powerfully manifested in sex . . . should surprise no one at home in Greek and especially Roman literature of the period; it will be equally familiar to readers of Jewish and Christian fulmination against the Gentile world, as well as of intra-Christian polemic. It is a rhetoric to which all subscribed."[56] Tacitus thus stood in a rhetorical tradition of ancient Greek and Roman moralists who utilized a discourse of sexuality to construct the Other.

Some Greek and Latin poets also weighed in on the subject of Jewish sexuality. Writing at the beginning of the first century BCE in Palestine, the Greek writer Meleager offered the following depiction of a "Sabbath-keeper's" love: "White-cheeked Demo, someone is next to you and is taking his delight, but my own heart groans within me. If thy lover is some Sabbath-keeper no great wonder! Love burns hot even on cold Sabbaths."[57] Over a century later, the Roman poet Martial wrote a poem to a certain Roman girl, Caelia, who, he noted, granted sexual favors to a variety of peoples, including Parthians, Germans, Dacians, Cilicians, and Cappadocians—nor did she "shun the lecheries of circumcised Jews."[58] It is worth noting that both Meleager and Martial link Jewish lust and lechery to other known Jewish practices, such as Sabbath observance (Meleager) and circumcision (Martial). For these poets, excessive and lascivious sexual behavior was one of several practices that marked Jewish identity.[59]

Not only did ancient Greek and Roman writers at times characterize Jews as hypersexual; Jewish writers, on occasion, depicted the Jewish people as subjects of *porneia*. When the rhetoric of sexual invective was deployed against other Jews, it often occurred in the context of inter-Jewish polemic. For example, in the *Testament of the Twelve Patriarchs*, Levi relates his vision of "the end of days" when Israel "will transgress against the Lord" and "become a scorn to all the Gentiles."[60] According to the Testament of Levi, part of Israel's transgression will include sexual sins: "Out of covetousness you will teach the commandments of the Lord, you will pollute married women, and you will defile the virgins of Jerusalem. With harlots and adulteresses you will be joined, and the daughters of the Gentiles you will take as wives, purifying them with an unlawful purification, and your union shall be like that of Sodom and Gomorrah."[61] Although it is difficult to identify the specific historical and social situation in which these Testaments were produced, it is most likely that this sexual invective originated in a community that opposed the Jewish leadership or priesthood of the time.[62]

Such inter-Jewish polemic echoed and developed accusations of sexual immorality found in the prophets. In Ezekiel, for example, the Lord accuses Jerusalem of abandoning her status as the beloved bride of God and turning instead to "play the whore" (Ezek 16:15). The Lord states that Jerusalem's lust and licentiousness exceeds that of the Egyptians and the Philistines (16:26–27); she is an "adulterous wife, who receives strangers instead of her husband" (16:32). In Hosea, the Lord brings similar accusations against the "people of Israel": "A spirit of whoredom has led them astray, and they have played the whore, forsaking their God. . . . [T]hus a people without understanding comes to ruin" (Hos 4:12, 14). In these passages, charges of adultery and prostitution function as ways in which the prophetic texts communicate God's anger at Israel's apostasy and idolatry. Deviant sexuality operates here as a proxy for deviant practices of piety. A discourse of sexuality is thus invoked to "convey what is 'really' going on elsewhere, at another political epicenter."[63]

When early Christian authors began to direct accusations of *porneia* against the Jews in the second century, they utilized these prophetic pronouncements against Israel as biblical "prooftexts" to make their case.[64] In the chapters that follow, I explore how early Christian representations of Jews as sexually licentious were caught up in Christian endeavors not only to appropriate biblical texts (including the prophets) for their own communities but also to formulate a Christian hermeneutic practice that differed from that of the Jews. While early Christian authors "made the difference" between Jewish and Christian biblical interpretive practices, they also strove to distinguish Christian sexual practice as different from (and superior to) that of the Jews. As Dale Martin has noted, albeit of a different context: "Anxiety about sex is coupled with anxiety about texts."[65]

Plan of the Book

In Chapter 1, I examine accusations of *porneia* from Paul's letters to the *Epistle of Barnabas* and Justin Martyr's *Dialogue with Trypho*. Paul reiterated traditional Jewish polemics against Gentiles to argue that *porneia* was linked inextricably to Gentile idolatry. In 1 Thessalonians, 1 Corinthians, and Romans, in particular, Gentiles (not Jews, and not humanity in general) were the objects of Paul's sexual slander. By contrast, two second-century texts—the *Epistle of Barnabas* and Justin's *Dialogue with Trypho*—identified Jews as the objects of sexual slander. In contradistinction to Paul and without reference to him, the author of *Barnabas* and Justin construed *porneia* as that which troubled Jews in particular. *Barnabas* and the *Dialogue with Trypho* both implicate these accusations of Jewish sexual immorality in the construction of Christian biblical hermeneutics.

Chapter 2 explores how Origen of Alexandria, a prolific and influential interpreter of the Bible, continued this co-construction of sexual ethics and biblical hermeneutics by construing Jewish identity, literal interpretation, and carnality as the counterparts to Christian identity, spiritual interpretation, and *sōphrosynē*. Unlike Justin and the author of *Barnabas*, however, Origen used Pauline dichotomies (flesh versus spirit; letter versus spirit) to associate Christian identity with the spirit and Jewish identity with the body. In Origen's hands, Paul became the ideal spiritual interpreter because he successfully subjugated the flesh to the spirit. According to Origen, Paul's subjugation of flesh by spirit served as a model for the subjugation of literal (Jewish) interpretive practices by spiritual (Christian) ones: in this way, the Christian "spirit" triumphed over the Jewish "letter." Origen's various performances of spiritual interpretation (in his *Commentary on the Epistle to the Romans*, homilies on Genesis, and *On First Principles*, in particular) reveal the ways in which he invokes Jewish literalism and carnality in the exposition of his interpretive theory.

Chapter 3 provides a "test case" for the examination of the interaction between hermeneutics and sexuality in early Christianity. Here I explore patristic interpretations of the story of Susanna and the elders, with particular attention to Hippolytus's interpretation in his *Commentary on Daniel* and Origen's interpretation in his *Letter to Africanus*. Their respective interpretations support the alignment of Christianness with chastity and Jewishness with sexual licentiousness. Origen and Hippolytus both portrayed Jews as a sexual threat to virtuous Christians, and both utilized categories of "male" and "female" in their constructions of the Christian interpreter as a "chaste" woman, vulnerable to Jewish attacks.

Chapter 4 analyzes John Chrysostom's sermons *Adversus Iudaeos*—sermons that contain some of the most explicit sexual slander against Jews in the early Christian period. In these sermons, delivered in Antioch in 386 and 387, Chrysostom used sexual stereotypes against Jews to produce Jewish-Christian difference and to urge members of his congregation to refrain from participating in Jewish fasts and festivals. He portrayed Jewish men variously as "soft" (*malakos*), licentious, predatory, and bestial. He depicted Jewish women as prostitutes (*pornai*) and compared the synagogue to a brothel. By contrast, he imagined Christians as pure, chaste, and modest. Chrysostom's accusations of the Jews' "undisciplined passion" functioned not only in his representation of Jewishness but also in the construction of gender and sexuality in fourth-century Antioch.

The Conclusion returns to the question of the relationship between representation and violence. Here I briefly explore how Christian leaders used sexual slander and stereotypes as ways to justify violent acts against Jews and Judaizing heretics. The Conclusion also returns to the question of the subject. In late antiquity, the Jewish subject was constituted, in part, through the address of its other, the Christian. This address was most often intended to be injurious, as in the case of slanderous hate speech and accusations of sexual depravity. Yet, as Foucault and Butler remind us, the site of injury can become the site of resistance. With this in mind, we might ask: What do the varieties of late ancient Jewish identities have to teach us about the opportunities for resistance, subversion, and freedom made possible in the very structures of subjection?

Chapter 1

The Making of Carnal Israel:
Paul, *Barnabas*, Justin

Paul is the earliest surviving writer to encourage believers in Christ to follow a stricter set of sexual guidelines than their non-Christian counterparts. In his earliest extant letter, Paul encouraged the members of the church in Thessalonica to "abstain from *porneia*," for "this is the will of God." He urged each member of the community to possess his "vessel" (*skeuos*) in holiness and honor, not in the passion of lust (*pathei epithymias*), like the Gentiles who do not know God" (1 Thess 4:3–5).[1] Believers in Christ gained sanctification and holiness by abstaining from fornication and controlling their bodily desires: "For God did not call us for impurity, but in holiness" (1 Thess 4:7). For Paul, "the passion of lust," like impurity, originated outside the community and was characteristic of nonbelieving Gentiles. His exhortation to self-mastery aimed to differentiate the community of believers on the basis of sexual practice. Gentiles provided the foil.

The object of these accusations of sexual immorality shifted in the first and second centuries of Christianity. In 1 Thess 4:3–5 and elsewhere, Paul had reworked previous Jewish polemics against Gentiles to craft an argument in which *porneia* was linked inextricably to religious idolatry. Instead of depicting *porneia* as a problem that afflicted humanity as a whole, Paul, like many Jewish polemicists before him, conceived of *porneia* and idolatry as the paradigmatic sins of Gentiles. Apart from Paul and in contradistinction to him, Christian writers of the second century began to identify *porneia* as a Jewish characteristic. Texts such as the *Epistle of Barnabas* and Justin Martyr's *Dialogue with Trypho* stood at the beginning of a tradition that not only distinguished Christian from Jew on the basis of sexual behavior but also constructed Jewish men, in particular, as lustful, carnal, adulterous, and polygamous. The sexual slander against the Jews developed, at first, without reference to Paul.

Such sexualized representations of Gentiles and Jews occurred within the context of ancient discourses of ethnicity. In the first-century Roman world, it was a commonplace in both texts and images to construct the ethnic Other as strangely and excessively sexual. The discourse of alterity that Paul participated in was one in which Otherness was defined in religious, ethnic, and sexual terms. As Denise Kimber Buell and Caroline Johnson Hodge note: "Ethnic identity, religious practices and loyalties, and moral standing are inextricable in Paul's description of 'others.'"[2] A focus on accusations of sexual immorality illuminates the ways in which sex and gender functioned in the production of religious and ethnic Others in early Christian texts.

Porneia as a Gentile Problem: 1 Thessalonians and 1 Corinthians

In 1 Thessalonians and 1 Corinthians, Paul refashioned traditional Jewish characterizations of Gentile impurity and combined them with Greek and Roman discourses of self-mastery.[3] Many ancient Jewish writers before him had warned against sexual immorality and impurity, which they imagined as symptomatic of Gentile culture. Greek and Roman writers, moreover, warned against indulging excessive pleasures and desires. Virtues such as *sōphrosynē* (bodily self-control) and *enkrateia* (self-mastery) served as antidotes to unrestraint.[4] Philo of Alexandria, who, like Paul, drew on Greek ideas about self-mastery to describe Jewish asceticism, stated that "the opposite of desire [*epithymia*] is *enkrateia*."[5] Paul's warnings about the dangers of sexual immorality and the benefits of bodily self-mastery built on these earlier Jewish, Greek, and Roman discourses. In 1 Thess 4:3–7, for example, Paul warns against the "passion of lust" associated with Gentile culture while encouraging his audience to practice sexual self-control.

In 1 Corinthians, Paul similarly admonishes the community of believers to "flee *porneia*" (1 Cor 6:18). To Paul's dismay, however, sexual deviance finds its way into the Corinthian congregation: "It is actually reported that there is *porneia* among you, and of a kind that is not found even among Gentiles; for a man is living with his father's wife. And you are arrogant! Should you not rather have mourned, so that he who has done this would have been removed from among you?" (1 Cor 5:1–2). In this passage, Paul denounces a man who has sexual relations with his stepmother, and he warns the Corinthian community against inclusion of such a licentious person in their church. The nature of this sexual sin is such that it "is not found even among Gentiles." Paul's underlying assumption here is that, in most cases, the worst sexual sins are indeed found among Gentiles.

A few lines later, Paul urges believers to flee from immorality within the community, even if they cannot escape its prevalence in the nonbelieving Gentile world: "I wrote to you in my letter not to associate with fornicators [*pornois*]—not at all meaning the fornicators of this world . . . since you would then need to go out of the world. But now I am writing to you not to associate with anyone who bears the name of brother who is sexually immoral [*pornos*], or greedy, or is an idolater, slanderer, drunkard, or robber" (1 Cor 5:9–11). In this list of vices, Paul associates sexual immorality with economic sins (greed and robbery), religious sin (idolatry), and other common vices that divide the community (drunkenness, slanderous speech). Paul warns against this behavior whether it occurs outside the community of believers (in Gentile culture) or inside (among brothers and sisters in Christ).

In 1 Corinthians 7, Paul advocates celibacy and, if necessary, marriage, as antidotes to sexual immorality such as that found in 1 Corinthians 5.[6] He promotes certain ascetic practices, or practices of self-mastery, by which believers in Christ distance themselves both ethnically and religiously from nonbelieving Gentiles and from the immoral bodily practices sanctioned by wider Gentile culture. These ascetic practices include virginity (1 Cor 7:8–9, 7:25–26), sexual self-control within marriage (1 Cor 7:3–6), avoidance of *porneia* and those who engage in it (1 Cor 5:9–11, 6:18), and disassociation with prostitutes (1 Cor 6:13–17). Again, the distinction between a believer in Christ and a nonbelieving Gentile depends upon a system of ethnic and sexual markers that caricatures the latter as the sexually immoral counterexample to the former.

Paul thus ascribes sexual immorality to Gentile identity and encourages believers to hold fast to a new identity in Christ—one that distances itself from *porneia*, idolatry, and other vices associated with Gentiles. In passages such as 1 Thess 4:3–7 and 1 Cor 5:1–2, Paul associates certain sexual practices and moral qualities with ethnicity (Gentile-ness) and argues that religious and ethnic identity is transformed (to being-in-Christ) by "fleeing" immoral Gentile practices. Sexual practice thus forms one of the cruxes of Paul's argument for religious and ethnic transformation to being-in-Christ.

Porneia and Idolatry in Paul's Vice Catalogs

In his letters, Paul often responds to practical concerns of the community of believers by offering a catalog of vices aimed at first identifying and then curtailing immoral behavior. As in 1 Cor 5:11, elsewhere in his letters he groups together certain sins to reiterate the association of *porneia* and Gentile idolatry. In so doing, he frustrates the boundaries between sexual and religious sins.[7] In the following two vice lists (from Galatians and 1 Corinthians), he places sexual sins such as *porneia, aselgeia* (licentiousness), and *moicheia* (adultery) alongside other (Gentile) sins such as idolatry and impurity:

> Now the works of the flesh are obvious: sexual immorality [*porneia*], impurity, licentiousness [*aselgeia*], idolatry, sorcery, enmities, strife, jealousy, anger, quarrels, dissensions, factions, envy, drunkenness, carousing, and things like these. I am warning you, as I warned you before: those who do such things will not inherit the kingdom of God. (Gal 5:19–21)

> Do you not know that wrongdoers will not inherit the kingdom of God? Do not be deceived! Sexually immoral people [*pornoi*], idolaters, adulterers [*moichoi*], "soft" men [*malakoi*], those who exploit others [*arsenokoîtai*], thieves, the greedy, drunkards, revilers, robbers—none of these will inherit the kingdom of God. (1 Cor 6:9–10)

The proximity of sexual sins (*porneia, aselgeia, moicheia*) and religious sin (idolatry) in these lists indicates how Paul attempts to "fix" Gentiles as especially susceptible to the perils of sexual vice. Such characterization of Gentile culture is central to his more general project of identifying practices that distinguish the believer in Christ from communities of nonbelievers.

Some of the earliest interpreters of Paul reiterated his association of sexual immorality and Gentile culture. The authors of Ephesians and Colossians, for example, echoed the Pauline and Hellenistic Jewish associations of sexual vice, practices of idolatry, and Gentile identity.[8] Writing in Paul's name, the author of Ephesians warns his audience: "No longer live as the Gentiles live, in the futility of their minds, darkened in their understanding, alienated from the life of God because of the ignorance that is in them and because of their hardness of heart." Gentiles, he continues, "have lost all sensitivity and have handed themselves over to licentiousness [*aselgeia*] so that in their greediness they practice each impurity. But you did not learn Christ in this manner!" (Eph 4:17–20). Similarly, the author of Colossians depicts Gentile sin as the old way of life that followers of Christ must abandon: "Put to death, therefore, the things which are earthly: *porneia*, impurity, passion, evil lust [*epithymian kakēn*], and greed; this is idolatry. . . . These are the ways you also once followed, when you were living that life. But now even you must get rid of these things" (Col 3:5, 7–8). Here, the author warns against an old way of life (Gentile-ness) that was characterized by idolatry, *porneia*, and other vices, and urges the community to adopt a new way of life (being-in-Christ) that "puts to death" lusts and passions. Vice lists such as those found in Galatians 5, 1 Corinthians 6, Ephesians 4, and Colossians 3 not only extend Jewish arguments that associate idolatry and *porneia* with Gentile identity but also define the new community of believers in Christ based on their disassociation with licentious behavior.

Gentiles, Idolatry, and "Dishonorable Passions": Romans 1–2

> Claiming to be wise, they became fools; and they exchanged the glory of the immortal God for images resembling a mortal human being or birds or four-footed animals or reptiles. Therefore God handed them over in the lusts of their hearts to impurity, to the degrading of their bodies among themselves, because they exchanged the truth about God for a lie and worshiped and served the creature rather than the Creator, who is blessed forever! Because of this God handed them over to passions of dishonor, for their women exchanged natural intercourse for unnatural, and in the same way also the men, giving up natural intercourse with women, were consumed with passion for one another. Men committed shameless acts with men and received in their own persons the due penalty for their error. And since they did not see fit to acknowledge God, God gave them up to a debased mind and to things that should not be done. (Rom 1:22–28)[9]

Paul's most vivid depiction of idolatrous Gentiles as sexually depraved occurs in Rom 1:18–32. In this passage, Paul contends that sexually immoral practices are a result of and punishment for Gentile idolatry. As in 1 Thessalonians and 1 Corinthians, here Paul builds on a Jewish tradition that associates the ethnic Other with idolatry and sexual sin. As Stanley Stowers has noted, Paul describes Gentiles in terms of an "ethnic caricature" that activates two cultural codes: "the ethic of self-mastery and a Jewish code of purity and pollution."[10] By depicting Gentiles as particularly susceptible to sexual sin, Paul contributes to a discourse of alterity that characterizes the ethnic Other as morally and sexually depraved.

Rom 1:18–32 draws on and contributes to a well-established Jewish tradition that identifies Gentiles with idolatry and sexual vice.[11] Paul does not consider the situation of Jews vis-à-vis sin until Romans 2. In Rom 1:18–32, Paul presents *porneia* (1:26–27) and other vices (1:28–31) as consequences of the Gentiles' rejection of God through their turn to worship mere "images resembling a mortal being" (1:23). This story of Gentile idolatry and vice would have been familiar to Jewish listeners.[12] Paul turns to an imagined Jewish interlocutor in Rom 2:17–29 after he has presented his message of God's impartial treatment of Jews and Gentiles alike in 2:6–16:

> But if you call yourself a Jew and rely on the law and boast of your relation to God and know his will and determine what is best because you are instructed in the law, and if you are sure that you are a guide to the blind, a light to those who are in darkness, a corrector of the foolish, a teacher of children, having in the law the embodiment of knowledge and truth, you, then, that teach others, will you not teach yourself? While you preach against stealing, do you steal? You that forbid adultery, do you commit adultery? You that abhor idols, do you rob temples? You that boast in the law, do you dishonor God by breaking the law? For, as it is written, "The name of God is blasphemed among the Gentiles because of you." (Rom 2:17–24)

Viewed in the context of Paul's focus on God's impartiality vis-à-vis Jews and Gentiles, this passage claims that Jews, like Gentiles, are capable of hypocrisy and pretension, especially when they preach against certain actions (robbery, adultery) yet persist in engaging in these activities themselves. Paul's mention of adultery (*moicheia*) in Rom 2:22 represents the only instance in his letters in which sexually immoral behavior is ascribed to a Jew.

Porneia, on Paul's model, is a Gentile problem. Since the primary ethnic-religious dichotomy in Paul's worldview is that between Jews and Gentiles, the charges of Gentile sexual immorality in 1 Thess 4:3–5, 1 Cor 5:1–2, and Rom 1:18–32 comprise a caricature of the ethnic and religious Other to the Jews. In these passages, Paul constructs a sexualized Gentile subject that functions as the negative counterpart of the sexually pure brother or sister in Christ.[13] His characterizations of Gentile *porneia* function not as theological commentary on human sin or as philosophical and anthropological speculation but, rather, as an "ethnic cultural stereotype" within an ancient discourse of alterity.[14]

"Israel According to the Flesh"

Passages such as 1 Thess 4:3–7, 1 Cor 5:1–2, and Rom 1:18–32 show that Paul consistently conceived of *porneia* as symptomatic of Gentile culture. He used accusations of *porneia* to create difference and distance between the community of believers in Christ and the wider Roman culture. In addition to acting as boundary markers, accusations of *porneia* also functioned as negative examples for Paul and his addressees. His condemnations of *porneia* had meaning in the context of Paul's own self-styling as an ascetic and his exhortations to self-mastery among community members. By contrast, his understanding of *sarx* (flesh) was neither consistent nor easily mapped onto the terrain of Jewish-Gentile difference. Rather, Paul alternated between valuing *sarx* negatively, often in radical opposition to *pneuma* (spirit), and utilizing *sarx* as a morally neutral term that signaled literal hermeneutics, historicity, kinship, ethnicity, or the body.[15] The various connotations of *sarx* become evident only in context.

Most of the time, Paul evaluated *sarx* negatively, opposing it to *pneuma* and using it to characterize "this world." In Gal 5:16–17, Paul instates a radical dualism between *sarx* and *pneuma*: "I say, walk by the spirit, and do not gratify the desires of the flesh. For the desires of the flesh are against the spirit, and the desires of the spirit are against the flesh."[16] Often, when Paul mentions *sarx*, *porneia* is not far behind: "Now the works of the flesh are obvious: *porneia*, impurity, licentiousness, idolatry, sorcery, enmities, strife, jealousy, anger, quarrels, dissensions, factions, envy, drunkenness, carousing, and things like these" (Gal 5:19–20). A way of life that gratifies desires of the flesh is one that is filled with unclean and divisive practices. Sexual immorality is among these. For Paul, the choice to conduct oneself according to the desires of the flesh is a grave one indeed, for it excludes the believer from inheriting the kingdom of God (Gal 5:21b).

Paul offers a more forceful association of *sarx* and sexuality in Rom 7:5–6. Here, *sarx* stands for a former way of life, one characterized by sexual reproduction and endless cycles of life and death ("bearing fruit for death"): "While we were living in the flesh, our passions of sin, aroused by the law, were at work in our members to bear fruit for death. But now we are discharged from the law, dead to that which held us captive, so that we are slaves not under the old written code but in the new life of the Spirit." Note that living "in the flesh" is rooted here in observance of the law, according to Paul.[17] The "new life of the Spirit" stands opposed to the life in the flesh and is achieved, in part, by putting to death sinful passions. Paul summarizes this dualism in Rom 8:4: "To set the mind on the flesh is death, but to set the mind on the spirit is life and peace."

Paul describes the movement from a life guided by observance of the law to life in Christ by referring to a corresponding movement from flesh to spirit. "Flesh" functions as a euphemism for the old way of life under the law—a life that privileged and safeguarded signs of kinship and ethnic difference (for example, circumcision) and cycles of procreation and death.[18] In addition to Rom 7:5–6, Phil 3:2–3 offers a glimpse into Paul's association of flesh with circumcision and confidence in the law. Referring to those who insist upon circumcision for all male believers in Christ, he warns: "Beware of the dogs, beware of the evil workers, beware of those who mutilate the flesh! For it is we who are the circumcision, who worship in the spirit of God and boast in Christ Jesus and have no confidence in the flesh." Caught up in Paul's privileging of spirit over flesh is his rejection of these signifiers of ethnic particularity and his extirpation of sexual desire.[19] As Daniel Boyarin suggests, Paul is disturbed by desire and ethnic exclusivity alike, and his turn to spirit enables his "escape" from both.[20]

In some cases, however, Paul's use of *sarx* is morally ambiguous. In his interpretation of Phil 1:22, 24 ("If I am to live in the flesh, that means fruitful labor for me . . . but to remain in the flesh is more necessary for you"), Robert Jewett claims that Paul uses "flesh" in a "neutral sense to depict the worldly sphere."[21] Moreover, Jewett argues that in 1 Cor 10:18 ("Behold Israel according to the flesh"), Paul "avoids drawing negative conclusions from the 'flesh' category."[22] Since Paul alternates between negative and morally neutral valuations of *sarx*, we must look to context for clues. As we have seen, in Gal 5:16–21, flesh functions as the site of desires gone awry—desires for excessive and polluting sex, magical cures, quarrels, and excessive drink and pleasure. Other times, as in Rom 9:3, flesh signals physical kinship and genealogy: "For

I could wish that I myself were accursed and cut off from Christ for the sake of my own people, my kindred according to the flesh." The latter usage is more morally neutral than the former.

Kata sarka also signifies a hermeneutic practice for Paul—one that attends to the literal, the "body" of the letter, as opposed to the spiritual or allegorical sense. For Paul, the dual structure of language—in which literal signals the outward meaning and spiritual the inward meaning—mirrors his understanding of the human body as spirit (inner) and flesh (outer).[23] This relationship between hermeneutics and the body helps to make sense of the function of *sarx* in the phrase "Israel according to the flesh" in 1 Cor 10:18. In 1 Corinthians 10, Paul warns against participation in the worship of pagan idols and the eating of idol meat. Because consumption of sacrificial food and drink affects not only the individual but also the corporate body, a believer should not "partake of the table of the Lord and the table of demons" (1 Cor 10:21). "Consider Israel *kata sarka*," he writes. "Are not those who eat the sacrifices partners in the alter?" (1 Cor 10:18). Here, the morally neutral phrase, Israel *kata sarka*, denotes the people of Israel who participate in a flesh(l)y observance (temple sacrifice), interpreted literally. This understanding of the phrase militates against an interpretation that would too easily align Jewishness (Israel) with sexual vice (flesh). For some late ancient interpreters of Paul, however, this supposed alignment of Jewishness with all things fleshly—neatly expressed by the phrase Israel *kata sarka*—is precisely the proof they need to differentiate Christians from Jews on the basis of fleshliness and sexuality.[24]

Although church fathers of the third and fourth centuries used Pauline dichotomies such as flesh and spirit to distinguish between Jews and Christians, Paul had other aims in mind. When Paul wrote, "Behold Israel according to the flesh," he did not identify Jewishness with fleshliness and sexuality; writers in the centuries following Paul burdened the verse with this weight. Rather, "Israel according to the flesh" was, for Paul, a hermeneutical idiom that indicated the literal/historical practices of Israel, especially circumcision and sacrifice.[25] The phrase served as a foil to spiritual, allegorical Israel, which included not only Jewish but also Gentile believers in Christ. With the advent of Christ, Israel *kata sarka* became subordinate to Israel *kata pneuma*; but for Paul, this subordination entailed no condemnation of Israel *kata sarka* as especially vulnerable to sexual immorality or inordinate "desires of the flesh." Paul simply did not recognize *porneia* as a problem that afflicted his Jewish contemporaries.

Examples in which Paul associated Jewish identity with sexual vice are scarce. As mentioned above, in one instance he accused an imagined Jewish teacher of practicing adultery while preaching against it (Rom 2:22), but here he focused his ire more on hypocrisy than on adultery. He did not view *porneia* as a particularly Jewish trait.[26] *Porneia*, for Paul, as for other Hellenistic Jewish writers before him, was a Gentile problem. Yet the dyadic (and often hierarchical) pairings of spirit and flesh, on the one hand, and Jew and Gentile, on the other hand, provided rich imagery for Paul's late ancient interpreters, who redeployed these pairings to form a dichotomous structure in which Jewishness, carnality, and *porneia* were set against Christianness, spirituality, and sexual renunciation. By the time John Chrysostom delivered his sermons against the Jews in the 380s, *porneia* had become the Jewish sin par excellence.

Whereas later writers such as Origen and John Chrysostom explicitly borrowed Paul's language and transformed Paul's categories in their respective constructions of "carnal" Jews, several writers of the second century were hesitant to appropriate Pauline language for their own purposes. Usage of Paul's letters, which were not yet universally authoritative, varied by region, and allegiance to Paul failed to fall neatly on orthodox/heretical lines.[27] The author of the *Epistle of Barnabas* and Justin Martyr's failure to mention Paul did not constitute a strategic rejection or avoidance of Paul. Rather, the incipient trope whereby Jews were represented as sexually deviant developed, at first, without reference to Paul. The later reemergence of Pauline language in Origen's sexualized representation of Jews thus constituted a departure from and radical transformation of Paul's thought.

The *Epistle of Barnabas*

> Moses received the three firm teachings about food and spoke in the
> Spirit. But [the Jews] received his words according to the desires of
> their own flesh, as if he were actually speaking about food.
> —The *Epistle of Barnabas* 10.9

The *Epistle of Barnabas* was a popular and revered document in some early Christian circles in the second and third centuries. One of the oldest manuscripts of the New Testament, Codex Sinaiticus, included *Barnabas* as one of the canonical writings, and Alexandrian church fathers such as Clement and Origen referred to *Barnabas* as scripture.[28] *Barnabas* is a treatise by an unknown author, presented in the form of a letter. The first part of the letter (chapters 1–17) claims that "Israel" misunderstands Hebrew scripture and its laws so that the "true" interpretation of scripture might lie solely with the followers of Christ. The second part of the letter (chapters 18–20) presents the "two ways" teaching, urging believers in Christ to follow the "path of light" by behaving virtuously.[29] Modern scholars hold different views of the date and provenance of the text, but most agree that it was written in the late first or early second century in the Greek-speaking Eastern Mediterranean, most likely in Egypt, Syria, or Palestine.[30]

In relation to Paul, *Barnabas* offered an alternative avenue for the construction of Jewishness and Jewish hermeneutics—one that was separate from Paul's construction but nevertheless engaged in similar work of identity formation, scriptural exegesis, and the strategic production of early Christian difference and distinction. The author of *Barnabas* used a discussion of biblical hermeneutics as an occasion to map differences between Jews and the community of interpreters that he addressed.[31] According to the epistle, the Hebrew Bible belongs not to Israel, whose people never interpreted scripture properly in the first place, but to believers in Christ, the true heirs of God's promises to the biblical patriarchs (*Ep. Barn.* 4.6–8; 14.1–4). There exists yet another group of interpreters against which the author of *Barnabas* writes: the adherents of a certain hybrid interpretive practice who hold that "the covenant is both theirs and ours" (4.6).[32] On the contrary, writes the author of *Barnabas*: "[I]t is ours." Upon receiving the covenant, the people of Israel promptly lost it: "But they permanently lost it, in this way, when Moses had just received it. For the scripture says, 'Moses was on the mountain fasting for forty days and forty nights, and he received the covenant from the Lord, stone tablets written with the finger of the Lord's own hand.' But when they turned back to idols they lost it. For the Lord says this: 'Moses, Moses, go down quickly, because your people, whom you led from the land of Egypt, has broken the law.' Moses understood and cast the two tablets from his hands. And their covenant was smashed—that the covenant of his beloved, Jesus, might be sealed in our hearts, in the hope brought by faith in him" (4.7–8). For the author of *Barnabas*, there is only one covenant, and its only legitimate interpreters are the followers of Christ.

The practices that Israel embraced as a result of misunderstanding the law are thus erroneous and indicative of Israel's allegiance to the "literal." Sacrifices (2.8), fasting (3), temple worship (6), circumcision (9), dietary regulations (10), and Sabbath observance (15) constitute the list of inappropriate and vain practices of Israel since the breaking of the covenant on Sinai. In the discussion of biblical dietary laws, the author aligns the scriptural interpretation of Israel with lust (*epithymia*) in order to denigrate Israel, its practices, and its biblical hermeneutics. Unlike Paul, who understood lust as that which troubled Gentiles in particular, the author of *Barnabas* conceived of *epithymia* as a problem for Israel that resulted from its mistaken adherence to literal interpretation.

In chapter 10, the author turns to Moses' commandments regarding the consumption of certain animals such as pigs, eagles, hawks, crows, certain types of fish, hares, hyenas, and weasels.[33] According to the author of *Barnabas*, "they" (the Jews) misunderstood these commandments, thinking they were really about food. "We" (believers in Christ) possess the true, spiritual understanding of these commandments. According to the spiritual understanding, these commandments warn against imitating or associating with certain types of people. For example, when Moses said, "Do not eat the pig," he meant: "Do not cling to such people, who are like pigs." In a stroke of imaginative exegesis, the author of *Barnabas* explains what kind of people these are: "That is to say, when they live in luxury, they forget the Lord, but when they are in need, they remember the Lord. This is just like the pig; when it is eating, it does not know its master, but when hungry it cries out" (10.3). By interpreting the commandment as truly about the consumption of food, Jews abide by the most literal—and, in this case, "carnal"—of readings and miss the spiritual truth of the commandment.

Writing in the first half of the first century CE, Philo of Alexandria (himself a Jew) anticipated *Barnabas*'s allegorical interpretation of the dietary laws in Leviticus and Deuteronomy. Philo argued that Moses' prohibitions of the consumption of certain animals symbolized a more general teaching on the extirpation of desires. For example, Moses prohibited the eating of the plumpest and fleshiest animals, like the pig, because these animals enticed the "most slavish of the senses—the taste" and produced "insatiate desire—an incurable evil to both soul and body" (*Spec. Laws* 4.100).[34] The "four-legged" and "many-footed" creatures prohibited in Lev 11:42 similarly represented the "slaves not of a single passion—*epithymia*—but of all passions" (4.113). Philo's allegorical interpretation associated the prohibited animals with dangerous passions, and the refusal to eat these animals signaled one's progress in *enkrateia* (4.101).

Barnabas replicated some of Philo's hermeneutical moves (and ironically, used them to denigrate Jewish hermeneutics) by interpreting biblical dietary laws as injunctions against illicit desires, more generally. For *Barnabas*, the consequences of Israel's literal interpretation became especially thorny where questions of sexuality were concerned. Prohibitions about three animals—the hare, the hyena, and the weasel—represented not a literal bar on eating such animals but warnings against improper sexual practices. *Barnabas* interprets Moses' teachings as follows:

> But also "do not eat the hare." For what reason? "You must not," he says, "be one who corrupts children or be like such people." For the rabbit adds an orifice every year; it has as many holes as years it has lived. "Nor shall you eat the hyena." "You must not," he says, "be an adulterer or a pervert nor be like such people." For what reason? Because this animal changes its nature every year, at one time it is male, the next time female. And he has fully hated the weasel. "You must not," he says, "be like those who are reputed to perform a lawless deed in their mouth because of their uncleanness, nor cling to unclean women who perform the lawless deed in their mouth." For this animal conceives with its mouth. (*Ep. Barn.* 10.6–8)[35]

According to the *Epistle of Barnabas*, the spiritual understanding of these commandments properly conveyed the divine injunctions against the sexual corruption of children, adultery, and oral sex. If Jews remained mired in the literal, they missed this important distinction between dietary and sexual regulations.

Immediately following this "spiritual" explication of Moses' commandments about animals, the author of *Barnabas* states the reason for Israel's misinterpretation: "And so, Moses received the three firm teachings about food and spoke in the Spirit. But [the Jews] received his words according to the desires of their own flesh, as if he were actually speaking about food" (10.9). In this passage, inordinate desire and fleshliness are associated explicitly with Jews and their interpretive practices. Sexuality and textuality are linked. Not only is the inferior, literal reading of the text rooted in the "lusts of the flesh," but it also produces an interpretation that leaves Jews vulnerable to the snare of illicit sex, since they do not properly understand the divine commandments regarding sex (and take them to be about food instead).

Followers of Christ, by contrast, live and interpret texts "according to the spirit," which accords them a virtue higher than that of Israel and enables them to achieve the correct interpretation of Mosaic laws (10; 19.4).[36] In chapter

10, the author of *Barnabas* consigns the Jews to more literal interpretive practices than Christians and argues that the root of Jewish misinterpretation lies
in their "lust of the flesh," a phrase that signals excessive desire for both food
and sex. The author of *Barnabas* "rewrites Jewishness for [his] own purposes"[37]
by aligning Jewishness with literal, fleshly interpretation, on the one hand,
and Christianness with spiritual interpretation, on the other.

Justin Martyr's *Dialogue with Trypho*

Another example of this correlation of Jewishness, fleshly desire, and literalist hermeneutics occurs in Justin Martyr's *Dialogue with Trypho*. This text
purports to record a conversation between Justin, a Christian convert from
"paganism," and Trypho, a Jew, in the town of Ephesus soon after the Bar
Kokhba revolt, in 135. Most likely, Justin composed the *Dialogue* in the 160s
in Rome, where he was later martyred during the reign of Marcus Aurelius.[38]

Like the author of *Barnabas*, Justin constructed "Judaism" for his own
heresiological purposes in the *Dialogue*. In his endeavor to delimit a single
orthodox Christianity, Justin pitted Christian against Jew and orthodoxy
against heresy, thus forming a homology between Judaism and heresy.[39] The
categories "Judaism" and "heresy" served as proxies for each other in Justin's
delineation of an orthodox Christianity. In this way, Justin participated in the
construction of the categories "Christian," "Jew," and "heretic," the very categories that he hoped would be read as natural, bounded, and dichotomous.
The attendant construction of the Other to Christianity—Judaism—occurred
within this nexus of heresiological representation, biblical interpretation, and
religious self-definition in the second century.

Throughout the *Dialogue*, Justin registered many ways in which Christians
had replaced Jews as heirs to God's promises to Israel. In his view, Christians
now constituted the "true people of Israel" and the "true seed of Abraham."[40]
Jewish practices (circumcision, Sabbath observance) and Jewish obedience
to the law were rendered obsolete by the advent of Christ (*Dial.* 92.3–4).[41]
Justin employed biblical examples to emphasize the disobedience, stubborn-
ness, false worship, and *porneia* of the Jews, and he leveled charges against his
Jewish interlocutors by redeploying prophetic injunctions against Israel and
stories of Israel's idolatry, apostasy (with the golden calf), and fornication with
the daughters of foreigners.[42]

One way in which Justin produced difference between Jews and Christians was by depicting the latter as morally superior to the former. In the following passage, he argues that his Jewish interlocutors should adopt Christian virtues (here symbolized by unleavened bread) and abandon the life of vice (the bad leaven): "Wash your souls free of anger, of avarice, of jealousy, and of hatred; then the whole body will be pure. This is the symbolic meaning of unleavened bread, that you do not commit old deeds of the bad leaven" (*Dial.* 14.2). Justin then turns on his Jewish interlocutors and accuses them not only of carnal interpretative practices but also of embracing lives of sin: "You, however, understand everything in a carnal way, and you deem yourselves religious if you perform such deeds, even when your souls are filled with deceit and every other kind of sin" (14.2). Here Justin constructs Jewish understanding of scripture as carnal—a construction he reiterates and embellishes in his exegesis of Hebrew Bible passages.

Near the end of the *Dialogue*, Justin constructs his Jewish interlocutors as lustful by contending that Jewish leaders of his day, because of their lust for women, misinterpret scriptural passages about Jacob's multiple marriages. Instead of reading for the "true" spiritual meaning of Jacob's marriages, which is found in the typological understanding of Leah and Rachel as types of the synagogue and church, Jews utilize scripture to justify the satisfaction of their desires. Justin addresses Trypho and his friends: "It would be better for you to obey God rather than your stupid, blind teachers, who even now permit each of you to have four or five wives; and if any of you see a beautiful woman and desire to have her, they cite the actions of Jacob . . . and the other patriarchs to prove there is no evil in such practices. How wretched and ignorant they are even in this respect" (*Dial.* 134.1). Justin claims that biblical exegetes cannot access the "divine" meaning of such texts apart from Christ. Jewish exegetes, he contends, "never considered the more divine in the purpose for which each thing was done, but rather what concerned base and corruptible passions" (134.2).

In this passage, Justin simultaneously constructs and rejects a Jewish interpretation of Jacob's marriages. His argument depends upon a tautology, one that is first developed in *Barnabas* and continued in Origen: Jewish misunderstanding of scripture is rooted in Jewish lust; simultaneously, Jewish lust is rooted in and authorized by Jewish (mis)understanding of scripture. For Justin, like *Barnabas*, the way out of both dilemmas—sexual desire *and* heterodox hermeneutics—lies in utilizing Christ as the necessary interpretive lens with which to read the Hebrew scriptures.[43] Justin's interpretation of Jacob's multiple marriages attempts to illustrate the superiority of Christian biblical interpretation, on the one hand, and associate Jewish identity with insatiable lust and plural marriages, on the other.

Justin presents the story of David's adulterous affair with Bathsheba in a similar fashion by using the interpretive moment not only to acquit biblical patriarchs of any sexual sin but also to slander present-day Jews. Turning to the story in 2 Samuel 11, Justin argues that the "one deed of transgression of David with the wife of Uriah shows that the patriarchs took many wives, not to commit adultery, but that certain mysteries might thus be indicated by them." In the next breath, Justin seizes the opportunity to slander his Jewish interlocutors: "For, had it been permissible to take any wife whomever, or as many as one desired (as women are taken under the name of marriage by your countrymen all over the world, wherever they live or are sent), David certainly would have been permitted this by much greater right" (*Dial.* 141.4). By suggesting that Trypho's "countrymen" marry as many women as they desire, Justin portrays Jewish men as excessively lustful and polygamous.[44] He claims, in effect, that whereas Jewish men have a wife in every port, Christian men restrict themselves and "live with only one wife" (110.3). Sexual slander such as this serves to distinguish Christians from Jews on the basis of the former's more stringent and controlled sexual practices.

Justin's *Dialogue with Trypho* thus fashioned Jewish men as "carnal," misguided interpreters of their own biblical traditions. According to Justin, Jews utilized stories of the sexual exploits of biblical patriarchs to justify deviant practices in the present, including polygamy. More so than in the *Epistle of Barnabas*, Justin's *Dialogue* presented a systematized representation of Jews as illicitly sexual and carnal—fitting counterparts to sexually restrained Christians. That Justin performed this reading of Jewishness with no reference to Paul is not surprising, for Paul offered no explicit association of Jewish identity and sexual immorality.[45] Justin, like the author of *Barnabas*, developed this caricature of "carnal" Jews apart from—and in contradistinction to—Paul.

Sexual Slander against Jews in the Century after Paul

Justin and the author of the *Epistle of Barnabas* stood at the beginning of a tradition that produced Jewish-Christian difference, in part, by distinguishing Christians as superior in sexual purity and chastity. Jews, by contrast, were portrayed as sexual deviants: carnal, lustful, adulterous, and polygamous. Apart from the examples in Justin's *Dialogue* and the *Epistle of Barnabas*, however, this sexualized representation of Jews was not widespread in the century after Paul's death. Ignatius's letters, the *Epistle to Diognetus*, and Melito of Sardis's Paschal homily, for example, bear little or no trace of an association of Jews and sexual vice. Justin and the author of *Barnabas* thus offer rare glimpses of an incipient (and insidious) trope that was more fully developed only in the third, fourth, and fifth centuries.

The representations of Jewishness in Ignatius's letters, the *Epistle to Diognetus*, and Melito's *On Pascha* set in context second-century representations of Jews such as those in the *Epistle of Barnabas* and Justin's *Dialogue*. Ignatius, bishop of Antioch in the early second century, wrote his letters en route to his martyrdom in Rome.[46] Like other Christian writers of the period, Ignatius encouraged his addressees to embrace a life of virtue that distinguished them from non-Christians: "In response to their anger, show meekness; to their boasting, be humble; . . . to their savage behavior, act civilized." This they should do, argues Ignatius, to "abide in Jesus Christ both in the flesh and in the spirit, with all holiness and self-control [*sōphrosynē*]" (Ign. *Eph.* 11.2–3). Ignatius also invokes this discourse of self-mastery to bolster his own authority not only as a leader but also as a renunciant: "My passion [*erōs*] has been crucified," he writes to the Romans, "and there is no burning love within me for material things" (Ign. *Rom.* 7.2).

Yet for all Ignatius's insistence on virtuous and ascetic behavior among Christians—and for all his anti-Jewish rhetoric—nowhere does he present Jews as sexually depraved counterparts to Christians. Rather, in Ignatius's mutual construction of Judaism and "Christianism" (Ign. *Phld.* 6.1), the former represents the "old way" of life whose beliefs and practices are to be cast aside to embrace "a new hope" in Christ (Ign. *Mag.* 9.1). For Ignatius, belief in Christ renders obsolete any observance of Jewish practices: "It is outlandish to proclaim Jesus Christ and practice Judaism. For 'Christianism' [Χριστιανισμός] did not believe in Judaism [Ἰουδαισμόν], but Judaism in 'Christianism'" (Ign. *Mag.* 10.3).[47] The proper prioritization of these two cultural formations is of absolute necessity to Ignatius. Although Ignatius works to create difference and distance between Christianness and Jewishness, he does so without characterizing Jews as carnal or licentious.

The *Epistle to Diognetus* likewise maintains that believers in Christ distinguish themselves, in part, by superior practices of sexual virtue.[48] Written in the middle of the second century, the author of the epistle maintains that Christians "share their meals but not their sexual partners. They are found in the flesh but do not live according to the flesh" (*Diogn.* 5.7–8). The author urges Christians to shun Jewish practices (anxiety over food, Sabbath, circumcision, fasting): "Christians are right to abstain from the vulgar silliness, deceit, and meddling ways of the Jews" (*Diogn.* 4.1, 6). Christian is distinguished from Jew here on the basis of practice and behavior; yet nowhere does the author of the epistle charge Jews with the sexual vices leveled against them in Justin's *Dialogue.*

Both the *Epistle to Diognetus* and Melito's *On Pascha* distinguish between a past that was marked by sexual depravity and a present marked by righteous behavior, but neither maps this "difference in times" as Jewish-Christian difference.[49] Rather, both authors present the unrighteous past as collectively owned—as "our past." The author of the *Epistle to Diognetus* writes: "And so, having arranged all things by himself, along with his child, he permitted us—while it was still the former time—to be borne along by disorderly passions, as we wished, carried off by our pleasures and desires. He took no delight at all in our sins, but he endured them. Nor did he approve of the former time of unrighteousness, but he was creating the present age of righteousness, so that even though at that time our works proved that we were unworthy of life, we might in the present be made worthy by the kindness of God" (*Diogn.* 9.1). For Melito, sexual depravity is part of the inheritance that Adam left to all his children: "The destruction of men upon earth," he writes, "became strange and terrible. For these things befell them: they were seized by tyrannical sin, and were led to lands of lusts [τοὺς χώρους τῶν ἐπιθυμιῶν], where they were swamped by insatiable pleasures, adultery [μοιχείας], *porneia*, licentiousness [ἀσελγείας], avarice, murders, bloodshed, evil and lawless tyranny."[50] For Melito, as for the author of *Diognetus*, the state of unrighteousness, *porneia*, and disorderly passion reigned over the entire human race until the coming of Christ, who inaugurated the period of righteousness and chastity. Although each author utilized anti-Jewish rhetoric in his articulation of Jewish-Christian difference, neither included sexual slander against Jews.[51]

In the second century, at least, the developing discourse of Christian sexual morality often operated apart from the discourse of Jewish-Christian difference. Where the two discourses coincided, as in Justin's *Dialogue*, Jews became objects of sexual invective. In the earliest examples of Christian sexualized representation of Jews (*Epistle of Barnabas* and Justin's *Dialogue*), sexual slander occurred within the framework of biblical exegesis. Unlike Paul and without reference to him, Justin and the author of *Barnabas* constructed the Jew as a literal, "carnal" interpreter of biblical texts and, simultaneously, as lustful, adulterous, and polygamous. Two subsequent readers of Paul—Origen and John Chrysostom—reworked and transformed key Pauline texts to construct, authorize, and "naturalize" the association of a "literalistic" Jewish hermeneutic with its paradigmatic practitioner: the carnal, lustful Jew.

Chapter 2

Origen Reads Jewishness

Born in 185 CE in Alexandria, Origen grew up in a city that was the center of intellectual life in the Roman empire and the seat of the Roman administration of Egypt. Alexandria was the home of the first-century Jewish Hellenistic philosopher Philo and the second-century Christian theologians and teachers Basilides, Valentinus, and Clement—all astute biblical interpreters themselves. With the support of his father, Origen studied Greek literature and philosophy, mathematics, astronomy, and the Christian scriptures. When Origen was a teenager, his father died during a persecution of Christians by the emperor Septimius Severus, leaving Origen as the responsible eldest son of a large family. Origen soon began to support himself and his family by teaching Greek literature. He later abandoned this position to teach, preach, and study the Bible exclusively.[1] When he died in the early 250s, he left behind a wealth of biblical commentaries, homilies, and apologetic works, many of which survive only in Latin translations by Rufinus of Aquileia, a fourth-century theologian and translator.[2]

Origen wrote his celebrated (and, later, controversial) exposition of Christian doctrine and biblical interpretation, *On First Principles*, while living in Alexandria.[3] The majority of Origen's biblical commentaries and homilies, however, were composed during the period when he was teaching and preaching in Caesarea Maritima, a cosmopolitan center of Roman rule in Palestine.[4] Origen relocated to Caesarea in 234, after a prolonged battle with Alexandria's bishop, Demetrius. By the third century, Caesarea boasted an unusually diverse population. As Lee Levine describes, in the later empire, "[f]our separate minority groups functioned within [Caesarea]: pagans, Jews, Christians, and Samaritans. . . . This diversity added immeasurably to the cosmopolitan nature of the city, a characteristic which in turn influenced the component communities."[5] Compared with Jerusalem, Caesarea "was the hellenized city of

Palestine par excellence," where Herod's temple to Augustus and Roma served as the "symbolic entrance" to the city.[6] In this site of cosmopolitan pluralism, economic and social contact among members of different religious groups was frequent.[7]

Cultural hybridity was unavoidable in such a site of contact and intermingling.[8] In several homilies, Origen struggled against a hybrid "Judaeo-Christianism" by warning his audience of the dangerous mixing of Jewish and Christian practices. For example, in a sermon on Leviticus, he states: "If you bring that which you learned from the Jews yesterday into the church today, that is to eat the meat of yesterday's sacrifice."[9] Similarly, in a homily on Jeremiah, Origen chastises Christian women, in particular, for observing the Jewish Sabbath. Women, he writes, "do not hear [the words about Sabbath] in a hidden way (Jer 13:15–17), but hear outwardly. . . . [T]hey go back to the 'poor and weak elements' (Gal 4:9), as if Christ had not yet appeared, he who perfects us and carries us across from the elements of the Law to the perfection of the Gospel."[10] Later in this same homily, he addresses those among his own congregation who fast with the Jews: "All of you who keep the Jewish fast so that you do not understand the Day of Atonement as that which is in accord with the coming of Jesus Christ, you do not hear the atonement in a hidden way, but only outwardly."[11] Here, Origen exhorts Christians to "hear in a hidden way," that is, attend to the spiritual meaning of the prophetic and legal texts. Using spiritual interpretation, Christians can avoid the error of the Jews (and errant Christian women), who, in Origen's rhetorical presentation, hold fast to the "letter" and thus regress to the "poor and weak elements" of religious practice. Confronted with this situation of cultural and religious overlap, Origen thus endeavored to construct (and subsequently naturalize) border lines between Christian and Jewish communities—lines that were drawn not only around interpretive practices but also around practices of piety such as observance of the Sabbath and participation in fasts and festivals.

Although Origen paid respect to his Jewish teachers and predecessors and acknowledged the value of Jewish biblical interpretations,[12] the homilies and commentaries of the Caesarean period reflect a more negative view of his Jewish contemporaries. Nicholas de Lange notes that Origen used the more positive term *Hebraioi* (Hebrews) to refer to contemporary Jews whom he consulted on philological and exegetical issues. By contrast, Origen used the term *Ioudaioi* (Jews) in contexts of conflict and polemic.[13] In his endeavor to draw a hard-and-fast line between Jewish modes of exegesis and Christian ones—a project he took up in many of his Caesarean sermons and biblical commentaries—Origen employed the more negative term, *Ioudaioi*.

In his representation of Jewish biblical exegesis, Origen consistently read Jewishness as aligned with carnality and literal interpretive practices. Such a reading of Jewishness is especially apparent in Origen's exegetical treatises and homilies on the Hebrew Bible. Origen developed his theory of Christian spiritual interpretation, moreover, with reference not only to the carnal hermeneutics of "Israel according to the flesh" but also to the ascetic practice and sexual chastity of his ideal Christian interpreter, Paul. Origen's scriptural justification for his construction of Jews as fleshly, literal readers lay in his rewriting (and misrepresentation) of Paul. Unlike Justin Martyr and the author of *Barnabas* (who figured Jews as carnal without any reference to Paul's letters), Origen was explicit in his use of Pauline dichotomies to spiritualize Christian identity and *em-body* Jewish identity. Origen's construction of the figure of the carnal Jew thus functioned as an insidious implication of the intertwining of his exposition of Christian spiritual interpretation, his reading and representation of Paul, and his exhortation to sexual chastity.

In his rhetorical production of Jewish literalism and his argument for Christian interpretive superiority, Origen formulated a certain "discourse of sexuality" that characterized Jews as more fleshly and sexually depraved than their Christian counterparts. His hermeneutical method was therefore imbricated with a theory of alterity that differentiated Christian identity from Jewish identity on the basis of relationship to the flesh. Five texts, in particular, illumine the associative lines that Origen drew between Jewishness, fleshliness, and literalism. His *Homilies on Exodus*, delivered in Caesarea in the late 230s or early 240s, provide a point of entry for thinking about Origen's differentiation of Christian interpretive practice from Jewish practice. *On First Principles*, a theological treatise written in Alexandria in 229, presents Origen's early theory of interpretation and reflection on allegorical method.[14] His *Homilies on Genesis*, delivered in Caesarea a decade or so after the composition of *On First Principles*, provide Origen with an occasion to appropriate biblical narratives in support of his construction of Jewish literalism and Jewish carnality, including the story of Abraham's circumcision and the story of Lot and his daughters. Origen's *Commentary on the Epistle to the Romans*, composed in Caesarea in 246, exemplifies the ways in which Origen "reconstructs" Paul not only to authorize the association of Jewish identity and literal reading practices but also to justify the superiority of Christian biblical interpretation and sexual practices. Finally, his *Commentary on the Song of Songs*, written in

Athens a year before the commentary on Romans, offers a theory of biblical interpretation that associates advanced spiritual understanding with sexual
chastity (*castitas*) and bodily self-control (*continentia*).[15]

Spiritual Christians, Literal Jews: Origen's *Homilies on Exodus*

"The question is," said Alice, "whether you can make words mean so
many different things."
—Lewis Carroll, *Through the Looking Glass*

I think each word of Divine Scripture is like a seed whose nature is
to multiply diffusely, reborn into an ear of corn or whatever its spe-
cies be, when it has been cast into earth. Its increase is proportionate
to the diligent labor of the skillful farmer or the fertility of the earth.
—Origen, *Homily on Exodus 1.1*

Origen begins his first homily on Exodus with a reflection on the proliferation
of meaning of the words of scripture. Instructing his congregation on spiritual
interpretive practices, Origen warns that the words of scripture can appear at
first "small and insignificant," but with the proper "cultivation," each seed of
scripture "grows into a tree and puts forth branches and foliage." All that these
seeds need is a "skillful and diligent farmer"—one who, like Origen himself,
adheres to "the discipline of spiritual agriculture."[16]

Paul, for Origen, is this "skillful and diligent farmer" who demonstrates
to the church how to cultivate "the seeds of spiritual understanding" (*Hom.
Exod.* 5.1; GCS 6, 184).[17] Paul is the first to gather the church "from the Gentiles" and teach the church the proper interpretation of "the books of the law."
According to Origen, one of Paul's signal contributions lies in distinguishing between Christian and Jewish interpretations of the law. Fearing that the
church may be confused about what to do with a "foreign" document such as
the Jewish law, Paul wished "to distinguish disciples of Christ from disciples
of the synagogue by the way they understand the law." The difference between
Jews and Christians is, for Origen, absolute: "The Jews, by misunderstanding
[the law], rejected Christ. We, by understanding the law spiritually, show that
it was justly given for the instruction of the church" (5.1; GCS 6, 183).

In his claim for Christian interpretive superiority with regard to the
Jewish law, Origen contends that the failing of the Jews is a result of their

"misunderstanding" of scripture. He develops this point a few lines later by indicating that Jewish "misunderstanding" is rooted in the Jews' literalist reading practices. He argues, for example, that whereas Jews understand the crossing of the Red Sea to be merely a crossing, Paul interprets this historical incident as a type of baptism (5.1; GCS 6, 185). Whereas Jews think that the manna from heaven is mere "food for the stomach," Paul calls the manna "spiritual food." The problem, for Origen, is not the literal meaning, per se, but the inability of the Jews to see beyond it.[18] In a homily on Noah and the ark, for instance, Origen defends the literal meaning of the ark's construction against the "heretic" Apelles, who uses this and similar passages to argue that the Hebrew scriptures contain no divine inspiration whatsoever (*Hom Gen.* 2.1; GCS 6, 23–24). In Origen's delineation of the true interpretation of the Hebrew texts, he must negotiate a fine line between those who reject Hebrew scriptures altogether (heretics) and those who fail to understand the Hebrew scriptures spiritually (Jews). Jews and heretics thus function as differentiated yet conterminous categories with which Origen contrasts the spiritual Christian interpreter.

According to Origen, Paul performs the proper "cultivation" of biblical texts by uncovering the spiritual meanings contained within the "small and insignificant" words of scripture. Yet within Origen's homiletic presentation of Paul and Pauline interpretive practices lies a simultaneous construction and denigration of Jewish interpretive practices as intrinsically literalistic. Origen frequently encourages biblical interpreters to imitate Paul by moving beyond the literal meaning to the "elevated sense" (ἀναγωγή) of scripture.[19] Drawing on Hellenistic rhetorical techniques,[20] Philo's discussions of allegory,[21] and Paul's figural interpretation of Abraham in Galatians 4,[22] Origen presents a theory of interpretation that privileges the inner, spiritual meaning of the text over the outward and literal. In his explication of his hermeneutical theory in book 4 of *On First Principles* and in many of his commentaries and homilies, he recommends that Christians attend to this "elevated" understanding of the biblical text and avoid the errors of the Jews, who concern themselves with base, literalistic interpretive practices.[23]

Jews, Flesh, Letter: *On First Principles*

In book 4 of *On First Principles*, Origen presents a theory of interpretation that consistently aligns literalist reading practices—reading according to the "bare letter"[24]—with Jewishness and carnality. Like Justin Martyr before him, Origen begins by arguing that the correct understanding of Old Testament passages is not possible until the coming of Christ: "[I]t was after the advent of Jesus that the inspiration of the prophetic words and the spiritual nature of Moses' law came to light. For before the advent of Christ it was not at all possible to bring forward clear proofs of the divine inspiration of the old scriptures" (*Princ.* 4.1.6; SC 268, 282).[25] Utilizing Paul's imagery of the veil in 2 Cor 3:15–16 ("To this very day whenever Moses is read, a veil lies over their minds, but when one turns to the Lord, the veil is removed"), Origen contends that the "light that was contained within the law of Moses" was at first "hidden away under a veil." This veiled light, however, "shone forth at the advent of Jesus, when the veil was taken away" (*Princ.* 4.1.6; SC 268, 282).[26]

According to Origen, Jewish readers persist in misunderstanding their own scriptures because they continue to read as if through a veil—a veil that obscures the light of the text's spiritual meaning, which is accessible only through Christ.[27] Because Jews do not utilize Christ as an interpretive lens, they never advance beyond the "bare letter" to the spiritual meaning of the text. Origen emphasizes the theologically devastating consequences of Jewish literalism when he writes that "the hard-hearted and ignorant members of the circumcision have refused to believe in our Savior because they think that they are keeping closely to the language of the prophecies that relate to him." The Jews, he continues, reject Christ because they "see that he did not literally 'proclaim release to the captives' or build what they consider to be a real 'city of God'" (*Princ.* 4.2.1; SC 238, 292–294). Jewish interpretive practice, for Origen, is the very thing that keeps Jews from believing in Christ. Later, in a homily on Jeremiah, Origen develops this idea by arguing that the Jews' "murder of Jesus" results from the fact that they are unable to "hear" scripture "in a hidden way." Because Jews hear scripture outwardly instead of inwardly, they continue to be "liable" for the death of Jesus. Origen claims that "this ordinary Jew killed the Lord Jesus and is liable today also for the murder of Jesus, since he did not hear in a hidden way either the Law or the Prophets" (*Hom. Jer.* 12.13.1; SC 238, 44–46). Unlike his Jewish counterpart, the Christian interpreter, in Origen's view, should approach scripture by "praying" that "the Lord might remove the veil of the letter and uncover the light of the Spirit" (*Hom. Gen.* 6.1.1; GCS 6, 66).

According to Origen's theory of interpretation, the "bare letter" of scripture represents the "bodily meaning," the messy "flesh" of the biblical text to which the Jews mistakenly cling.[28] He posits that the "divine character of scripture" functions as the "hidden splendor" of biblical teachings, yet this "splendor" remains "concealed under a poor and humble style"—an "earthen vessel" composed of the "bare" words and phrasings of the biblical text.[29] Echoing Paul's phrase in 2 Cor 4:7 ("We have this treasure in earthen vessels"), Origen offers a corresponding characterization of the relationship between the spiritual and literal meanings of scriptural texts: "A treasure of divine meanings," he writes, "lies hidden within the 'frail vessel' of the poor letter" (*Princ.* 4.3.14; SC 268, 392). For Origen, the literal words of scripture constitute a "shameful text," to use Virginia Burrus's phrase.[30] Jews, unlike Christians, attend solely to these "fleshly" aspects of scripture and thus prove themselves to be not only carnal interpreters but also performers of shameful acts, more generally, as Origen argues in later texts.

Origen's representation of Jewish literalism depends upon his (mis) representation of Paul's language. Reworking Paul's language and inventing phrases such as "the flesh of scripture," Origen draws upon Pauline statements about the "flesh" to crystallize the connection between Jewish literalism and the "works of the flesh" (*Princ.* 4.2.4; SC 268, 310). As Ruth Clements has shown, Origen's use of "the appellation 'fleshly,' drawn from Paul, increased the rhetorically negative casting thus given to the literal sense."[31] By linking Paul's distinction between spirit and flesh to the (post-Pauline) distinction of Christian and Jew, respectively, Origen recasts Paul's understandings of "letter" and "flesh" to produce Jewish-Christian difference and to subordinate Jewish identity and interpretation.

Paul's phrase in 1 Cor 10:18—"Behold Israel according to the flesh"—lies at the heart of Origen's alignment of literalist reading practices with Jewishness and carnality. Origen uses this Pauline phrase as shorthand to conflate Jews, whom he identifies as "God's former people," with the flesh: "Let not 'Israel after the flesh,' which is called by the apostle 'flesh,' 'glory before God,'" he writes in the fourth book of *On First Principles* (4.1.4; SC 268, 274).[32] He includes a similar conflation of Jewishness and fleshliness in his *Commentary on Romans* when he interprets Rom 8:5: "'Those who are according to the flesh set their minds on the things of the flesh'; that is, the Jews whom he calls Israel according to the flesh. They set their minds upon the fleshly aspect of the law in that they understand the law according to the flesh" (*Comm. Rom.* 6.12.6 and 6.12.9). Here Origen reads Jews into Paul's argument about "flesh" versus "spirit" by identifying "those who live according to the flesh" as Jews. In other words, Origen *imports* the Jewish/Christian dichotomy to make meaning of Paul's flesh/spirit dichotomy.

Later in *On First Principles*, Origen turns again to the phrase "Israel according to the flesh" and adds a corresponding phrase that is not present in Paul's letters—"Israel according to the spirit"—to highlight the opposition between Jews and Christians (*Princ.* 4.3.6; SC 268, 366). Origen contends that "Israel after the flesh" represents Jews of his own day who embrace a literalist hermeneutic and attend solely to the bodily meaning of the text. "Israel according to the spirit," by contrast, represents followers of Christ, who recognize that "the whole of divine scripture . . . has a spiritual meaning" that "raises apprehension to a high level." Again, Origen mobilizes Paul's dyadic structure of flesh/spirit to construct a hierarchy between Jewish and Christian modes of interpretation. Such a construction depends upon a redeployment of Paul's language and categories that strategically aligns "Israel according to the flesh" with Jews of Origen's own day and assigns to the latter a particular "fleshly" mode of biblical interpretation—a misplaced devotion to "the letter that kills."

Circumcision and Jewish Flesh: Origen's *Third Homily on Genesis*

> We, therefore, instructed by the apostle Paul, say that just as many
> other things were made in the figure and image of future truth,
> so also that circumcision of flesh was bearing the form of spiritual
> circumcision about which it was both worthy and fitting that "the
> God of majesty" give precepts to mortals. Hear, therefore, how Paul,
> "a teacher of the Gentiles in faith and truth," teaches the Church of
> Christ about the mystery of circumcision. "Behold," he says, "the
> mutilation"—speaking about the Jews who are mutilated in the
> flesh—"for we," he says, "are the circumcision, who serve God in
> spirit and have no confidence in the flesh."
> —Origen, *Homily on Genesis* 3.4

Origen finds in the Jewish practice of circumcision an exemplary correspondence of fleshly interpretive practices, literal observance of the law, and Jewish sexual depravity. He utilizes circumcision as a vivid example of the way in which Jewish hermeneutics are mapped onto the Jewish body. In his third homily on Genesis, Origen mines the story of Abraham's circumcision in Genesis 17 and discovers there the spiritual meaning "behind" God's commandment to Abraham to circumcise himself and all his male offspring as a sign of God's covenant.³³ Such a fleshly commandment troubles Origen and prompts him to ask whether "the omnipotent God, who holds dominion of heaven and earth, when he wished to make a covenant with a holy man put the main point of such an important matter in this, that the foreskin of his flesh and of his future progeny should be circumcised" (*Hom. Gen.* 3.4; GCS 6, 43). In response to his own query, Origen castigates Jewish leaders for putting their faith in the flesh: "These [fleshly concerns] indeed are the only things in which the masters and teachers of the synagogue place the glory of the saints" (3.4; GCS 6, 43).

As is his common practice, Origen turns to Paul to delineate the spiritual meaning behind God's commandment to circumcise. In the quotation above, Origen employs Paul's statement in Phil 3:2–3 ("Beware of those who mutilate the flesh") to argue against the Jewish practice of fleshly circumcision (which he, following Paul, describes as "mutilation") and for "spiritual" circumcision, which befits those "who serve God in spirit." Rom 2:28–29³⁴ also serves Origen in a similar regard. He uses this passage to contend that true circumcision is "inward": "He is a Jew who is one inwardly with circumcision of the heart in the spirit, not in the letter" (*Hom. Gen.* 3.4).³⁵

Reading Phil 3:2–3 together with Rom 2:28–29, Origen thus depicts Jews as literalist interpreters of God's commandment to Abraham to circumcise himself and his male offspring. Whereas Jews interpret this commandment to be about the flesh, and hence "mutilate" their flesh, Christians understand this commandment to be about the spirit. To support his argument for an allegorical understanding of circumcision, Origen introduces examples from the prophets and the Pentateuch that invoke circumcision in reference to other parts of the body, including the heart (Ezek 44:9 and Jer 9:26), ears (Jer 6:10), and lips (Exod 4:13).³⁶ If one uses allegorical interpretation to understand these passages, he posits, why not also understand the command to circumcise the foreskin allegorically? Origen claims that if Jews understand the circumcision of the heart, ears, and lips allegorically, they should understand circumcision of the foreskin allegorically as well (*Hom. Gen.* 3.5; GCS 6, 45).

For Origen, circumcision signifies not a practice of bodily "mutilation" (as Jews, he claims, understand it) but a practice of asceticism and bodily self-mastery.³⁷ In outlining his allegorical interpretation of circumcision, Origen (ironically) builds on the work of Philo (a first-century Jew).³⁸ In *On the Migration of Abraham*, Philo argues that the recognition of a spiritual meaning to scripture does not abrogate the commandments to follow the literal law. He offers circumcision as an example: "It is true that circumcision reflects the cutting out of pleasure and all passions, and the putting away of impious conceit . . . but let us not on this account repeal the law laid down for circumcising."[39] In another work, *The Special Laws*, Philo rehearses the benefits of circumcision handed down by previous interpreters of Moses, and adds his own understanding of circumcision as a symbol for the "cutting out of excessive and superfluous pleasure," most notably sexual pleasure.[40]

As in Philo's allegorical interpretation, Origen associates circumcision with ascetic practices that distance the "spiritual" biblical interpreter from the realm of the flesh and prepare him to hear the word of God in its spiritual sense. With this line of argument, he endeavors to appropriate circumcision for exclusive Christian purposes. Origen compares spiritual circumcision to sexual chastity within marriage: "Let us see how, according to our promise, circumcision of the flesh ought to be received. There is no one who does not know that this member, in which the foreskin is seen to be, serves the natural functions of coitus and procreation. If anyone, therefore, is not troubled in respect to movements of this kind, nor exceeds the bounds set by the laws, nor has known a woman other than his lawful wife, and, in the case of her also, makes use of her in the determined and lawful times for the sake of posterity alone, that man is to be said to be circumcised in the foreskin of his flesh" (*Hom. Gen.* 3.6; GCS 6, 46–47).

Conversely, uncircumcision is aligned with lust and licentiousness: "But that man is uncircumcised in the foreskin of his flesh who falls down in all lasciviousness and everywhere loiters for diverse and illicit embraces, and is carried along unbridled in every whirlpool of lust!" (3.6; GCS 6, 47). Here Origen understands uncircumcision as an abandonment of oneself to lust and shameful passions, whereas he reads circumcision as a discipline of sexual chastity that prepares one for (and is a result of) the proper understanding of scripture. "True circumcision of the foreskin of the flesh" is, for Origen, the exclusive domain of the pure and chaste "virgin brides of Christ" (3.6; GCS 6, 47).

Origen develops this theme by noting that the circumcision of the lips and heart signify bodily chastity and uncircumcision signifies sexual depravity: "Let the eye also be circumcised lest it lust for things belonging to another, lest it look 'to lust after a woman.' For that man is uncircumcised in his eyes whose gaze, lustful and curious, wanders about in respect to the figures of women" (3.6; GCS 6, 47). Later in the same homily, he warns: "If there is anyone who burns with obscene desires and shameful passions and, to speak briefly, who 'commits adultery in his heart,' this man is 'uncircumcised in heart.' But he also is 'uncircumcised in heart' who holds heretical views in his mind and arranges blasphemous assertions against knowledge of Christ in his heart" (3.6; GCS 6, 47). In this last passage, Origen firmly links heresy with "obscene desires," "shameful passions," and adultery. A degeneration from the virtue of *sōphrosynē* to the shame of *porneia* signifies the fall from orthodoxy to heresy, from Christian spiritualism to Jewish literalism.

A few lines later in this same homily on Genesis, Origen challenges a hypothetical Jew to "compare" the Christian "spiritual" account of circumcision to the "Jewish fables and disgusting stories" (3.6; GCS 6, 47): "See whether in those stories of yours or in these which are preached in the Church of Christ, circumcision is observed according to God's command. Do not even you yourself perceive and understand that this circumcision of the church is honorable, holy, worthy of God; that that of yours is indecent, foul, shameful, and displayed as obscene (κακέμφατον) both in condition and appearance!" (3.6; GCS 6, 48–49).

Here Origen contends that circumcision as observed by the Jews constitutes an obscene gesture and exposes their debased sexuality. He urges Christians to shun this Jewish practice and instead observe a "spiritual" circumcision that, in its highest form, takes the form of sexual renunciation.

In his fifth homily on Luke, Origen uses the story of the silence of Zechariah (Luke 1:22) as another occasion to castigate the Jews for the "mute and dumb" ways in which they interpret scriptural commandments about circumcision. Jewish practices, he writes, "lack words and reason." Jewish circumcision "is like an *empty sign* . . . a mute deed." Indeed, he continues, "[t]he people who rejected the Word from their midst could not be anything but mute and dumb" (*Hom. Luc.* 5.2).[41] Here Origen strategically links the (fleshly) practice of circumcision to the (fleshly) practice of literalist interpretation by depicting Jewish circumcision as an "empty sign." Because Jews interpret circumcision according to the "bare letter," he claims, the deed is void of meaningful content, and thus it fails to signify any spiritual truth. According to Origen, this futile observance of the Jews is akin to their scriptural interpretation: in the end, it remains "mute and dumb," producing no meaning and conveying no truth—a waste. In this way, Origen maps what he views as the futility of Jewish interpretation onto the Jewish body.

By depicting the fleshly and material consequences of Jewish literalism, Origen thus theorizes Jewish hermeneutics as a fruitless carnal practice. Similarly, by positing a correspondence between Jewish circumcision and Jewish interpretation, Origen theorizes Jewish difference as simultaneously theoretical and embodied. His mapping of Jewish interpretive practice onto the body serves in this instance to naturalize Jewish difference. Moreover, his use of Phil 3:2–3 and Rom 2:28–29, in his third homily on Genesis, indicates how he can use select Pauline phrases to authorize the distinction he draws between Jewish and Christian interpretations of circumcision.

Origen Rewrites Paul

Origen was the first Christian writer to present Paul as the authorizing figure for this particular construction of Jewish-Christian difference as a difference of praxis—both interpretive and embodied. Origen repeatedly reworked Pauline ideas in order to depict Paul as the original and legitimating source for his representation of Jewish literalism and Jewish carnality. In his homilies and commentaries, Origen frequently presented Paul's spiritual interpretation as the foil to Jewish interpretations. Paul, in Origen's hands, became that "diligent farmer" who exposed Jewish misunderstandings and sowed the seeds of Christian spiritual understanding.[42]

In a sermon on the story of Abimelech's pursuit of Sarah in Genesis 20, Origen advises those who wish to "understand these words literally" to "gather with the Jews." But to him who wants to "be a Christian," Origen recommends that he listen to "Paul saying that 'the Law is spiritual' and declaring that these words are 'allegorical' when the law speaks of Abraham and his wife and sons" (*Hom. Gen.* 6.1; GCS 6, 66). Origen here cites Paul's figural interpretation of Hagar and Sarah in Galatians 4 to authorize his own method of allegorical interpretation and to differentiate this method from that of the Jews.

Origen's hierarchical structuring of the relation between Christian and Jewish biblical interpretation depends, in part, upon his (mis)representation of Paul as a Christian supersessionist. Origen synchronizes phrases from a variety of Paul's letters and letters attributed to Paul in an effort to authorize his "displacement" of Jewish interpretive practices and his portrayal of Jews as "fleshly."[43] In his commentary on Romans, Origen juxtaposes several Pauline (and so-called Pauline) dyadic pairs (from Romans, 2 Corinthians, Hebrews) that he wishes to associate with the Jewish/Christian dichotomy.[44] He utilizes this juxtaposition to depict Paul as the original "author" of the rhetorical association of Jewishness with literalism and fleshliness. Origen writes: "In the entire preceding text of the epistle [to the Romans] the Apostle had shown how religion has been transferred from the Jews to the Gentiles, from circumcision to faith, from the letter to the spirit, from shadow to truth, from carnal observance to spiritual observance" (*Comm. Rom.* 9.1.1; FC 22). Origen here associates Jews with the subordinated term of each pair: circumcision, the "letter," shadow, and "carnal observance," but he links Gentile (glossed as Christian) identity to the privileged term of each pair: faith, spirit, truth, and "spiritual observance." His strategic collapsing of separate Pauline passages thus transforms Paul's dyadic pairs into a hierarchical structure in which Jews are systematically associated with the devalued terms (flesh, shadow) and Gentiles/Christians are, by contrast, consistently linked with terms of more positive valence (spirit, truth).[45]

Origen frequently draws attention to Paul's negative statements about Jews and Israel while downplaying Paul's more positive statements about Israel. In a detailed analysis of Origen's Pauline quotations and his censorship of texts concerning the priority of Israel, John McGuckin argues that "Origen has clearly been ready to alter the tenor of St. Paul himself, his master theologian, to firm up the apologetic at those instances the Apostle might be seen to have given too much away because of his love and respect for Judaism."[46] Writing in defense of Christian interpretive methods as well as the Christianization of Jewish scripture, Origen transforms Pauline language in his endeavor to invalidate the interpretive practices of his Jewish contemporaries.[47] The effect of his rhetoric is to drive a wedge between Jewish and Christian identities, practices, and hermeneutics.

Paul, the Ascetic Interpreter: *The Commentary on Romans*

Thus far, we have seen how Origen contends that Jews live and read "according to the flesh" and thus misinterpret scripture and the Jewish law by attending to the "fleshly aspect of the law." Christians, by contrast, have replaced Jews as the rightful heirs of the law of Moses because of (Christian) spiritual understanding of the law, he argues (*Comm. Rom.* 6.12.6). Origen also reshapes Paul's language to shore up his association of Jewish identity with literalist interpretation, on the one hand, and Christian identity with spiritual interpretation, on the other. Select passages from Origen's *Commentary on the Epistle to the Romans* and his homilies on Genesis and Luke suggest that Origen understands Paul not only as the paradigmatic biblical exegete but also as an exemplary ascetic.[48] Indeed, for Origen, Paul's capacity to subject his flesh to the spirit lies at the root of his spiritual interpretive practice. On Origen's model, spiritual understanding of scripture is linked inextricably to a practice of spiritual discipline. Origen's encomium to Paul and Paul's spiritual discipline, however, often coincides with his denigration of Jewish exegesis and Jewish sexual praxis.

In Origen's *Commentary on the Epistle to the Romans*, Paul serves as the paradigmatic spiritual interpreter who refuses to be seduced by the literal and the carnal. Drawing on Pauline phrases in 2 Corinthians and Galatians, Origen writes of Paul: "In him who was always carrying around the death of Jesus in his own body, certainly the flesh never lusted against the spirit, but rather the flesh had been subjected to him since it had been put to death in the likeness of Christ's death."[49] For Origen, Paul's subjugation of the flesh by the spirit, accomplished by "carrying around the death of Jesus in his body," serves as a model for the subjugation of literal Jewish interpretive practices by spiritual Christian ones. Such a subjugation of flesh by spirit is necessary for Christian biblical interpretation, for, as Origen explains, "it is the flesh that lusts against the spirit; and as long as the flesh pours forth its lusts, it impedes the purity of the spirit and it clouds the sincerity of prayer" (7.6.4). On this model, Paul's ability to capture and convey the spiritual meaning of the biblical text derives from his ascetic practice. That is, Paul's personal subjugation of the flesh enables his hermeneutic subjugation of (fleshly) Jewish interpretive practices. Correspondingly, Paul's adherence to spiritual hermeneutics informs his bodily practice because it enables him to interpret problematic biblical passages (such as those dealing with sex and reproduction) allegorically.

Origen suggests that by imitating Paul's spiritual discipline, Christians of his own day can learn to replicate Paul's spiritual interpretive practice. Indeed, for Origen, these two projects—the subjugation of fleshly interpretation and the subjugation of one's flesh—go hand in hand. Such is the case in Origen's allegorical and ascetic interpretation of "sacrifices" in Leviticus: "Those who put to death their own members from the incentive of lust and rage, and who possess actions in their body that are pleasing to God are offering in a rational manner a sacrifice that is living, holy, and pleasing to God" (9.1.3). In this passage, Origen privileges a spiritual, "rational," and ascetic interpretation of the Levitical sacrifices over a literal one. This spiritual interpretation, moreover, is borne out by a bodily practice: "putting to death" one's members from the dangerous passions of "lust" and "rage." Here Origen closely relates spiritual interpretation to a practice of bodily self-control (*sōphrosynē*) such that a spiritual hermeneutics is theorized, in part, as a bodily discipline.[50] *Allēgoria* is *askēsis.*

Often Origen's exhortation to follow Paul in his spiritual bodily discipline and allegorical interpretive practices is accompanied by a denigration of corresponding Jewish practices. For example, in a homily on the Gospel of Luke, Origen praises Paul for his capacity for spiritual understanding while, simultaneously, slandering Jews for literalist interpretive practices that promote sexual licentiousness. Origen claims that, due to their affinity for the flesh, Jews often interpret scripture to legitimate indulgence in sex and to promote human reproduction. Origen comments on the story in Luke 20:27–36 in which the Sadducees pose a question to Jesus about a woman with seven husbands (to which Jesus responds, "In the resurrection . . . they shall neither marry nor be given in marriage, but will be like angels in heaven"). Origen uses this story as an occasion to castigate Sadducees, that is, Jews, for their biblical interpretive practices, claiming that they interpret statements such as "Blessed are the sons of your womb" (Deut 7:13) and "Your wife is like a fruitful vine" (Ps 128:3) as applicable to the time of the resurrection.[51] According to Origen, "Jews understand all of [these scriptural blessings] corporeally" (*Hom. Luc.* 39.3–4). Paul, by contrast, interpreted these biblical blessings spiritually and thus serves as a positive example to later Christian exegetes: "Paul," writes Origen, "interpreted all of these blessings, which have been placed in the Law, spiritually. He knew that they are not carnal" (*Hom. Luc.* 39.3).

Elsewhere in his *Commentary on the Epistle to the Romans,* Origen further develops this theme of Jewish "fleshliness" and Jewish sexual indulgence by linking it with accusations of Jewish *porneia.* Commenting on Rom 2:22 ("You who forbid adultery, do you commit adultery?"), Origen creates an analogy between Jewish hermeneutics and Jewish sexual practices. Addressing Jewish exegetes, he writes: "You who forbid adultery commit adultery in the synagogue of the people of God by introducing a corrupt and adulterous word of doctrine to it; and you join that doctrine to the letter of the law, which is outward. . . . You therefore who forbid adultery, you commit such a grave adultery that you introduce an adulterous understanding to it" (*Comm. Rom.* 2.11.5–6). Here, Origen understands the word "adultery" as referring to Jewish deviance not only in sexual matters but also in textual matters, and he plays on the double meaning. Considered in this way, adultery is imagined not only as something Jews do with their bodies but also as something they do with their sacred texts. For Origen, Jewish understanding is an "adulterous understanding"; it entails literalist readings, false interpretations, and flagrant misuse of texts. Origen thus reworks Paul's language to construct Jews as sexually and textually corruptive. Jewish exegetes are, on Origen's model, guilty of "adulterating" scripture (being "unfaithful" to the word of God) on the basis of their literalist interpretation and textual interpolation.[52] For Origen, such fraudulent treatment of sacred texts also produces a "lax" morality in regard to sexuality and marriage.

Accusations of Jewish *porneia* also lie at the heart of Origen's figural interpretation of the story of Lot and his daughters in his fifth homily on Genesis. Origen contends that this troublesome story necessitates a spiritual interpretation, for "the law is spiritual" and the things that happened to the ancients "happened figuratively" (*Hom. Gen.* 5.2; GCS 6, 59–60).[53] On Origen's model, Lot represents "the rational understanding and the manly soul"; he is a "figure of the Law" itself. Lot's wife, however, who cannot resist the temptation to look back, "represents the flesh," which "always looks to vices" and "looks backward and seeks after pleasures."

Origen turns to another biblical intertext—the allegory of the two prostituting sisters, Oholah and Oholibah, in Ezekiel 23—to interpret Lot's daughters. Ezek 23:4 states that the names of these two sisters who "played the whore in their youth" stand for places: "Oholah is Samaria, and Oholibah is Jerusalem." By reading Oholah and Oholibah as figures of Lot's daughters, Origen draws the link between Lot's daughters and "Judah" and "Samaria"— "the people divided into two parts made the two daughters of the Law." Elaborating the links between Judah and Samaria, on the one hand, and Lot's incestuous daughters, on the other, Origen casts Judaeans and Samaritans as carnal interpreters: "Those daughters desiring carnal offspring . . . depriving their father of sense and making him sleep, that is, covering and obscuring his spiritual understanding, draw only carnal understanding from him." By this carnal understanding "they conceive; by this they give birth to such sons as their father neither perceives nor recognizes. For that was neither the understanding nor the will of the Law to beget carnally" (*Hom. Gen.* 5.5; GCS 6, 64). Origen thus associates the sexual deviance of Lot's daughters with the interpretive deviance of Jews and Samaritans, who "obscure" the spiritual and rational interpretation and produce "carnal offspring" in its place. As in *On First Principles* and the *Commentary on the Epistle to the Romans*, Origen here develops and embellishes his rhetorical association of Jewishness, carnal interpretive practice, and sexual licentiousness.

In his interpretation of the story of Lot and his daughters, in particular, Origen associates spiritual interpretation of scripture with rationality and masculinity (Lot, "the manly soul") and "carnal" interpretation with flesh and femininity (Lot's wife and daughters). Indeed, Origen's presentation of this story introduces gender into the hierarchical structuring of Christian spiritual interpretation over Jewish literalism. Read as feminine, fleshly, and sexually deviant, Jews, with their literal interpretative practices, stand in stark contrast to the masculine rationality of Christians and their spiritual hermeneutics. On this model, practices of spiritual discipline, bodily self-control, and figural interpretation represent a stylized performance of masculine *sōphrosynē*. Adherence to a spiritual hermeneutic and a corresponding discipline of the body constitute, in Origen's view, a practice of masculinity (in which Paul serves as the exemplary model).[54] Here, Origen utilizes gender "to think with" insofar as he deploys gendered categories to naturalize the distinction between Jewish and Christian identity and between Jewish and Christian hermeneutics.[55]

Gender, Power, and Jewish-Christian Difference

Origen thus appealed to differences in gendered performances, sexual practices, and interpretive methods to describe the difference between Jews and Christians. His claim for Christian superiority with regard to Jews, moreover, was imbricated in a corresponding claim for Christian rationality, spirituality, subjugation of the flesh, and bodily self-control. What seemed at first to be a defense of the merits of allegorical interpretation over literal interpretation is exposed here as part of a larger project to create power relations and produce differences in identity. As we have seen, Origen's representation of Jewish literalism constructed Jews as sexually depraved, feminized, and misguidedly attached to "works of the flesh." Since Origen was writing within a situation of cultural hybridity and religious mingling, where the lines between Christian and Jew were blurred and contested, his multiple appeals to Jewish-Christian difference were part of his attempt to establish fixed boundaries between Jewish and Christian communities. His turn to a "discourse of sexuality" thus functioned as a way to fortify these boundaries and depict Jews as sexual and textual corruptors.

Discourses of sexuality—with their images of permeability, penetration, and adulteration—provide a particularly useful way to theorize cultural interaction in ancient times as well as modern. As theorists of colonialism have argued, discourses of sexuality often are invoked to sexualize religious and cultural borderlines and to heighten the threat posed by border-crossing.[56]

Moreover, as Ann Laura Stoler has argued in her work on colonial cultures, sex is often deployed as a polyvalent symbol for other (not necessarily sexual) asymmetrical power relations: "Sexuality, then, serves as a loaded metaphor for domination. . . . Sexual asymmetries convey what is 'really' going on elsewhere, at another political epicenter. They are tropes to depict other centers of power."[57] Taking up Stoler's idea that discourses of sexuality serve as overdetermined modes by which to express differences of power, and applying this idea to Origen's reading of Jewishness, we find that Origen utilized a discourse of sexuality to produce cultural difference between Jews and Christians. That is, he produced Jewish-Christian difference, in part, by recourse to more entrenched and "naturalized" notions of sexual virtue and vice. The distinction of spiritual Christian reading practice was displaced onto a distinction of sexual morality.

The Seduction of the Literal: *The Commentary on the Song of Songs*

In closing this chapter, I wish to problematize the absolute distinction that I have been drawing between "literal" and "spiritual" interpretation by attending to some of the passages in which Origen appeals to the "bare letter" of scripture. Although Origen consistently prefers "spiritual" interpretations over those "according to the bare letter," literal, bodily, and historical readings are not to be shunned entirely.[58] Often the literal language of scripture demands no spiritual interpretation whatsoever: "We must assert," writes Origen, "that in regard to some things the historical fact is true; as that Abraham was buried in the double cave at Hebron . . . and that Jerusalem is the chief city of Judea." Indeed, he continues, "the passages which are historically true are far more numerous than those which are composed with purely spiritual meanings" (*Princ.* 4.3.4; SC 268, 356–360). According to Origen's theory of interpretation, the "bare letter" of scripture itself is capable of seducing "simple" readers by its beauty. This charm of the literal, however, can mislead the reader. Luckily, Origen explains, scripture contains "certain stumbling blocks . . . and hindrances and impossibilities [that are] inserted in the midst of the law . . . in order that we may not be completely drawn away by the sheer attractiveness of the language [ἵνα μὴ πάντη ὑπὸ τῆς λέξεως ἑλκόμενοι τὸ ἀγωγὸν ἄκρατον ἐχούσης]" (*Princ.* 4.2.9; SC 268, 336).

On Origen's model, this seduction of the literal constitutes a danger for the interpreter, especially one who lives according to the flesh. Nowhere is this danger more present than in a text like the Song of Songs. In the prologue to his *Commentary on the Song of Songs*, Origen writes:

> If any man who lives only after the flesh should approach [this text—the *Song of Songs*], to such a one the reading of this Scripture will be the occasion of no small hazard and danger. For he, not knowing how to hear love's language in purity and with chaste ears, will twist the whole manner of his hearing of it away from the inner spiritual man and on to the outward and carnal; and he will be turned away from the spirit to the flesh, and will foster carnal desires in himself, and it will seem to be the divine scriptures that are thus urging and egging him on to fleshly lust! For this reason, therefore, I advise and counsel everyone who is not yet rid of the vexations of flesh and blood and has not ceased to feel the passion of his bodily nature, to refrain completely from reading this little book and the things that will be said about it.[59]

In this passage, Origen maintains that proper spiritual interpretation of scripture, especially of an "advanced" and dangerous text such as the Song of Songs, requires a proper behavior and attitude toward the body. Practices of sexual chastity and bodily purity prepare the mind for hearing "love's language" in a spiritual way. Danger arises when the interpreter has abandoned the spirit for the flesh. For the carnally minded, the Song of Songs will serve not as an occasion to advance spiritual understanding but as a provocation to fleshly passion. The "simple" reader of this "little book" will, in Origen's words, "rush into carnal sins and down the steep places of immodesty, either by taking some suggestions and recommendations out of what had been written . . . or else by using what the ancients wrote as a cloak for their own lack of self-control" (*Comm. Cant.* 2.2; SC 375, 90). Although Origen does not specifically associate this dangerous reading with Jewish interpretive practices in this passage, he does argue that spiritual understanding depends upon the proper preparation of the body through chastity.[60] For him, allegorical practice, which stakes the Christian claim to the spiritual meaning of the text, is linked to a restrained and renounced sexuality.

Origen makes this link between chastity and allegory explicit in his discussion of the Song's use of *amor* (ερώς). First he argues that "divine Scripture" wants to avoid mentioning *amor* because it becomes "an occasion of falling for its readers." Instead, scripture usually prefers the term *caritas* (ἀγάπη) (Prol. 2.22–24; SC 375, 106–108). Then Origen notes that although scripture can speak of becoming a "passionate lover [*amator*] of the beauty" of Wisdom, it never describes Isaac's love of Rebecca as passionate. If this were the case, "some unseemly passion on the part of the saints of God might have been inferred from the words, especially by those who do not know how to rise up from the letter to the spirit" (2.23; SC 375, 108). By yielding to the seduction of the "letter," the literalist interpreter risks a carnal reading of scripture, and this carnal reading, in turn, propels him into licentious acts (2.2; SC 375, 90). The spiritual reader, however, rises above the ignoble letter and indecorous acts. For this one, practices of bodily self-control and practices of spiritual interpretation mutually reinforce each other.

According to Origen, the Song of Songs represents one of the most "advanced" texts of scripture and must be read only by the spiritually mature: "[A] man may come to it when his manner of life has been purified, and he has learned to know the difference between things corruptible and things incorruptible" (3.16; SC 375, 138). A seductive text such as this is inappropriate for simple, literalist readers, but for the spiritual interpreter, it provides the occasion to "purify" the soul "in all its actions and habits" and to advance to "the contemplation of the divine with sincere and spiritual love" (3.16; SC 375, 138). Yet even here, the trace of the literal remains as the site of the initial seduction of the exegete—the beginning point of spiritual transformation through language.[61]

Origen's inscription of the literal as a site of the initial seduction of the reader parallels his inscription of Jewishness in his hermeneutical theory. The trace of the literal signals the "remains" of the Jews in his texts.[62] Jewishness, consistently figured in images of (desirable) flesh and language, overflows the not-quite-bounded space that Origen inscribes for it in his hierarchical structure of Christian/Jew, figural/literal, spirit/flesh. For all his endeavors to circumscribe Jewishness as absolute Other, as outside the boundaries of Christianness, he cannot suppress it enough.

The social and cultural function of Origen's sexualized representation of Jews thus involves not only a mapping of religious and hermeneutic difference as sexual difference but also a simultaneous inscription and deferral of this difference.[63] The Other, constructed here as "the Jew," is preserved in Origen's hermeneutical writings as the necessary "remainder" of the literal text of scripture—the site of the "seduction" and "sheer attractiveness" of language. As Andrew Jacobs has recently claimed, "Christianity must be constantly reminded of the remainder of Jewishness at its origins even as it persists in pushing an increasingly supersessionist line."[64] Origen, I suggest, reads this "remainder of Jewishness" not only as a marker of carnal, "adulterous" understanding to be superseded by Christian spiritualism but also as a textual *provocateur* that continues to seduce and attract the Christian reader. In Origen's interpretive theory, Jewishness thus signals a necessary, if inferior, stage in Christian hermeneutical and spiritual development—one that through its "sheer attractiveness" persistently presents the body and the "bare letter" as forces to be reckoned with by Christian exegetes.

Chapter 3

Sexual/Textual Corruption: Early Christian Interpretations of Susanna and the Elders

In the Catacomb of Priscilla in Rome, three scenes from the Jewish apocryphal story of Susanna and the elders line the walls of the *cappella greca*.[1] Painted around 250 CE, these frescoes depict the public accusation of Susanna by the elders (Figure 1), the intervention of Daniel (Figure 2), and the prayer of Susanna after her exoneration (Figure 3). The first fresco (Figure 1) visually interprets the two elders' violation of Susanna during her trial. The text known from the ancient Greek versions of Susanna states: "As she was veiled, the law-less ones ordered her to be uncovered so that they might sate themselves with her beauty. Those who were with her and all who saw her were weeping. Then the two elders stood up before the people and laid their hands on her head. Through her tears she looked up toward Heaven, for her heart trusted in the Lord" (Susanna 32–35).

Visualizing this incident in the story, the fresco presents two licentious elders flanking Susanna. Each lays one hand on her head in a gesture of accu-sation, and with the other hand he grasps her bare arm. The interplay of sight, touch, and *porneia* depicted here would not be lost on the early Christian viewer. Commenting on this scene in the narrative, Hippolytus, a Christian theologian and presbyter living in Rome in the late second and early third centuries,[2] imagined that as the elders laid their hands upon Susanna's head, they satisfied their lust (*epithymia*) through touch.[3]

Some early Christian authors appropriated this story of Susanna and the elders to define Christians as chaste and their religious opponents, including Jews, as sexually licentious. Third-century writers such as Hippolytus and Ori-gen located the narrative force of this story in its description of an attempted

Figure 1. Susanna and the elders. Catacomb of Priscilla, Rome (Pontificia Commissione di Archeologia Sacra, Rome, photo no. Pri C 41).

sexual violation of a chaste and pious woman, and they used this theme to plot differences between the church and its opponents. Casting the church's "enemies" in the role of sexual predators, Hippolytus and, to a greater extent, Origen presented Jews as a sexual threat to virtuous Christians. In this way, both authors employed a narrative of attempted sexual violence to describe the situation of Christians in the third century.

Susanna and the Elders: Two Versions

The story of Susanna is one of three Greek additions to the book of Daniel, along with "The Prayer of Azariah and the Song of the Three Jews" and "Bel and the Dragon."[4] Since the time of Origen, several issues have engaged commentators on Susanna, including original language, genre, purpose, canonicity, date of composition, provenance, and relation to the book of Daniel. Although there exists no external evidence of an early Semitic version of the story, many scholars (Origen among them) argue that Susanna was originally a Hebrew or an Aramaic composition.[5] For all the debates about the provenance

Figure 2. Susanna, Daniel, and the elders. Catacomb of Priscilla, Rome (Pontificia Commissione di Archeologia Sacra, Rome, photo no. Pri C 40).

Figure 3. Susanna and Daniel. Catacomb of Priscilla, Rome (Pontificia Commissione di Archeologia Sacra, Rome, photo no. Pri C 42).

of Susanna, there exists much more information about the history of Susanna after the Greek compositions than before them.[6]

The earliest surviving version of Susanna is the Old Greek, which scholars date to the late second century BCE (135–100).[7] The second version, which Origen and later church fathers attributed to Theodotion, is dated to the first half of the first century CE, over a century before the time of Theodotion (late second century). Readings and references to the Theodotion additions to Daniel occur in several first-century texts, including books of the New Testament.[8] The Theodotion version of Susanna is longer than the Old Greek; over a third of it contains new material, while a quarter of it repeats the Old Greek verbatim.[9] Theodotion additions include biographical details in the beginning (verses 1–5), an emphasis on the role of Daniel (verses 45–50), and several dramatic embellishments (verses 11, 15–18, 20–21, 31b, 36b, 39). The Theodotion text changes and adds to the Old Greek in order to present the story in a smoother style, emphasize the erotic and psychological elements, individualize and historicize the characters, and offer a new conclusion to the narrative. The Theodotion version also accentuates and embellishes the eroticized elements of the story by depicting the elders as violent, lustful voyeurs and Susanna as their innocent victim.[10] These embellishments rendered the Theodotion version particularly useful for Christian writers who redeployed the story to deprecate Jewish leadership and construct Jews as sexually depraved.[11]

The appropriation of the Theodotion text by third-century writers such as Hippolytus and Origen supported the production of Jewish-Christian difference insofar as it claimed the chaste protagonist as a prototype of the church while imagining "the enemies of the church" (including Jews) in the role of the sexually licentious elders. Christian authors employed the Theodotion text, with its emphasis on the villainous elders and its avoidance of positive Jewish associations, in the service not only of Christian self-definition but also of anti-Jewish ideology. By the third century CE, the Susanna narrative had been "Christianized," for Christian writers recontextualized the story as one that pertained not to Jewish diasporic history but to Christian history.[12]

Susanna as Church: Hippolytus's *Commentary on Daniel*

Whereas the mid-third-century frescoes in the Catacomb of Priscilla constitute the earliest surviving visual interpretation of Susanna and the elders, Hippolytus offers the earliest extant commentary on the story. Writing from Rome at the beginning of the third century, Hippolytus composed a four-volume commentary on the book of Daniel and devoted the entire first volume to an interpretation of Susanna and the elders. The allegorical method that he employed in his exegesis staked a Christian claim to the story by fashioning Susanna as a prefiguration of the church. Correspondingly, the licentious elders represented, for Hippolytus, those who preyed upon the church and sought to oppress her. With this allegorical reading, Hippolytus capitalized on the narrative force of the story by redeploying it to portray the church as innocent sufferer and the church's opponents as licentious predators.

Hippolytus introduces his allegorical method early in his commentary when he argues that "this history [of Susanna] will happen later, although it is written first in the book. For it is a custom of the writers to set down in the scriptures many things that come about later" (*Comm. Dan.* 1.5; GCS 7, 12).[13] By thus imploding the temporality of the story, he appropriates the biblical past for the Christian present and argues that what is narrated in Jewish history realizes its existence in Christian history.[14]

In the following passage, Hippolytus presents an allegorical interpretation of Susanna by identifying the ways in which characters, objects, and the setting of the story prefigure the history of the church: "For what the elders did *then* to Susanna is similarly accomplished *now* by the leaders who are presently in Babylon. For Susanna is a figure of the church, and Joachim her husband, of Christ. And the garden is the calling of the saints, who are like fruitful trees planted in the church. Babylon is the world. And the two elders are presented as a type of the two peoples who plot against the church—one of the circumcision and one of the Gentiles. For the words 'appointed' leaders and 'judges' of the people mean that in this age they exercise power and rule, these unjust judges of the just" (1.15; GCS 7, 36).

Extending the allegorical reading, Hippolytus contends that Susanna's bath signifies baptism (1.17; GCS 7, 38–40); this, too, solidifies her prefiguration of the church, for "the church, like Susanna, is washed and presented as a pure young bride to God" (1.17; GCS 7, 38–40).[15] This alignment of Susanna and the church is invoked again when Hippolytus calls upon Christian women to imitate the story's heroine on account of her "faith," "discretion" (εὐλαβὲς), and "self-control of the body" (σῶφρον περὶ τὸ σῶμα) (1.23; GCS 7, 52).

Just as Hippolytus's allegorical understanding of Susanna defines Christian identity in terms of faithfulness, piety, feminine chastity, and suffering, his interpretation of the elders attempts to circumscribe the identity of his religious opponents. Here, he compares Jewish and Gentile "persecutors of the church" to the scheming and voyeuristic villains of the story. Hippolytus uses a particular passage from Susanna 10–12 to make his point:

> But the verse—"eagerly they watched each day" Susanna walking
> in the garden—this means that until now the Gentiles and the Jews
> of the circumcision closely watch and meddle in the affairs of the
> church, wishing to bring false witness against us. . . . For how did
> these oppressors of and conspirers against the church become capa-
> ble of justly judging, raising their eyes to heaven with a pure heart,
> enslaved as they are by the leaders "of this age"? "And they were
> both overwhelmed by passion for her, but they did not tell each
> other of their distress, for they were ashamed to disclose their lust-
> ful desire to seduce her" (Susanna 10–11). These words are easy to
> understand: Always these two peoples, enflamed by Satan at work
> in them, desire to harass and stir up oppressions against the church,
> striving to corrupt [διαφθείρωσιν] her. (1.16; GCS 7, 36–38)

In this passage, Hippolytus's analogy between the lustful elders, on the one hand, and Jewish[16] and Gentile oppressors of the church, on the other, frames the relationship between the church and its opponents as one of unjust domi-nation inflected with sexual threat. The church is imagined here as an ob-ject of sexual violence, while her enemies are portrayed as instigators of this violence.

Hippolytus develops this imagery of sexual domination by employing violent verbs such as διαφθείρω (to corrupt) and μιαίνω (to defile)—terms that signal not only patterns of unjust domination but also practices of sexual exploitation.[17] Hippolytus deploys this vocabulary to enhance his depiction of his opponents as sexually threatening to the integrity of the church. With reference to the elders' illicit proposition of Susanna in Susanna 19–21, he writes:

> When the blessed Susanna heard these words she was troubled
> in her heart and she shielded her body because she did not wish
> to be defiled [μιανθῆναι] by the lawless elders. . . . You might
> find this fulfilled now in the church. For when the two peoples
> agree to corrupt [διαφθεῖραι] the souls of the saints, they watch
> closely "for a fitting day" and enter into the house of God. While

all there are praying and praising God, they seize them and drag some of them about and prevail over them, saying, "Come, submit [συγκατάθεσθε] to us and pay homage to our Gods. And if not, we will bear witness against you." And when they are not willing, they bring them to the courts and accuse them of acting in opposition to Caesar's decrees, and they condemn them to death. (1.21; GCS 7, 48–50)

Here, Hippolytus compares Susanna's fate to that of the Christian martyr.[18] Like her, the martyr is subjected to voyeurism, meddling, seizure, domination, unjust litigation, false testimony, and a death sentence. The Christian martyr, like Susanna, is faced with an impossible choice: either she submits (συγκατάθεσθε) to her oppressors, or she faces death. Moreover, like the wicked elders, the Jewish and Gentile "persecutors of the church" propagate violence by corrupting and bearing false witness against the church.

With this allegorical interpretation of Susanna, Hippolytus inventively configures Jewish and Gentile persecution of Christians as a type of sexual exploitation. Such a presentation not only accentuates the construction of religious Others as licentious predators but also contributes to the developing discourse of Christian asceticism by depicting the church as a vulnerable victim for which *sōphrosynē* serves as a necessary shield against external defilement.[19] Writing in the early third century—a time when Christians wielded little social or political power within the empire—Hippolytus capitalized on this narrative of attempted violence, condemnation, and redemption to fashion the church's enemies (Jewish and Gentile) as powerful persecutors (φθόριες) of the innocent. What is at stake in such a gendered and sexualized construal of the church's relationship to its enemies?

Mapping Gender, Mapping Power

In the ancient world, as today, gender difference provided a useful metaphor for describing power relationships.[20] In her examination of the uses of gender among orators in the Second Sophistic, Maud Gleason notes that ancient rhetoricians deployed categories of "male" and "female" to connote authority and activity (male) and powerlessness and passivity (female). Drawing on this rhetorical tradition of gendered imagery in ancient Roman thought, Hippolytus employed feminine metaphors for the church to define Christian identity in terms of chastity, vulnerability, and victimization.[21] In this way, he invoked gender to position Christians as paradigmatic (and feminized) sufferers.[22]

Hippolytus also deployed sex to construct a particular relation of power between his Jewish and Gentile opponents and Christians. He drew on language of voyeurism, seduction, defilement, and attempted sexual violation to represent the violent and unjust use of power by his religious opponents. With this sexualized representation of power relations, Hippolytus contributed to a developing Christian discourse of alterity that constructed religious, ethnic, and cultural Others as sexual predators who preyed upon the innocent.[23]

Hippolytus's reading of Susanna also aligned non-Christian Jews and Gentiles with Roman imperial power, thereby consigning them to the position of leonine aggressors. Moreover, by securing Susanna as a figure for the church, Hippolytus associated Christian identity with feminine vulnerability and thus strategically located Christians as victims of imperial violence.[24] For Hippolytus, and for Origen after him, scenes of seduction and exploitation— vividly depicted in the story of Susanna—proved to be a particularly apt way to describe the relationship between the imperiled church and the wider, non-Christian empire. Unlike Hippolytus, who identified his opponents as "Gentiles" and "Jews of the circumcision," Origen singled out Jews as his primary objects of sexualized representation.

Sexualized Representation in Origen's *Letter to Africanus*

In his *Letter to Africanus*, and in some of his other works as well, Origen modeled Jewishness after the lustful elders in the Susanna story.[25] Like Hippolytus, Origen claimed Susanna for Christian use by comparing her predicament to that of the Christian exegete—"hemmed in on every side" (Susanna 22). He employed the Susanna narrative to produce difference not only between Jewish and Christian sexual behavior but also between Jewish and Christian exegetical practices.

Origen differentiated between Jewish and Christian modes of reading scripture by suggesting that Jewish interpretation adhered more closely to the world of bodies and desires. For Origen, not only did Christians have a different understanding of biblical texts than did Jews; they also had a different relationship to the body and sexuality. Here he inextricably linked exegetical strategies to attitudes toward the body. To borrow a phrase from Daniel Boyarin, "hermeneutics becomes anthropology."[26] One effect of Origen's linkage of hermeneutics and anthropology was the creation of an image of the Jewish interpreter as "fleshly" and sexualized—an image neatly illustrated by the gawking elders in the story of Susanna. Origen's reading of Susanna thus provides an occasion for analyzing the overlapping construction of gender and Jewish-Christian difference in late antiquity.

Origen wrote his *Letter to Africanus* while on a trip to Nicomedia, in Asia Minor, in 249, a little before the persecution of Christians under Emperor Decius.[27] Caesarea had been Origen's residence for almost twenty years. He wrote in response to a letter from another Christian writer and philosopher, Julius Africanus, that contested his inclusion of the story of Susanna in the book of Daniel, and thus ensued the debate over the canonicity of the story. Africanus claimed that because Susanna was found only in Greek versions of the Bible, it was most likely a Greek "forgery."[28] He appealed to the fact that the Jews have not retained the story in their scriptures to support his claim. For evidence that the Susanna story represented a Greek forgery, Africanus pointed to a play on words that exists only in Greek: there are two puns relating types of trees to forms of punishment—πρῖνος (evergreen/oak) and πρίζειν (to saw); σχῖνος (mastic tree) and σχίζειν (to cleave)—such wordplay, for Africanus, would not "work" in Hebrew. Moreover, Africanus argued that the style of the Susanna story differed from that of the book of Daniel. These factors, argued Africanus, should demonstrate that Susanna was a "more modern" addition to Daniel and should not be considered an authentic part of scripture.

Origen defended the canonicity of Susanna in several ways, exhibiting much exegetical finesse in the process. He registered numerous occasions in which the Greek version of the Bible contained words or phrases that were not found in Hebrew versions and other occasions in which the Hebrew version contained phrases not present in the Greek. Indeed, his compilation of the Hexapla (a multi-language translation of the Hebrew Bible in six columns) had armed him with several examples of the discrepancies between Greek and Hebrew versions. Regarding the wordplay, Origen reported that he had consulted "not a few Jews about it," yet he remained undecided. Because the Hebrew words for the trees named in Greek were unknown, he claimed that one could not determine whether the puns would have translated (*Ep. Afr.* 10; SC 302, 538). Origen also allowed that whoever translated Susanna into Greek might have transposed the pun so that it would retain the wordplay if not the literal translation (18; SC 302, 558). Furthermore, he dismissed Africanus's last objection, that the style was different. "This I cannot see," wrote Origen (22; SC 302, 572).

In the middle section of his letter, Origen defends the canonicity of Susanna, as well as its origins in Hebrew, by contending that Jewish leaders of his own day, like the wicked elders before them, have engaged in illicit activity by hiding the story of Susanna and the elders from the people. After registering the differences between the Greek and Hebrew versions, and after exploring the implications of the wordplay, Origen argues that some Jewish sages do know the Susanna story but have excluded it on account of its shameful content. He knows of one sage who recalls a tradition about the elders in the story, and he describes this man as "a Hebrew fond of learning, said among themselves to be the son of a wise man, and educated to succeed his father" (11; SC 302, 538). This Jewish sage identifies the licentious elders of the Susanna story with the wicked elders of Jeremiah 29, Zedekiah and Ahab, who are accused of both false prophecy and committing adultery with their neighbors' wives (11; SC 302, 538).[29] Interweaving the elders of the story of Susanna with those of Jeremiah 29, Origen depicts "these men, who bore the title Elder but who performed their service wickedly" (11; SC 302, 540). Quoting Susanna 53–56, Origen asserts that one of these elders "condemned the innocent, and let the guilty go free," while the other was seduced by beauty; "lust led his heart astray" (11; SC 302, 540). From a different Hebrew sage, Origen learns another tradition about these elders:

> I know another Hebrew who related the following traditions about these elders: When the people were in captivity and hoping to be liberated from slavery under their enemies by the coming of the Messiah, these elders pretended to know revelations about the Messiah. Each for his own part, whenever he met a woman whom he wished to seduce, told her in secret that *he* had been given the ability by God to beget the Messiah. Then the woman, deceived by the hope of begetting the Messiah, gave herself freely to her deceiver. And thus the elders Ahab and Zedekiah committed adultery with the wives of their fellow citizens. Therefore, Daniel rightly called one an "old relic of wicked days" (Susanna 52), and of the other he said, "Thus you did to the daughters of Israel, and out of fear they consorted with you; but a daughter of Judah would not tolerate your wickedness" (Susanna 57). Perhaps deceit and fear had a power over these women to make them offer their bodies to those who called themselves elders. (12; SC 302, 540–542)

Origen here performs an intertextual reading of Susanna, Jeremiah 29, and rabbinic legends about Zedekiah and Ahab that shapes and expands the understanding of these wicked elders. They have become multilayered characters, with an even seedier past than the story of Susanna suggests.

Origen adds another layer to these traditions about the lustful elders when he aligns them with his Jewish contemporaries—with the elders of his own day—and charges the latter with concealing this sacred, albeit embarrassing, story from their people. How does Origen accomplish this more complex reading? First, he accuses his Jewish contemporaries of hiding "from the knowledge of the people as many of the passages which contained any accusation against the elders, rulers, and judges, as they could" (13; SC 302, 542). Instead of being included in scripture, these stories were passed down as apocryphal legends, and, hence, they ceased to carry the authoritative status of a biblical text. Second, Origen accuses Jewish interpreters of his own day of expurgating scriptural passages in order to portray their predecessors in a more favorable light. For example, he claims that Jewish elders have hidden the story of the martyrdom of Isaiah, relegating it to apocryphal status, because it accuses Jews of killing a prophet.[30] According to Origen, the Jews also corrupted this story of martyrdom by adding illegitimate words and phrases: "purposefully reckless," they "interpolat[ed] phrases and words that were ill-fitting in order to discredit the whole" (13; SC 302, 544).

Third, and finally, Origen collapses the difference between the sexually corruptive elders in the Susanna story and the textually corruptive elders of his own day: "Therefore I know of no other explanation but that those who bear the titles of sages, leaders, and elders of the people excised all the texts that might discredit them among the people. Therefore it is no wonder if this story about the licentious elders plotting against Susanna is true, but was concealed and removed from the scriptures by those whose purpose is not far removed from that of the elders" (14; SC 302, 546–548).

Here, Origen suggests that the Jewish elders of his own time are no different from the elders who wickedly solicited Susanna. He claims that the deceptive interpretive practices of his Jewish contemporaries attest to the authenticity and historicity of Susanna. These deceptive interpretive practices include interpolating, editing, expurgating, and hiding the text. Origen thus links the duplicitous and corruptive textual practices of Jewish exegetes with the illicit, predatory sexuality of the elders in the story. He concludes: "I think I have demonstrated that it is not absurd to say that the story [of Susanna and the elders] took place, and that the elders of that time dared to commit against Susanna that act of licentious cruelty, and that it was written down by the providence of the Spirit, but it was excised, as the Spirit said, by 'the rulers of Sodom' " (15; SC 302, 550).[31]

It is curious that in these passages, Origen offers two paradoxical images of Jewish sages. On the one hand, he presents his Jewish informants as erudite and trustworthy, conveyors of important information and traditions that Origen puts to good use in his argument for an original Hebrew version of Susanna. On the other hand, he claims that Jewish sages are deceptive, hiding from the people any scriptural accounts that might discredit their authority.[32] By accusing Jewish sages of expurgating, hiding, interpolating, and misinterpreting biblical texts, Origen attempts to establish primacy for his Christian mode of interpretation. In this way, he simultaneously legitimizes his own interpretation through references to Jewish knowledge and delegitimizes Jewish interpretation by comparing the sages' illicit textual practices to the lascivious behavior of the elders of the past.

To summarize, I highlight the *work* that the licentious elders of the Susanna story do for Origen in his *Letter to Africanus*. The elders provide him with an opportunity both to utilize information he has gleaned from "learned Hebrews" and to construct a sexualized image of Jewish masculinity that he can deprecate. In an intertextual reading of the elders of the Susanna story that alludes to the wicked elders Zedekiah and Ahab in the book of Jeremiah, Origen depicts Jewish elders of the past as aggressively lustful, duplicitous, and exploitative of women. These wicked elders of the past, in turn, provide him with an opportunity to chastise Jewish leaders and exegetes of his own day and implicate them in the crimes of the past—the very crimes that they wished to conceal from the masses. By collapsing the difference between past and present elders, Origen blurs the lines between sexual and textual corruption.

Constructing the Christian Interpreter: Origen's First *Homily on Leviticus*

In his first *Homily on Leviticus*, delivered a few years before he writes his *Letter to Africanus*, Origen uses the Susanna story to distinguish between proper and improper readings of scripture. In this homily, Origen configures the text as a body,[33] all the while drawing upon incarnational themes in which the Word of God becomes "clothed in the flesh of Mary."[34] As the "veil of the flesh" covered the human body of Christ, so, too, he writes, the "veil of the letter" clothes the Word of God: "[T]he letter is seen as flesh but the spiritual sense hiding within it is perceived as divinity" (*Hom. Lev.* 1.1; SC 286, 66).

With this introduction to allegorical exegesis in his first *Homily on Leviticus*, Origen proceeds to offer a reading of the Levitical laws, attending to their literal and spiritual interpretations. Here is his vision of the Christian exegete who penetrates to the deeper, hidden meaning of the text: "I myself think that the priest who removes the hide 'of the calf' offered as 'a whole burnt offering' and pulls away the skin with which its members are covered is the one who removes the veil of the letter from the word of God and uncovers its interior parts which are members of spiritual intelligence" (1.4; SC 286, 78–80). The Christian exegete, or priest, in this case, does more than unveil a hidden meaning; he flays the beast. Sacred text is imagined here as a sacrificial calf whose skin is drawn back to reveal the arteries and veins of a "spiritual intelligence." For Origen, this represents the proper way to handle the text of Leviticus, whose literal meaning masks a deeper, spiritual one.

To describe the improper, Jewish way of reading the Levitical laws, Origen turns to the story of Susanna and the elders. Here, his complaint is lodged against Jewish interpreters who insist upon the literal sense of scripture: "For they do this who force us to be subject to the historical sense and to keep to the letter of the law. But it is time for us to use the words of the holy Susanna against these shameless elders, which indeed those who repudiate the story of Susanna excise from the list of divine books. But we both accept it and aptly use it against them when it says, 'Everywhere there is distress for me.' For if I shall consent to you to follow the letter of the law, 'it will mean death for me'; but if I will not consent, 'I will not escape from your hands. But it is better for me to fall into your hands without resistance than to sin in the sight of the Lord'" (1.1; SC 286, 68).

The passage that Origen quotes here is from Susanna 22–23. It is the part of the story in which the elders have just surprised the innocent bather and told her that she could either submit to their wishes, or they would testify against her and accuse her of adultery with another young man (Susanna 19–21). Finding herself in a perilous bind, Susanna groans and says, "I am hemmed in on every side. For if I do this, it will mean death for me; if I do not, I cannot escape your hands. I choose not to do it; I will fall into your hands, rather than sin in the sight of the Lord" (Susanna 22–23).

Origen likens this perilous bind of Susanna to that of the Christian exegete. Like Susanna, the spiritual Christian exegete is offered only two negative choices: either he submits to the Jews and follows the literal sense of the law, or he follows the spirit of the law and is persecuted by Jews on account of it. Origen suggests that Christians, like Susanna, should make the latter choice: "Therefore, let us fall, if it is necessary, into your [the Jews'] detractions so long as the church, which has already turned to Christ the Lord, may know the truth of the word, which is completely covered under the veil of the letter" (1.1; SC 286, 70). Here, Origen interprets the Christian exegete as a woman—and a Jewish woman, at that—who is afflicted by the Jews, represented by the licentious elders of the story.

In his *Letter to Africanus* and first *Homily on Leviticus*, Origen asserts that the story of Susanna fittingly illustrates the predicament of the Christian exegete. Like Susanna, the Christian exegete is chaste, faithful, and imperiled, the lamb to the Jewish lion.[35] By positioning Christian identity and Christian exegesis as akin to a vulnerable, persecuted, yet chaste woman, Origen participates in the common discourse of "powerlessness and suffering" that characterized much Christian writing of the time.[36] As in Christian martyr acts, Origen's text redeploys the discourse of suffering to define Christian subjectivity and produce Jewish-Christian difference. For Christians, vulnerability transforms into triumph, and the discourse of vulnerability and suffering intersects in various ways with the reconfiguration of gender in the third and fourth centuries.

Mapping Gender, Mapping Difference

In separate works, Daniel Boyarin and Virginia Burrus have traced the "reimagination of manhood" in the later Roman empire by examining texts ranging from second-century martyr acts to late fourth-century Trinitarian treatises.[37] Building on the work of Maud Gleason, Boyarin, for example, shows how definitions and performances of masculinity shifted as "ideal male identity" became "secured in part via cross-gender identification with female virgins."[38] We can plot Origen's interpretation of Susanna on this shifting landscape by indicating how he identifies the plight of the Christian exegete with that of the Jewish heroine. Origen's reading of the Susanna story, in particular, illuminates the ways in which the mapping of gender intersected with the mapping of Jewish-Christian difference in the third century.

The terrain of gender definition shifted between the second and fourth centuries, so that by the late fourth century, in Burrus's words, idealized "masculinity incorporated characteristics or stances traditionally marked as 'feminine,' "[39] whereas, in the second and third centuries, the female martyr is measured, in part, by her ability to perform as a man. In the second and third centuries, a courageous and virile masculinity signifies spiritual strength in female heroines (Thecla and Perpetua are examples).[40] Yet by the fourth century, a shift in the mapping of gender has occurred, and "a much more complex structure of gender" develops in which idealized manhood is produced in part by feminized performances of passivity, virginity, and retreat.[41] As Burrus indicates: "Empire had reshaped the city into a stage for agonistic performances of a multifaceted manhood distinguished by its power to turn vulnerability—frequently figured as a capacity for feminization—to advantage."[42]

Origen's feminization of Christians and his hyper-masculinization of Jews operate on this trajectory of gender reconfiguration. In his *Letter to Africanus* and first *Homily on Leviticus*, he imagines the Christian exegete not as a female virgin but as a chaste Jewish matron who is threatened on all sides by the detractions of those who possess more power than she does. In Origen's texts, this comparison of the Christian exegete to Susanna is imbricated with his definition of Christian exegesis: allegorical practice, which stakes the Christian claim to the spiritual meaning of the text, is linked to a restrained and renounced sexuality. The literal and duplicitous exegesis of the Jews, by contrast, is associated with hyper-masculinity and excessive lust, represented here by the elders in the story. Here, Origen's idealized Christian man adopts the posture of the chaste female while the role of the virile and domineering man is consigned to Jews.

Origen thus produced Jewish-Christian difference by recourse to the more entrenched and naturalized difference between male and female, and in so doing he constructed the relationship of Jews to Christians as one fraught with overtones of sexual domination and violence. Like that of Hippolytus before him, his reading of the Susanna story redeployed ancient notions of a "violent and invasive" male sexuality in order to portray Christians as victims of Jewish power.[43] Considered in this way, Origen's sexualized representation of Jewish-Christian relations pitted Christians, the archetypal sufferers, against Jews, their aggressive and leonine oppressors. In his complex reading of the Susanna story, Origen used accusations of carnality and illicit sexuality to define religious Others.

Susanna as a Model of Chastity: Clement, Methodius, Asterius, Pseudo-Chrysostom

Susanna frequently appeared as a model of chastity and *sōphrosynē* in the work of other Greek fathers of the second, third, and fourth centuries. Like Origen and Hippolytus, many early Christian writers used the story of Susanna and the elders to align Christian identity with the preservation of bodily integrity and purity in the face of exterior threat. Origen and Hippolytus were distinctive, however, in their allegorical interpretations of the wicked elders.[44] After Origen, few writers focused on identifying the elders with present-day opponents of the church. Rather, third-, fourth-, and early fifth-century writers such as Methodius of Olympus, Asterius of Amasea, and an anonymous author writing under the name of John Chrysostom (Pseudo-Chrysostom) upheld Susanna as an example of chastity to be imitated by Christian women, in particular.[45]

Clement of Alexandria (Origen's predecessor, teacher, and fellow Christian Neoplatonist) was one of the first Christian writers to identify Susanna as a model of *sōphrosynē*. In book 4 of his *Stromata*, he lists women from ages past who demonstrated a capability for perfection and includes Susanna among these. For Clement, Susanna's "extraordinary dignity" establishes her as an "unwavering martyr of chastity" (μάρτυς ἁγνείας ἀρρεπής).[46] In his *Symposium*, an ode to Christian virginity written in the early fourth century, Methodius, bishop of Olympus in Lycia, urges ascetic Christian women to imitate Susanna's rejection of sexual advances. He has the character Thecla, the "chief of virgins," offer the following hymn to Susanna:

> *Thecla*: Seeing the fair figure of Susanna, the two judges, maddened with desire, said, O lady, we have come longing to lie secretly with you, beloved; but she, trembling, cried:
> *Chorus*: I keep myself pure for you, O Bridegroom, and holding a lighted torch I go to meet you.
> *Thecla*: It is better for me to die than to give myself to you, O men who are mad for women, and to suffer eternal justice by the fiery vengeance of God. Save me now, O Christ, from these things.[47]

In this passage, Methodius associates Susanna's (marital) chastity with the Christian virgin's purity and fidelity to her bridegroom. Just as Daniel saves

Susanna from death by exposing the elders' false accusation against her, Christ saves the female Christian virgin who maintains her purity, by interceding on her behalf.

Writing around the year 400, Asterius, bishop of Amasea in northern Asia Minor, delivered a sermon on Susanna in which he associated her *sōphrosynē* with that of Joseph. Like Joseph, who refused the sexual advances of Potiphar's wife, Susanna rejected the elders' illicit proposition.[48] Asterius encouraged his auditors to emulate Joseph and Susanna, for both were "tutors of bodily self-mastery" (παιδαγωγοὺς σωφροσύνης) (*Hom.* 6.4). Like Methodius before him, Asterius encouraged women, in particular, to imitate Susanna: "Women, emulate Susanna; in this way you will guard [your] *sōphrosynē* with courage, as she did hers" (*Hom.* 6.7).

Pseudo-Chrysostom (who was most likely a Cappadocian writer who lived in Constantinople and wrote under Chrysostom's name) composed a sermon on Susanna around the same time as Asterius's sermon,[49] in which he presented her as a model of chastity, a suffering victim, and a courageous victor over her enemies. He vividly depicted Susanna as a lamb between two wolves. For Pseudo-Chrysostom, her struggle against these "wolves" established not only her *sōphrosynē* but also the elders' licentiousness (ἀκολασία). Her fight, argued Pseudo-Chrysostom, was more glorious than that of Joseph: "Susanna endured a violent battle, more severe than that of Joseph. He, a man, contended with one woman; but Susanna, a woman, had to contend with two men."[50] In contrast to Origen and Hippolytus, Pseudo-Chrysostom did not elaborate on the identity of the two "wolves," but like his predecessors, he configured the Jewish heroine of the story as a suffering "lamb." In his rhetorical presentation, Pseudo-Chrysostom transformed this suffering "lamb" into a Christian victor, a glorious champion of courage, fidelity, and chastity.

The portrayal of Susanna as a lamb between two wolves appeared not only in text but also in visual form (Figure 4). In the *arcosolium* of Celerina in the Roman Catacomb of Praetextatus, a fresco dated to the early fourth century offers a figurative interpretation of Susanna and the elders. She is depicted as a lamb standing between two wolves, and the identification is certain because "SVSANNA" is inscribed over the head of the lamb and "SENIORIS" over the back of one of the wolves. In the visual and textual imagination of these fourth-century Christians, the story of Susanna and its attendant themes of chastity, piety, violence, and deliverance functioned as a way to theorize Christian identity. She represented the "paradigmatic sufferer"

Figure 4. Susanna and the elders. Catacomb of Praetextatus, Rome (Pontificia Commissione di Archeologia Sacra, Rome, photo no. Pre C 20).

who nevertheless triumphed over her enemies by holding fast to the virtues of purity, chastity, and piety. The Susanna narrative thus fittingly applied to the formation of Christian identity both before and after the imperial sanction of the church. In the second and third centuries, writers invoked Susanna to describe the struggle of the church against her more powerful adversaries. In the later fourth century, writers utilized Susanna to encourage Christians to renounce sexual relations or practice marital chastity. For these later authors, Susanna's *sōphrosynē*, even in the face of death, enabled her transformation into a triumphant victor over her licentious adversaries.

To summarize, Hippolytus and Origen constructed Jews as a sexual threat to virtuous Christians in their independent interpretations of Susanna and the elders. Their interpretations expressed the concurrent proximity and distance between "Christianity" and "Judaism," and each author attempted to draw a border between Christians and Jews by depicting the former as chaste and pure and the latter as lascivious and violent. Origen, in particular, employed the story of Susanna as an occasion to produce difference between Jewish and Christian modes of reading scripture. He used sexual stereotypes not only to distinguish the Christian from his or her Others but also to forge a link between proper Christian sexual behavior and proper Christian hermeneutical practice. As the Susanna story entered the service of the im- perial church, the focus shifted away from sexualized representations of the wicked elders and toward the co-optation of Susanna as exemplar of chastity. Church fathers of the fourth century and beyond reiterated the link between

Christians and the chaste Jewish matron in order to regulate sexual morality within Christian communities. Such diverse interpretations of Susanna and the elders thus illuminate the variety of ways in which sexualized representation functioned in the production of anti-Jewish ideology and early Christian self-definition.

Chapter 4

"A Synagogue of *Malakoi* and *Pornai*": John Chrysostom's *Sermons against the Jews*

> [T]he borders between Christianity and Judaism are as constructed
> and imposed, as artificial and political as any of the borders on
> earth. . . . Rather than a natural-sounding "parting of the ways,"
> such as we usually hear about with respect to these two "religions,"
> I will suggest an imposed partitioning of what was once a territory
> without border lines.
> —Daniel Boyarin, *Border Lines: The Partition of Judaeo-
>   Christianity*

> It is against the Jews that I wish to draw up my battle line.
> —John Chrysostom, *Fourth Sermon against the Jews*

John Chrysostom's *Sermons against the Jews* contain many sexual stereotypes
of Jews—including insidious images of Jewish men as "soft" (*malakoi*), lustful, and bestial; Jewish women as prostitutes (*pornai*); and the synagogue
as a brothel (*porneion*).[1] Yet in the story of the Christian woman who was
dragged to the synagogue—the story with which the Introduction to this volume opens—it was the "Judaizing" man who suffered Chrysostom's verbal
attack. Like Hippolytus and Origen before him, Chrysostom used a narrative
of male violence against a woman to define a boundary between orthodoxy
and heresy, between a "pure" Christianity and a Christianity adulterated by
Jewishness. And like Hippolytus and Origen, Chrysostom depicted Jews and
"Judaizers" as wolves in pursuit of Christian sheep. He boasted that he himself was the shepherd who protected the sheep from their Jewish predators.[2]

Facing a situation in which some of his Christian congregants were visiting synagogues and joining in Jewish celebrations—a veritable "territory without border lines"—Chrysostom invoked a narrative of attempted exploitation of a woman to "draw up" his battle line and drive a wedge between Christianity and Judaism.[3]

In his sermons against the Jews, Chrysostom characterized Jews as sexual deviants and Judaizers as sexual aggressors. These caricatures functioned as devices by which he could sexualize religious and cultural border lines and heighten the threat posed by border-crossing. With his accusations of sexual excess, violence, and general immorality of Jews and Judaizers, Chrysostom endeavored not only to delegitimize the authority of his religious opponents but also to shore up his own authority and the links between Christian orthodoxy and sexual virtue.

Chrysostom delivered his first sermon against the Jews in Antioch in September 386, and he resumed this topic again in autumn 387 at the approach of the Jewish holidays, preaching six additional sermons.[4] Chrysostom's congregation comprised people who lived in close proximity to Jews and pagans. There were at least two important synagogues in the area—one within the city of Antioch and one nearby in the suburb of Daphne. The close proximity and interconnection of the Christian and Jewish communities troubled Chrysostom, and he used the occasion of the approaching Jewish holidays to chastise members of his congregation for flocking to the synagogue to receive special healings, make oaths, hear the scriptures, and celebrate Jewish holidays.

In the past, scholars such as Marcel Simon, Wayne Meeks, and Robert Wilken examined Chrysostom's sermons *Adversus Iudaeos* to identify the "reality" behind the impassioned rhetoric of the sermons.[5] More recently, Isabella Sandwell has explored the ways in which Chrysostom's sermons against the Jews functioned in relation to the formation of religious identity—as well as the formation of the category "religion"—in fourth-century Antioch.[6] In contrast to these previous studies, my concern lies with how Chrysostom's rhetoric functions in the construction of reality—the creation and contestation of identities, differences, communities, and boundaries in late fourth-century Antioch. In his effort to define a Christian orthodoxy, Chrysostom used the stereotype as a targeted device to construct Jewishness as the *negation* of Christianness. In Chrysostom's hands, stereotypes of Jews as licentious and immoral functioned to cordon off "pure" Christians from their heretical (that is, more Jewish) counterparts.

In his analysis of how stereotypes operate in modern colonial contexts,

Homi Bhabha argues that "the stereotype is a complex, ambivalent, contradictory mode of representation, as anxious as it is assertive, and demands not only that we extend our critical and political objectives but that we change the object of analysis itself."[7] In his sermons at Antioch, John Chrysostom "anxiously and assertively" repeats stereotypes of Jews in his effort to construct Jewish and Christian identities as antithetical and mutually exclusive. In an illustrative passage from his fourth sermon, Chrysostom demands of his audience: "The difference between the Jews and us is not a small one, is it? Is the dispute between us over ordinary, everyday matters, so that you think the two religions are one and the same? Why are you mixing what cannot be mixed? They crucified Christ, whom you adore as God. Do you see how great the difference is?" (*Adv. Jud.* 4.3.6; PG 48, 875). Despite his repeated attempts to disavow Jewishness and portray it as antithetical to Christianness, Chrysostom's construction of Jewish identity and behavior as the negation of Christian identity and behavior is neither complete nor absolute, for it is continually troubled by the *proximity* of Jews, the overlap of identities, and the porosity of borders. Bhabha's work on the stereotype in colonial discourse helps to theorize the ways in which Chrysostom's frantic attempts to "fix" Jewish identity expose (and, perhaps, create conditions for) the complexity, richness, and fluidity of religious identity in late ancient Antioch.

Chrysostom's Accusations against the Jews

Chrysostom's sermons *Adversus Iudaeos* include several caricatures of Jews and Jewish practices as immoral, base, and demonically inspired. Like Justin Martyr, Melito of Sardis, and other Christian heresiologists before him, Chrysostom accuses Jews of bearing responsibility for the murder of Christ, and he connects this murder to past Jewish aggression against the prophets: "You murdered Christ, you lifted violent hands against the Master, you spilled his precious blood. . . . In the old days your reckless deeds were aimed against his servants, against Moses, Isaiah, and Jeremiah. . . . But now you have put all the sins of your fathers into the shade" (6.2.10; PG 48, 907).[8] Chrysostom then justifies the suffering of Jews in his own day as divine punishment for Jewish aggression against Christ. The Jews' "present disgrace," he insists, is linked inextricably to their treatment of Christ: "Your mad rage against Christ . . . is why the penalty you now pay is greater than that paid by your fathers" (6.2.10; PG 48, 907). Echoing Justin Martyr, Chrysostom depicts the destruction of Jerusalem in 70 CE as divine punishment for the murder of Christ.[9] He claims that after Jesus died on the cross, God "then destroyed your city; it was then that he dispersed your people; it was then that he scattered your nation over the face of the earth" (5.1.7; PG 48, 884). With these descriptions of divine punishment of Jews, Chrysostom represents his Jewish contemporaries as subjects of violence—subjects in the double sense that they perpetrate violence and are subject to (a divinely sanctioned) violence.

In a further effort to vilify and dehumanize Jews, Chrysostom depicts not only their synagogues but also their souls as "dwelling places . . . of demons" (1.3.1 and 1.4.2; PG 48, 847, 848–849).[10] Comparing the synagogue with other Greek places of worship (such as the shrine of Matrona and the temple of Apollo), Chrysostom argues that Jews are a more dangerous influence on Christians than are pagans (1.6.4; PG 48, 852). Describing the synagogue, Chrysostom writes: "Here the slayers of Christ gather together, here the cross is driven out, here God is blasphemed, here the Father is ignored, here the Son is outraged, here the grace of the Spirit is rejected. Does not greater harm come from this place since the Jews themselves are demons?" (1.6.3; PG 48, 852). To avoid encountering the devil in the synagogue, Chrysostom recommends that upon entering a synagogue, Christians should "make the sign of the cross on your forehead" so that "the evil power that dwells in the synagogue immediately takes to flight" (8.8.7; PG 48, 940).[11] Of the Judaizers, Chrysostom demands: "How do you Judaizers have the boldness, after dancing with demons, to come back to the assembly of the apostles?" (2.3.5; PG 48, 861). To associate with Jews, share in their ritual practices, and enter their sacred spaces is, in Chrysostom's view, to come into contact with the sphere of the demonic. Such contact, moreover, jeopardizes the "purity" of the body of the church.[12]

Images of disease and pollution also color Chrysostom's description of the threat of Jews and Judaizers to the Christian community in Antioch.[13] In the beginning of his first sermon against the Jews, Chrysostom states that he is interrupting his series of sermons against the Anomoeans because "[a]nother very serious illness calls for any cure my words can bring, an illness which has become implanted in the body of the church. . . . What is this disease? The festivals of the pitiful and miserable Jews are soon to march upon us one after the other and in quick succession" (1.1.4–5; PG 48, 844). A few moments later, Chrysostom informs his congregation that although "the greater portion of the city [of Antioch] is Christian, . . . some are still sick with the Judaizing disease" (1.4.4; PG 48, 849). By depicting those who promote Jewish practices as diseased and polluting agents within the Christian community, Chrysostom theorizes the border line between Christianity and Judaism as a line between health and sickness, life and death. In Chrysostom's presentation, the threat of Jewishness could not be direr.

Chrysostom further embellishes his invective against Jews by accusing them of drunkenness and gluttony.[14] He introduces this theme in his first sermon by quoting Stephen in Acts 7:51, who accuses Jews of being a "stiff-necked people" (1.2.4; PG 48, 846).[15] Chrysostom then inquires about the "stiffness" and "hardness" of the Jews: "What is the source of this hardness?" he asks. "It comes from gluttony and drunkenness. Who says so? Moses himself. 'Israel ate and was filled and the darling grew fat and frisky'" (1.2.5; PG 48, 846).[16] A few moments later, Chrysostom utilizes this accusation of excess in food and drink to delegitimize Jewish fasting: "Now when [the Jews] fast, they go in for excesses and the ultimate licentiousness, dancing with bare feet in the market place. The pretext is that they are fasting, but they act like men who are drunk" (1.2.7; PG 48, 846).

Chrysostom returns to the theme of Jewish drunkenness in his final sermon against the Jews, delivered in September 387. Here he claims that Jews are drunk but not on wine. He supports this claim by registering other instances in which a man may be considered a "drunkard": for example, if he "nurtures some other passion in his soul," if he is "in love with a woman who is not his wife," if he "spends his time with prostitutes," or if he is "filled with the strong wine of his undisciplined passion." This type of drunkard, continues Chrysostom, is "[l]ike a deranged man or one who is out of his wits; he imagines he sees everywhere the woman he yearns to ravish" (8.1.2; PG 48, 927). Drunkenness is theorized, here, as *porneia*, and Jews, because of their indulgence of licentious desires, are guilty of crimes of both drunkenness and *porneia*. Given these broader definitions of "drunkenness," Chrysostom claims that "the Jews are drunk but do not know they are drunk" (8.1.2–4; PG 48, 927).

Accusations of drunkenness, gluttony, and *porneia* were part of a wider rhetorical project in which ancient moralists denounced opponents by characterizing them as pursuers of base pleasures. For Roman moralists, excess in food and drink signaled a lack of bodily self-control and a tendency to choose vice over virtue. Often when ancient moralists accused opponents of drunkenness and gluttony, charges of sexual immorality were not far behind.[17] Such is the case in regard to Chrysostom's accusations against the Jews. By associating drunkenness with practices of *porneia* (adultery, prostitution, and

promiscuity) and, then, by associating Jewishness with drunkenness, Chrysostom constructed Jews as particularly vulnerable to the lure of base pleasures,
and, thus, morally reprehensible. His depiction of Jews as morally debased in
regard to sexuality and bodily self-control continued throughout the entire
series of his sermons against the Jews but is particularly evident in his first and
second sermons.

Sexual Stereotypes in Chrysostom's First Sermon *Adversus Iudaeos*

Of his eight sermons against the Jews, Chrysostom's first sermon contains the
most frequent and derogatory invective, including the most frequent sexual
slander. His first sermon—which he probably delivered a full year before the
rest of his sermons *Adversus Iudaeos*—was highly polemical and "excessive"
in its language.[18] After introducing the immediate problem that this sermon
addresses—the "disease" of the "pitiful and miserable Jews" and the approach
of their festivals and fasts (1.1.4–5; PG 48, 844)—Chrysostom invokes Paul's
image of the olive tree in Rom 11:17–24. Whereas Paul utilized the image of
the olive tree to argue for Gentile humility in regard to Jews and the eventual
salvation of Jews ("how much more will these natural branches be grafted
back into their own olive tree"), Chrysostom reverses Paul's logic by suggesting
that the "Jewish" branches have been severed permanently and the "Christian"
branches have replaced them. He misrepresents Paul as a proponent of complete Christian supersessionism: "The morning sun of justice arose for [the
Jews], but they thrust aside its rays and still sit in darkness. We [Christians],
who were nurtured by darkness, drew the light to ourselves and were freed
from the gloom of their error. They were the branches of that holy root, but
those branches were broken. We had no share in the root, but we reaped the
fruit of godliness" (1.2.1; PG 48, 845). Here Chrysostom twists the meaning
of Paul's words to bolster his anti-Jewish claims.[19] Unlike Paul, he equates
Christians with Gentiles, distancing Christians entirely from their Jewish
"root." In the remainder of the sermon, Chrysostom argues that the Christian
replacement of Jews as recipients of God's promises is justified, in part, by the
continued immoral practices (including *porneia*) of Jews.

After his interpretation of the olive tree in Romans 11, Chrysostom turns
to the Gospel of Matthew for another image with which he can disparage
Jews. Matt 15:21–28 tells the story of a Canaanite woman who asks Jesus to
help her and her daughter, who is "tormented by a demon." Jesus refuses the

woman's request by stating that he has come to help only "the lost sheep of the house of Israel." She persists in her request, and Jesus responds: "It is not fair to take the children's food and throw it to the dogs" (Matt 15:24–26). In this passage, the "dogs" represent Gentiles, whereas Jews are the "children." As he did with Rom 11:17–24, Chrysostom strategically reverses the terms of this Matthean story to suit his own purposes: "Although those Jews had been called to the adoption of sons, they fell to kinship with dogs; we who were dogs received the strength, through God's grace, to put aside the irrational nature, which was ours, and to rise to the honor of sons. How do I prove this? Christ said: 'It is not fair to take the children's bread and to cast it to the dogs.' Christ was speaking to the Canaanite woman when he called the Jews children and the Gentiles dogs. But see how thereafter the order was changed about: They became dogs, and we became the children" (1.2.1–2; PG 48, 845).[20]

Chrysostom then combines the image of dogs from Matthew 15 with that of Phil 3:2–3 ("Beware of the dogs, beware of the evil workers, beware of those who mutilate the flesh"), claiming that Paul also understood Jews as "dogs": " 'Beware of the dogs,' Paul said of [the Jews], 'Beware of the evil workers, beware of the mutilation. For we are the circumcision.' Do you see how those who at first were children became dogs? Do you wish to learn how we, who at first were dogs, became children?" (1.2.2; PG 48, 845). As with the story of the olive tree, Chrysostom utilizes the texts of Matt 15:24–26 and Phil 3:2–3 to argue that Christians have fully replaced Jews as both the "children of God" and the proper recipients of the "bread."[21] Jews, by contrast, have replaced Gentiles as "dogs." With this image of Jewish dogs, Chrysostom introduces a theme that he will interweave throughout the remainder of his sermons *Adversus Iudaeos*: the sustained caricature of Jews as animals. Chrysostom's choice of animals is telling—he consistently compares Jews to animals known for licentious, promiscuous, and brute behavior: dog, heifer, hyena, and stallion.[22]

To lend authority to his depiction of Jews as brute animals, Chrysostom turns to the Hebrew prophets. Using the language of Hosea 4, he compares the obstinacy of the Jews to that of a "stubborn heifer" (1.2.5; PG 48, 846). Similarly, drawing on the language of Jeremiah 31, he depicts Jews as "untamed calves" (1.2.5; PG 48, 846).[23] In the midst of an argument in which he accuses Jews of murdering their own children, Chrysostom compares Jews to the "amorous stallion" of Jeremiah 5: "Wild beasts often lay down their lives and scorn their own safety to protect their young. No necessity forced the Jews when they murdered their own children with their own hands to pay honor to the avenging demons, the foes of our life. . . . Because of their licentiousness, did they not show a lust beyond that of irrational animals? Hear what the prophet says of their excesses. 'They are become as amorous stallions. Every one neighed after his neighbor's wife' (Jer 5:8), but he expressed the madness which came from their licentiousness with the greatest clarity by speaking of it as the neighing of brute beasts" (1.6.8; PG 48, 852–853).

In this passage, Chrysostom strategically combines sexualized images (stallions lusting after their neighbors' wives) with stereotypes of Jews as promiscuous animals and murderers of their own children. In addition, he attempts to legitimate these accusations against the Jews by quoting phrases from the prophets.[24]

Chrysostom's most explicit use of sexual slander to vilify Jews occurs soon after his depiction of Jews as "stubborn heifers" and "untamed calves" and immediately after his portrayal of Jewish fasts as exercises in "excess" and "licentiousness" (1.2.5–7; PG 48, 846). In the context of these accusations, Chrysostom adds the following caricature of Jews as sexually deviant: "But these Jews are gathering choruses of 'soft' men [*chorous malakōn synagagontes*] and a great trash heap of prostituting women [*peporneumenōn gynaikōn*]; they drag into the synagogue the whole theater, actors and all. For there is no difference between the theater and the synagogue" (1.2.7; PG 48, 846–847).[25] Chrysostom's first move is to depict Jewish men as *malakoi*. Dale Martin explains that in ancient texts, the term *malakos* "can refer to many things: the softness of expensive clothes, the richness and delicacy of gourmet food, the gentleness of light winds and breezes. When used as a term of moral condemnation, the word still refers to something perceived as 'soft': laziness, degeneracy, decadence, lack of courage, or, to sum up all these vices in one ancient category, the feminine."[26] In Chrysostom's case, such "gendered invective" functions as a strategy to denigrate Jews by challenging their ability to perform as males.[27] By associating Jewish men with the realm of the "feminine," via the label *malakoi*, Chrysostom aligns Jewishness and gender deviancy and, in so doing, challenges Jewish status and power in general. He thus articulates Christian dominance over Jews, in part, by challenging Jewish masculinity. Gender handily becomes a way to signify power.[28]

Second, Chrysostom identifies Jewish women as *pornai*. If the charge of "softness" and effeminacy presented a challenge to the late ancient Antiochene male and his performance of masculinity, charges of "prostitution" presented congruent challenges to Antiochene women. Accusations of female prostitution functioned not only as an insult to the chastity and gender performance of the community's women but also as an affront to men and their ability to enforce "proper" sexual hierarchies. As Blake Leyerle argues: "What is especially reprehensible in prostitution, then, is the perversion of the 'natural' sexual hierarchy in which men are to lead and women to follow."[29] By caricaturing Jewish men as *malakoi* and Jewish women as *pornai*, Chrysostom suggests that Jews fail in their proper gender performances. With sexualized and gendered invective such as this, Chrysostom aims not only to humiliate Jews and "Judaizers" in regard to gender and sexuality but also to call into question their status, social standing, and authority in religious and cultural domains.

Finally, Chrysostom depicts the synagogue as a theater (indeed, he argues for the complete identification of synagogue and theater) and compares Jews to actors. To grasp how devastating an insult this was in the context of Chrysostom's late fourth-century congregation, we must understand his attitude toward the theater in general. In his denunciations of the theater, Chrysostom consistently associates the theater and actors with *porneia*. In a homily on Matthew, Chrysostom portrays the theater as a place where "there are adulteries and stolen marriages. There are female prostitutes, male 'companions,' and pleasure boys: in short, everything that is illegal, monstrous, and full of shame." He demands: "Tell me, for instance, from where do those who plot against marriages come? Is it not from this theater? From where do those who undermine bedrooms come? Is it not from that stage? Is it not from there that husbands become burdensome to their wives? Is it not from there that wives become easily despised by their husbands? Is it not from there that most people are adulterers?"[30] In this passage, Chrysostom represents the theater as disruptive of social hierarchies and "natural" order. The theater troubles the gendered hierarchy within marriage, in particular. With this negative portrayal of the theater, Chrysostom resembles Roman moralists more so than Greek ones, who tended to hold the theater and actors in higher regard.[31] His depiction of the synagogue as a theater functions as sexualized invective that bolsters his claims that Jews are sexually licentious and lustful.

In supporting his rhetorical invective against the Jews, Chrysostom again draws on the language of the prophets in an attempt to legitimate, first, his charges of Jewish sexual immorality and, second, his description of the synagogue as a theater and brothel. Claiming that he "speaks" not in his own words but in "the words of the prophet" (*Adv. Jud.* 1.2.7; PG 48, 847), he utilizes a passage from Jeremiah to support his claim that the synagogue is "no better than" a theater or brothel: "Many, I know, respect the Jews and think that their present *politeia* is a venerable one. This is why I hasten to uproot and tear out this deadly opinion. I said that the synagogue is no better than the theater and I bring forward a prophet as my witness. Surely the Jews are not more deserving of belief than their prophets. What, therefore, did the prophet say? 'You had a harlot's brow; you became shameless before all' (Jer 3:3). Where a harlot has set herself up, that place is a brothel" (1.3.1; PG 48, 847).

Chrysostom continues this line of attack by depicting the synagogue as a "lodging place" of hyenas. This charge is especially vilifying since many ancients understood hyenas as sexually indecent because of their supposed ability to change between male and female.[32] He writes: "But the synagogue is not only a brothel and a theater; it is also a den of robbers and a lodging place for wild beasts. Jeremiah said, 'Your house has become for me the den of a hyena' (cf. Jer 7:11, Jer 12:9). He does not simply say, 'of a wild beast,' but 'of a filthy wild beast'" (1.3.1; PG 48, 847).[33]

At this point in his sermon, after maligning Jews as brute animals and sexual deviants, Chrysostom begins to focus his ire on so-called Judaizers or half-Christians—those who, according to Chrysostom, not only worship with Christians but also visit the synagogue and participate in Jewish fasts and festivals. It is at this moment in the sermon that he relates the story (discussed above) of the "faithful" Christian woman who is violently pursued by a "defiling" Judaizing man. He then admonishes Christians who fast with the Jews by invoking the rhetoric of shame: "Do you fast with the Jews? Then take off your shoes with the Jews, and walk barefoot in the agora, and share with them in their indecency and laughter. But you would not choose to do this because you are ashamed and apt to blush. Are you ashamed to share with them in outward appearance but unashamed to share in their impiety? What excuse will you have, you who are only half a Christian?" (1.4.7; PG 48, 849).

Chrysostom here depicts Jewish behavior as indecent and shameful. In his view, Jews lack bodily self-control and social dignity: they walk barefoot in public, they laugh, they "dance with demons" (2.3.5; PG 48, 861). For a Christian to join Jews in this disgraceful performance is to compromise not only her piety but also her honor and shame.[34] By embracing the hybrid status of half-Christian/half-Jew, she relinquishes her claims to faithfulness, modesty, and sexual purity.

Taken together, these accusations of sexual licentiousness, shameful indecency, effeminacy, prostitution, and bestiality heighten the rhetorical force of Chrysostom's argument that Jewish practice and behavior are inferior to Christian practice and behavior—indeed, that Jews, by their very nature, are inferior to Christians. By creating stereotypes of Jews and Judaizers as agents of *porneia* and pollution, he raises the stakes of "mixing" what he views as two mutually exclusive religious formations.[35] He contends that by joining Jews in their worship and celebrations, a Christian man compromises his masculinity and thereby his power and status in the community. Likewise, a Christian woman compromises her bodily integrity, chastity, and shame. By claiming that Jewish men are *malakoi*, Jewish women are *pornai*, and the synagogue is a *porneion*, Chrysostom endeavors to naturalize Jewish-Christian difference by appealing to popular moral attitudes toward gender and sexuality. In his subsequent sermons against the Jews, delivered in the following year, he returns to and develops many of these stereotypes.

Sexual Stereotypes in the Second Sermon *Adversus Iudaeos*

In his second sermon against the Jews, delivered a full year after the first, Chrysostom argues that by continuing to follow the Jewish law, Jews and Judaizers, first, flagrantly disregard the salvation brought about by Christ and, second, transgress biblical law itself, namely, the instruction to restrict sacrifices to the temple.[36] In regard to the first claim, Chrysostom follows Paul's argument in Galatians and Romans to demonstrate that Jews and Judaizers go astray because they continue to regard the law as effecting salvation after the coming of Christ. In regard to the second claim, Chrysostom garners evidence from Leviticus 17 and Deuteronomy 16 to prove that any Jewish sacrifice or worship practice that does not take place in the Jerusalem Temple is not only invalid but also sinful. Since the Jerusalem Temple has been destroyed by Romans, he argues, any continuation of Jewish practice outside of the temple transgresses God's law.[37] In other words, Chrysostom insists that the error of Jews and Judaizers lies in temporal *and* spatial violations. Those late fourth-century Antiochenes who continue in Jewish practices have not only arrived at the game too late (after the coming of Christ); they also show up at the wrong place (outside Jerusalem).

It is in his argument for the spatial violation of continuing Jewish practice that Chrysostom develops a sexualized representation of the synagogue. Chrysostom argues that the law requiring sacrifices to be brought to the entrance of the tent of meeting (Lev 17:1–10)—and, later, the temple—indicates that God drew the Jews together in one place so that they would have no occasion for impiety. Chrysostom likens this situation of isolation to one in which a master isolates his unruly female slave in order to train her in *sōphrosynē* :

"When a noble and free man has a licentious [*akolaston*] female slave (who draws in all the passersby for licentiousness), he does not allow her to go out into the street, to be seen in the narrow way, or to rush into the marketplace; instead, he shuts her in the house, and chaining her with iron, he orders her to remain indoors all the time, in order that the narrowness of the place and the force of the chains will be her foundation for bodily self-control [*sōphrosynē*]" (124ra).

This whorish, shackled slave woman, Chrysostom maintains, represents the synagogue, "gaping after every demon and every idol." Because of the licentiousness and impiety of the synagogue, God confined the Jews to Jerusalem and their worship to the temple so that this single holy place might train them in the "law of piety" (124rb). But even in their confinement, he claims, they continued in impiety and prostitution.

Chrysostom continues to exploit this association of Jewish impiety and *porneia* by using the prophets Hosea, Jeremiah, and Ezekiel as biblical proof-texts. He turns to Ezekiel 16 to drive home his point. In Ezek 16:33–34, the prophet compares Jerusalem to an adulterous wife. Chrysostom uses this comparison to argue that the Jews (substituted here for Jerusalem) engaged in the worst form of prostitution—a "perversion beyond all women": rather than accepting payment in exchange for sex, the Jews "paid money for their own prostitution" (125ra). To summarize, Chrysostom characterizes the Jews en masse as a rebellious slave/whore whom God keeps in iron shackles to keep her from promiscuity and to train her in the ways of *sōphrosynē*. One of Chrysostom's central points in this sermon is to insist that Jews and Judaizing heretics advance from the "milk" of Judaism to the "solid food" of Christianity, and his portrayal of the synagogue as a promiscuous slave in need of ascetic training further solidifies his linkage of Judaism with *porneia* and Christian orthodoxy with sexual renunciation and bodily self-control. Moreover, Chrysostom's depiction of God as a cruel slave driver who shackles the Jews in iron chains suggests to the audience that the transformation of Jews and Judaizers into proper Christians necessitates certain acts of violence.

Halfway through his second sermon, Chrysostom turns from discussing the transgressions of Jews to addressing the transgressions of so-called Judaizers—specifically, Christians in his congregation who are going off to hear the trumpets hailing the festivals of the "delirious and mad Jews." He aligns this "impious" hearing of the Jews' trumpets with an adulterous gaze, quoting Jesus' teaching in the Sermon on the Mount: "The one who looks at a woman to desire her has already committed adultery with her in his heart"

(Matt 5:28). Chrysostom explains his analogy of hearing and sight: "For just as a licentious gaze produces adultery, so also ill-timed hearing works impiety" (128rb). Instead of committing this adultery of the ears, those who have strayed from the church to the festivals of the Jews should heed the trumpet of Paul—that "spiritual trumpet" who "leads you out to the battle against the demons" (128va).

Chrysostom constructs women, in particular, as vulnerable to the designs of predatory Judaizers. He develops this portrayal of women as acutely susceptible to Judaizing heresies in his second sermon, especially, and he remarks that most of those drawn to the synagogue are women (128vb–129ra).[38] Chrysostom argues that if a man is outraged by his wife's infidelity and punishes her accordingly, how much more he should be infuriated by the fact that she cavorts with demons (129ra). Husbands, he exhorts, should control their wives by preventing them from "running off" to join the Jews in their fasts and festivals. Drawing on the language of Paul in 1 Corinthians 14, Chrysostom states: "This is why he made you to be head of the wife . . . so that you, like a teacher, a guardian, a patron, might urge her to godliness. Yet when the hour set for the services summons you to the church, you fail to rouse your wives from their sluggish indifference. But now that the devil summons your wives to the feast of Trumpets and they turn a ready ear to his call, you do not restrain them. You let them entangle themselves in accusations of ungodliness; you let them be dragged off into licentious ways. For, as a rule, it is the prostitutes, the 'soft' men, and the whole chorus from the theater who rush to that festival" (*Adv. Jud.* 2.3.4; PG 48, 860–861).

Chrysostom here depicts women as particularly prone not only to Judaizing aggression (the call of the devil) but also to licentiousness in general. He encourages husbands to imitate Paul (and, by proxy, himself) in guarding, teaching, and admonishing women so as to prevent them from going astray. Sexualized invective lurks under the surface of Chrysostom's warnings to husbands: strong Christian men, he suggests, maintain control over their wives and keep them from falling into licentious ways. Jews and Judaizers, by contrast, illicitly "prey" upon women and encourage them to participate in shameless, indecent acts, such as the festivals and fasts of the Jews.

After urging Christian husbands to guard their wives from Judaizing aggressors, he adds one further warning: "Why do I speak of the *porneia* that goes on there [at the Jewish festivals]? Are you not afraid that your wife may not come back from there after a demon has possessed her soul? Did you not hear in my previous discourse the argument which clearly proved to us that demons dwell in the very souls of the Jews and in the places in which they gather?" (2.3.5; PG 48, 861).[39] By adding the threat of demon possession, Chrysostom accentuates the danger of female contact with Jews, and he links Jewish *porneia* to the sphere of the demonic.

Because of the heightened danger and defilement of Jews, their sacred spaces, and their ritual practices, Chrysostom cautions Christian men to keep their wives at home. In his fourth sermon, he warns: "If you refuse to let [your wives] go to the theater, you must refuse all the more to let them go to the synagogue. To go to the synagogue is a greater crime than going to the theater. What goes on in the theater is, to be sure, sinful; what goes on in the synagogue is godlessness" (4.7.3; PG 48, 881). As in his first sermon against the Jews, here Chrysostom compares the synagogue to a theater in order to shore up his claim that the synagogue is a locus of sexual promiscuity and shamelessness. It is, in his view, no place for a chaste and modest Christian woman to enter.

Sexual Stereotypes in the Remaining Sermons *Adversus Iudaeos*

Chrysostom depicts Jewish places of worship as sites of *porneia* twice more, in his sixth and seventh homilies. In his sixth sermon, he describes the former Jerusalem temple as a "brothel, a stronghold of sin, a lodging-place for demons, a fortress of the devil, the ruin of the soul, the precipice and pit of all perdition" (6.7.6; PG 48, 915). Similarly, in his seventh sermon, he describes the "licentiousness" of the festival of Sukkot: "Their trumpets were a greater outrage than those heard in the theaters; their fasts were more disgraceful than any drunken revel. So, too, the tents which at this moment are pitched among them are no better than the inns where harlots and flute girls ply their trades" (7.1.2; PG 48, 915).

As he does in his first sermon, in his sixth sermon Chrysostom turns to prophetic writings in an attempt to authorize his claims about Jewish *porneia*. For example, he refers to the allegory of the two sisters, Oholah and Oholibah, in Ezekiel 23 to associate Jews of his own day with biblical prostitutes.[40] He addresses his Jewish contemporaries: "It is not only now that your people are living sinful lives. Did you, in the beginning, live your lives in justice and good deeds? Is it not true that from the beginning and long before today you lived with countless transgressions of the law? Did not the prophet Ezekiel accuse you ten thousand times when he brought in the two harlots, Oholah and

Oholibah, and said, 'You built a brothel in Egypt; you were mad after barbarians, and you worshiped strange gods'?" (Ezek 23:5–9) (6.2.5; PG 48, 906). In this passage, Chrysostom utilizes the passage from Ezekiel to argue that Jews are not only licentious in present times but also in former times. By accentuating the continuity of Jewish *porneia* over time, Chrysostom endeavors to "naturalize" Jewish behavior as indelibly and inescapably sinful.

Another example of this association of present Jewish sins and past (biblical) sins occurs in Chrysostom's fourth sermon, when he interprets the story of Sodom and Gomorrah by arguing for the resemblance of Jews to the sinful inhabitants of these cities. Quoting Isa 1:10 ("Hear the word of the . . . Lord, you rulers of Sodom, give ear to the law of our God, you people of Gomorrah"), Chrysostom argues that the prophet spoke "not to those who lived in Sodom and Gomorrah, but to the Jews . . . because, by imitating their evil lives, the Jews had developed a kinship with those who dwelt in those cities" (4.6.2; PG 48, 879). Following this linkage of Jewish sins to the sexual sins of Sodom and Gomorrah, Chrysostom deploys prophetic images to reiterate and reify the relation between Jews and lustful animals. He claims that "the prophet" (without specifying which prophet) "thus called the Jews dogs and sex-crazed stallions—not because they suddenly changed natures with those beasts but because they were pursuing the lustful habits of those animals" (4.6.3; PG 48, 879).[41] Combining the image of the "dog" (Isa 56:10) with that of the "lustful stallion" (Jer 5:8), Chrysostom strives to legitimate his identification of Jews with licentious beasts by, first, referring to carefully selected (and decontextualized) biblical images of animals and, second, associating such animals with Jews of the biblical past and late ancient present. In these passages, Chrysostom intertwines accusations of sexual immorality with images of Jews as animals in order to paint Jews as subhuman pursuers of base pleasures.

Chrysostom's exegetical technique in these passages is to take prophetic denunciations out of their historical contexts, apply them to his Jewish contemporaries, and therefore establish an "eternal type": Jews of fourth-century Antioch, he argues, are as debased and immoral as their biblical counterparts whom the prophets condemned. According to Chrysostom's caricature, Jewish licentiousness and immorality are natural, self-evident, uncontestable, total, and consistent over time.[42] Chrysostom himself claims that he has "made the prophets [his] warriors against the Jews and routed them" (8.1.6; PG 48, 928). His construction of the Jew as a brute animal not only enhances his rhetoric of violence but also functions as a foil for his formulation of orthodox Christian (ascetic) identity.

Jewish Bodies, Christian Bodies

In an insidious turn in his first sermon against the Jews, Chrysostom utilizes prophetic images of animals to depict Jews as subjects of justified violence. In the following passage, he associates Jews with slaughtered animals by drawing on Hosea's image of the "stubborn heifer" and Jeremiah's image of the "untamed calf": "Although such beasts are unfit for work, they are fit for slaughter. And this is what happened to the Jews: while they were making themselves unfit for work, they grew fit for slaughter. This is why Christ said: 'But as for these my enemies, who did not want me to be king over them, bring them here and slaughter them' (Luke 19:27)" (1.2.6; PG 48, 846). In this passage, Chrysostom introduces the Greek term *sphazō*—to slaughter or butcher—and draws on passages from Hosea, Jeremiah, and the Gospel of Luke to embellish his characterization of Jews as animals deserving of death. Using biblical language as "proof," he thus imagines the Jewish body as a sacrificial animal body, "unfit for work" but "fit for slaughter."

According to Chrysostom, Jewish proclivities for gluttony and lasciviousness contribute to their bestial condition and their continual subjection to suffering and violence. He claims that "living for their bellies, [the Jews] gape for the things of this world, their condition is no better than that of pigs or goats because of their licentious [*aselgeias*] ways and excessive gluttony. They know but one thing: to be punched in the belly and to be drunk, to be cut up for the sake of dancing and to be wounded for the sake of charioteering" (1.4.1; PG 48, 848). Jews, in his representation, are preoccupied with the sphere of the *carnal*, and thus they should be treated as *carne*.[43]

In a dramatic reversal of his use of animal imagery to describe Jews, Chrysostom portrays *himself* as a ravenous beast, thirsty for confrontation with Jews. At the start of his sixth sermon, he exclaims: "Wild beasts are less savage and fierce as long as they live in the forests and have had no experience fighting men. But when the hunters capture them, they drag them into the cities, lock them in cages, goad them on to do battle with beast-fighting gladiators. Then the beasts spring upon their prey, taste human flesh and drink human blood. After that, they would find it no easy task to keep away from such a feast but they avidly rush to this bloody banquet. This has been my experience, too. Once I took up my fight against the Jews and rushed to meet their shameless assaults . . . I somehow acquired a stronger yearning to do battle against them" (6.1.1–2; PG 48, 903).[44]

Similarly, in his second sermon, he compares his pursuit of Jews and Judaizers to the hunt: "Like a pack of hunting dogs, let us circle about and surround our quarry; let us drive them together from every side and bring them into subjection to the laws of the church" (2.1.4; PG 48, 857). In these passages, Antiochene Christians are encouraged to follow their priest's lead and join the "hunt" to rout out Judaizing heretics within the church and subject them to Christian discipline ("the laws of the church"). Chrysostom justifies the use of force, then, by characterizing Jews as "animals fit for slaughter."[45]

Not only does Chrysostom encourage Christians to exercise a militant vigilance over the borders between Christianity and Judaism, but he also describes Roman imperial violence against the Jews as orchestrated by God. In his second sermon, Chrysostom argues that the Roman destruction of Jerusalem in 70 CE, for example, functioned as part of God's overarching plan to prod the Jews to follow Christ. Like a mother forcibly weaning her nursing child from milk (Judaism) to solid food (Christianity), God used Roman soldiers to force the Jews away from their holy city so that they would cease their inane sacrifices and recognize the "true sacrifice," Christ. Chrysostom states: "God, wishing to lead them to more solid food, but then seeing them continuously fleeing for refuge back to Jerusalem and the civic life there, cut off and fortified the city (like a mother [who weans her child] by putting bile and the bitterest juice on her nipple); with the fear of the Romans and imperial decrees, he made Jerusalem inaccessible to them, in order that, because of the desolation and the soldiers' weapons, the Jews would stay away from their fatherland and little by little become accustomed to casting off their desire for milk and falling upon a love and longing for solid food. For the emperors caused the desolation, but God set it in motion."[46]

By depicting the Roman destruction of Jerusalem as part of God's (motherly) direction and discipline of her children, Chrysostom suggests that violence against Jews is not only justified but theologically necessary. This cruelty is, after all, for the Jews' own good. In addition, Chrysostom aligns the work of the church with the work of the empire, especially as concerns the subjection of Jews. Christians of the late fourth century, he implies, could summon the power, glory, and triumph of first-century Romans as they despoiled Jerusalem, assured that they were united with the empire in their hatred of a common foe, the Jews.

If Chrysostom imagines the paradigmatic Jewish body as glutted, drunk, carnal, and fit for suffering, cruelty, and death, then how does he imagine the perfect Christian body? How does his representation of Jewish bodies in his sermons *Adversus Iudaeos* compare with his depiction of idealized Christian bodies in other sermons? When Chrysostom describes the spiritual Christian body, he accentuates its absolute distance from the realm of the carnal. Such is the case in his thirteenth homily on Romans, where he states: "The one who lives rightly is not even in the body . . . for the spiritual man was not even in the flesh from then on, having become from that moment an angel, and ascended into heaven, and from then on lightly carrying the body about" (*Hom. Rom.* 13.7; PG 60, 517–518). Whereas the Jewish body, on Chrysostom's model, is weighted to the earth, burdened with food, drink, and excessive desires, the Christian body is light and luminous. The spiritual Christian, trained in the discipline of worldly renunciation, can expect her "flesh" to become "entirely spiritual, crucified in all parts." Her body "flies with the same wings as the soul" (13.8; PG 60, 518).[47]

Through the discipline of worldly renunciation, the spiritual Christian offers her body as "living sacrifice" to God (Rom 12:1). Chrysostom elaborates on this "living sacrifice" by contrasting it with Jewish sacrifice. Whereas Christian sacrifice is spiritual, he argues, Jewish sacrifice is carnal. He argues that "to distinguish [this sacrifice] from the Jewish, [Paul] calls it 'holy, acceptable to God, your reasonable service.' For theirs was a bodily one, and not very acceptable" (20.1; PG 60, 595). In contrast to the carnal Jew, the spiritual Christian becomes "the light of the world." Waking each day before the sun—"healthy, wakeful, and sober"—she lives as angels live in heaven (*Hom. Matt.* 68.3; PG 58, 635).[48] The idealized Christian body becomes unspeakably beautiful, styled as it is after the image of Christ (*Hom. Col.* 8; PG 62, 353).

These themes of sexuality and renunciation loom so large in Chrysostom's sermons precisely because the fourth-century priest theorized orthodox Christian identity, in large part, by its relation to sexual chastity.[49] The purity of the idealized Christian ascetic functioned as a mirror for the purity of Christian orthodoxy in general. Although the pure Christian body was vulnerable to the invasion of various "diseases," this body refused to be adulterated by Jewish, pagan, and heretical practices. Chrysostom asserted, moreover, that the perfect spiritual body was free from pain, as the apostle Paul's body was when he endured "hunger, beatings, and prisons" (*Hom. Rom.* 13.8; PG 60, 518).[50] Paul's suffering, Chrysostom claimed, was "slight" and "momentary" precisely because he had successfully "trained the flesh to be in harmony with the spirit" (13.8; PG 60, 518).

Whereas Chrysostom imagined the idealized Christian body to be light, ascendant, and spiritual—incapable of feeling passion or bodily suffering—he constructed the Jewish body as the opposite of these things. It was a burdened, fat, inebriated body, continually subjected to oppression and pain on account of its indulgence of bodily appetites. By this vivid comparison of the spiritual Christian and the carnal Jew, Chrysostom endeavored to elaborate the absolute difference between Jewish and Christian identity. Religious identity was thus forged and "naturalized" through this very process of mapping difference onto the body.

Fixing Jewishness

Chrysostom utilized a variety of stereotypes to produce the Jew as Other—both as the (desiring and seductive) negation of the chaste Christian and as the carnal counterpart to the person of spirit. In particular, by his use of sexual stereotypes—including his characterizations of Jews as *malakoi* and *pornai* and Judaizers as sexual aggressors—he deployed categories of sexuality to denigrate Jewishness while, simultaneously, producing an orthodox Christianness as pure and sexually chaste. Chrysostom's sexualized portrayal of Jews functioned as a discursive strategy to "fix" the identity of the Other.

The work of postcolonial theorist Homi Bhabha helps to illuminate some of the dynamics at play in Chrysostom's sexualized representation of Jews.[51] In *The Location of Culture*, Bhabha analyzes how the stereotype functions as "the major discursive strategy" of colonial discourse.[52] According to Bhabha, the stereotype functions in a similar way to the concept of "fixity": "Fixity, as the sign of cultural/historical/racial difference in the discourse of colonialism, is a paradoxical mode of representation: it connotes rigidity and an unchanging order as well as disorder, degeneracy and daemonic repetition."[53] Using this theoretical frame, we find that Chrysostom's effort to "fix" Jewish identity betrays itself as such a "paradoxical mode of representation" because it attempts to construct the Jew as an "unchanging," "eternal" type—wholly differentiated from the Christian—while simultaneously gesturing to the disordered overlap and dangerous proximity of Jewish and Christian identities in his own congregation. Chrysostom's repeated attempts to erase the space of hybridity attest to the vulnerability of the very border lines that he wishes to defend, namely, the lines between Christianity and Judaism, orthodoxy and heresy.

According to Bhabha's understanding of the operations of colonialist discourse, the stereotype "is a form of knowledge and identification that vacillates between what is always 'in place,' already known, and something that must be anxiously repeated . . . as if the essential duplicity of the Asiatic or the bestial sexual license of the African that needs no proof, can never really, in discourse, be proved."[54] In this latter example, racial and sexual stereotypes combine to construct the African as subhuman—indeed, "bestial"—in comparison with his or her white colonialist counterparts. Building on the work of Frantz Fanon and Jacques Lacan, Bhabha contends that, in colonial discourse, difference is frequently articulated in terms of race *and* sexuality.[55] Indeed, the construction of colonial subjectivity and power depends, in part, upon such "anxiously repeated" representations of difference. Bhabha continues: "[E]pithets racial or sexual come to be seen as modes of differentiation, realized as multiple, cross-cutting determinations, polymorphous and perverse, always demanding a specific and strategic calculation of their effects. Such is . . . the moment of colonial discourse. It is a form of discourse crucial to the binding of a range of differences and discriminations that inform the discursive and political practices of racial and cultural hierarchization."[56]

Applying this theory of the stereotype in colonial discourse to Chrysostom's sermons *Adversus Iudaeos*, we find that the fourth-century Antiochene's use of sexual stereotypes in his own "ideological construction of otherness" functions in congruent fashion to that of nineteenth-century European colonizers. The Jews—configured by Chrysostom as the religious, cultural, and ethnic Other[57]—are said to embrace practices of *porneia* so abhorrent that any pure (orthodox) Christian should shun and denounce them entirely. In his sermons, Chrysostom "anxiously repeats" this point while gesturing to the very real experience of overlap, complexity, and hybridity within his community. At one point, Chrysostom even admits his own frustration with the dangerous intimacy of Jewish and Christian identities: "This is my strongest reason for hating the synagogue," he states. "[I]t has the law and the prophets. And now I hate it more than if it had none of these" (*Adv. Jud.* 6.6.9; PG 48, 913).[58] Faced with such a "territory without border lines"—where Christian-Jews share sacred texts, mingle in sacred spaces, and dance and feast together on holy days—Chrysostom resorts to the fierce rhetorical weapon of sexualized invective to delineate clear borders and construct rigid hierarchies between "Judaism" and "Christianity." In clarifying boundaries between religious identities, Chrysostom endeavors to "fix" Jewishness as indelibly licentious and debased.

The Introduction to this volume opened with a narrative of violence—a story related by Chrysostom that rhetorically aligned "Judaizing" heresy with violence toward women. But another form of violence was inscribed in and enabled by Chrysostom's text: Christian violence against Jews. Chrysostom's stereotypes of Jews and Judaizers—as licentious, predatory, sexually deviant, diseased, defiling, animalistic, carnal, and immoral—constituted a vicious rhetoric that created the conditions for (as well as the ecclesiastical justifications of) physical violence against Jews. Bhabha suggests that, in our analysis of stereotypes, we should move beyond "the ready recognition of images as positive or negative." Instead, our efforts should aim at "understanding the *processes of subjectification* made possible (and plausible) through stereotypical discourse."⁵⁹ According to Bhabha, we should engage with the image's "effectivity, with the repertoire of positions of power and resistance, domination and dependence that constructs . . . both colonizer and colonized."⁶⁰

What were the "processes of subjectification" made possible through Chrysostom's sermons *Adversus Iudaeos*? What were the possible (and plausible) material effects of his stereotypical discourse? What positions of "power and resistance, domination and dependence" were produced in and by this particular construction of Jewish and Christian identities? The Conclusion takes up some of these questions by exploring the material and social consequences of Christian anti-Jewish ideology in the decades immediately following Chrysostom's tenure in Antioch.

Conclusion

> The critique of violence must begin with the question of the representability of life itself.
> —Judith Butler, *Frames of War*

The representation of a person or groups of people as sexually abject—as sexually heretical—so often functions as a way to justify the use of force against those persons. We need look no further than the atrocities committed by members of the U.S. military at the prison in Abu Ghraib to find that the construction of the subject of violence relies, in part, upon the sensationalism of sexualized representation. The use of sexualized representation and violence as a means of cultural differentiation has a long history. Sexual heresy—however defined at a particular cultural moment—serves as a way to rationalize the domination, disenfranchisement, torture, or obliteration of the heretic.

In her 2009 book, *Frames of War*, Judith Butler reminds us that "the critique of violence must begin with the question of the representability of life itself."[1] I want to use this insight to draw some concluding thoughts and questions about Christian representations of Jews and Christian violence against Jews in late antiquity. I have argued here that the Christian portrayal of Jews as carnal and prone to sexual vice began not with Paul but with second-century writers such as Justin Martyr and the author of the *Epistle of Barnabas*, who (apart from and in contradistinction to Paul) maintained that *porneia* presented a crisis for the Jews because it interfered with their practices of biblical interpretation. Jews' inability to control bodily appetites contributed to their inability to interpret biblical texts properly, and vice versa. Justin and *Barnabas*'s constructions of Jewish *porneia* and carnality marked a sharp divergence from Paul's understanding of *porneia* as a problem of idolatrous Gentiles.

Over half a century after Justin's death, Origen developed his representation of Jews as carnal and licentious and, in the process, reintroduced Paul into the discussion to confer apostolic legitimacy on his particular construction of

Jews as literal (fleshly) interpreters. Like Justin and *Barnabas*, Origen imagined *porneia* as a peculiar hindrance to biblical interpreters; yet unlike Justin and *Barnabas*, he turned to Paul to prove his point. Paul's dyadic pairings of spirit/flesh and spirit/letter loomed large in the early Christian imagination, especially by the time of Origen. In Origen's hands, the positive category of "spirit" came to signify Christianness, while Jewishness was associated with the "flesh" and the "letter that kills" (2 Cor 3:6).[2] Jewish-Christian difference was theorized, in part, as the difference between flesh and spirit.[3]

In various performances of "spiritual" biblical interpretation, Origen reshaped Paul's language to bolster his claim that Jews are carnal interpreters of their own sacred texts. For Origen, Paul's phrase in 1 Cor 10:18—"Israel according to the flesh"—came to designate Jews of both past and present, especially those who clung to "outdated" literalist interpretations of scripture. In Origen's view, Jewish literalism and carnality functioned as foils for Christian spiritualism and *sōphrosynē*. Origen's formulation of a Christian exegetical practice thus coincided with his construction of Jewish exegesis as carnal, literal, and obsolete. Likewise, his formulation of a Christian practice of *askēsis* coincided with his construction of Jews as inescapably licentious.

Over a century after Origen's death, John Chrysostom denounced Jews and Judaizers as dangerously and perversely sexual. In more pronounced rhetoric than that of Origen, Justin, or *Barnabas*, Chrysostom accused Jews of sexually immoral practices and behaviors, including prostitution, effeminacy, and sexual violence. In his sermons, he invoked images of disease and contagion to depict Jews and Judaizers as polluting agents within the community. Jewishness was an "illness" threatening the "body of the church." Turning prophetic language and sacrificial imagery against the Jews, Chrysostom depicted them as beasts "fit for slaughter."

Stereotypes of Jews as sexually licentious, bestial, defiling, and diseased combined in Chrysostom's sustained construction of Jews as subjects of violence, where Jews were portrayed both as perpetrators of violence and as subject to a justified—even necessary—Christian violence. Such a rhetorical construction of Jews as licentious and polluting agents within the community occurred not only in theological treatises and sermons of the late fourth century but also in imperial laws of the period. Legal texts of the late fourth and fifth centuries associated Jewishness with "deformity and illness, pestilence, filth, abomination, death, infamy, and madness."[4] In 409 CE, for example, Honorius issued a law in the name of Theodosius II that condemned Christian conversion to Judaism, ruling that "those imbued in the Christian mysteries shall not be forced to adopt the Jewish perversity" (*Cod. Theod.* 16.8.19; SC 497, 397). In a law from 438, Theodosius II described Judaism as an "abominable sect" that "proliferates licentiously."[5] In addressing practical concerns of Jewish participation in Roman society (such as slave ownership, public administration, military service, and proselytism), many imperial laws of the late Roman era drew on certain negative stereotypes of Jews to justify limitation and diminishment of Jewish status. The ideology of Christian anti-Judaism mutually informed the legal regulations of Jewish participation in the civic life of the empire.[6] The rhetoric of anti-Jewish stereotypes shaped and produced the reality of Jewish disenfranchisement. Religious and legal representations of Jewish Otherness in these texts thus contributed to the production of the Jewish subject as worthy of Christian regulation and domination.

At the same time, some of the legislation from this era inaugurated protections for the Jews and placed limits on the destruction of synagogues and anti-Jewish rioting. In a series of laws issued during the end of the fourth century and the beginning decades of the fifth century, Roman legislators consistently recognized synagogues as sites worthy of some form of governmental protection.[7] In a law from 393, for example, Emperor Theodosius states that "the sect of the Jews is prohibited by no law," and thus the destruction of synagogues should be prevented: "[R]epress with due severity," orders Theodosius, "the excess of those who presume to commit illegal deeds under the name of the Christian religion and attempt to destroy and despoil synagogues" (*Cod. Theod.* 16.8.9; SC 497, 382–383). Arcadius (397), Honorius (412), and Theodosius II (420 and 423) issued similar edicts that condemned the "injuring and persecuting of Jews" and the "occupation" and burning of synagogues by Christians.[8] Several laws from the 420s and after, however, prohibited the building of new synagogues.[9]

Analyzing these laws, Amnon Linder notes: "Such relatively frequent legislation indicates that the government was not entirely effective in enforcing these laws." He goes on to indicate that from 415 on, "it is apparent that the authorities gradually yielded to the pressure of fanatical Christians."[10] The prohibition on the building of new synagogues represented a "concession to the apparently numerous bishops and monks who opposed the imperial protection of synagogues," as Seth Schwartz has observed.[11] In this context, the relationship between the rhetoric of legal texts and the reality of violence is complex, but one can infer from the number of laws concerning violence against Jews and destruction of synagogues that such violence did occur and that it prompted diverse and impassioned responses from governors, emperors, bishops, and monks.

One such bishop who famously opposed imperial protection of synagogues was Ambrose, bishop of Milan in the late fourth century. After Christians burned a synagogue in 388 in Callinicum, a city on the eastern frontier of the empire, Ambrose openly opposed Theodosius's ruling that the Christian community of Callinicum rebuild the synagogue at its own expense. In a letter to the emperor, Ambrose argues that the burning of a synagogue is a divinely sanctioned act, since "God himself" condemns the synagogue as a "home of perfidy, a house of impiety, and a refuge of madness."[12] Indeed, Ambrose states that he himself would gladly take the blame for the burning of the Callinicum synagogue, since such an act forcefully displays "the judgment of God" against those places "where Christ [is] denied."[13]

In his plea to the emperor, Ambrose calls to mind instances of Jewish violence against Christians in order to defend the current destruction of the Callinicum synagogue. He reminds the emperor that Jews burned Christian basilicas in Damascus, Gaza, Alexandria, and elsewhere during the reign of Julian.[14] Ambrose then insists that if the emperor concedes to the wishes of dishonest Jews, the latter will not cease in their accusations of Christians: "Whom will they not accuse," he asks, "even though they do not know them at all, so that they can witness innumerable files of chained members of the Christian community, see the necks of the faithful people yoked in captivity, so that the servants of God are buried in darkness, smitten with axes, delivered to the flames?"[15] Here Ambrose appeals to an image of Christian victimization at the hands of Jews in order to sway the emperor to side with the Christian bishop and militants of Callinicum.[16] Past Jewish violence against Christians is exploited (or invented) to justify present Christian violence against Jews.

Ambrose's rhetorical conjuring of images of imperiled Christian victims was nothing new. We have seen this strategy employed before by Justin, Hippolytus, Origen, and Chrysostom. What was new—and what Origen and Hippolytus, to a lesser extent, introduced to a Christian audience—was the image of the sexually imperiled Christian. Origen envisaged the Christian as a vulnerable and chaste *matrona* besieged by her (male) Jewish detractors. In this way, he used gender as a tool to map Jewish-Christian difference while simultaneously accentuating and, more importantly, sexualizing the threat that Jews pose to Christians. Over a century after Origen's death, John Chrysostom embellished this image of the sexually vulnerable Christian to justify his harsh stance against the Judaizing presence within his congregation. He conceived of

Jewishness not merely as a disease but as a contagious epidemic that spread by means of illicit Judaizing men who preyed upon innocent Christian women. Origen and Chrysostom thus used sexuality—that "dense transfer point for relations of power"—to depict Jews as "lions" who abused their power to exploit vulnerable Christian "lambs."

Whereas Ambrose's letter to Theodosius and imperial legislation of the late fourth and early fifth centuries attested to material violence against Jews perpetrated at the hands of Christians, the church fathers' sexualized caricatures of Jews enacted a kind of discursive violence. The anti-Jewish stereotypes of early Christian theological discourse—from *Barnabas* to Chrysostom—and the Christian attempts to erase Jewish space at the end of the fourth century and beginning of the fifth were not merely coincidental. Rather, the stereotypes of Jews in Origen's commentaries and Chrysostom's sermons contributed to a climate in which acts of violence against Jews were made thinkable, meaningful, even endorsed. Early Christian leaders' recourse to sexual and gendered invective in their production of Jewish-Christian difference marked an insidious "process of subjectification"—one that helped to create the conditions for programs of dehumanization and violence. The sexualized representation of Jews promulgated by church fathers at the close of the fourth century and the beginning of the fifth attested to the fathers' efforts to "seize absolute control" over the construction of the subject of violence: the Jew, the Judaizer, the heretic.[17]

Michael Gaddis has remarked that "discourse about violence affected the ways in which violence could be used in practice," signaling a complex, interactive relationship between the ideology and practice of violence in the late ancient Roman empire.[18] Gaddis recommends that historians identify the "ideas and communities of support" that underlay violent acts perpetrated by Christians against Jews, pagans, and "heretics."[19] He suggests, moreover, that "[i]n the late antique context, it is less important to tie particular violent acts to particular individuals than it is to explore the larger complex of attitudes, values, and prejudices that could give rise to such violence."[20] The present study has sought to demonstrate how sexual slander fit within the "larger complex of attitudes, values, and prejudices" toward Jews in late antiquity. To comprehend the anti-Jewish violence of this era, we must first understand the "representability" of Jewish life in early Christian discourses.

Sites of Injury, Sites of Resistance

Christian representations of Jews as debased subjects of justified violence constituted sites of injury. The discourses of stereotype, name-calling, and sexual slander examined here functioned not merely as linguistic devices of ancient invective but as performative acts that themselves produced reality for late ancient Jews and Christians. In her 1997 book, *Excitable Speech: A Politics of the Performative*, Judith Butler notes that "being called a name can be the site of injury," but she also maintains that name-calling can function, paradoxically, as the site of subversion and resistance. She writes that "this name-calling may be the initiating moment of a countermobilization. The name one is called both subordinates and enables, producing a scene of agency from ambivalence, a set of effects that exceed the animating intentions of the call."[21] In this way, Butler points to potentialities and possibilities that are opened up within the act of name-calling and within the language of hate speech.

Butler's observation here serves as a correlate to the Foucauldian understanding of the subject as constituted through practices of subjection that are potentially (and simultaneously) practices of freedom. The recognition that the subject is produced over time through practices of subjection may, at first, sound disheartening. Yet this recognition also means that the self can intervene (subversively, parodically, creatively) in its own formation.[22] In the case of hate speech, the injurious address ("Jew," "Judaizer," "*malakos*," "queer") is not assured success in injury, for these categories of identity (insofar as they are historically constituted and repeated over time) remain open to reinscription and remobilization.[23]

The Christian sexual slander against Jews that I have examined here was and is not the last word. In fact, the anti-Jewish rhetoric of the late ancient church fathers is exposed as vulnerable, limited, unstable, and unsuccessful precisely at those points in which it attempts to be most totalizing. Origen, for example, anxiously and repeatedly tries to typify the Jew as a carnal and literal reader of scripture, yet his claims founder insofar as Jewishness and the literal remain, in Origen's texts, as the founding site of the Christian reader's seduction through language. Origen's claim for the depravity of "fleshly" Jewish exegesis, moreover, unravels when faced with the fact that his "spiritual" interpretations of scripture so often derive from those of a Jewish exegete, Philo. Over a century after Origen, Chrysostom's rhetorical efforts to "fix" the Jew and Judaizing heretic as sexually deviant, lascivious, emasculated, bestial, and contagious are exposed as faulty and vulnerable, for these stereotypes must be repeated over and over again to counter the slippage between Christianity and Judaism, orthodoxy and heresy. The hybrid—the Christian-Jew-Judaizer-heretic—troubles Chrysostom's neat categorization of religious identity. The hybrid exposes the ambivalence and instability at the core of Christian orthodox attempts to circumscribe Christianity and Judaism as pure and mutually exclusive categories.[24] Despite desperate efforts, the church fathers who preached against Jews and Judaizers were never able to "seize absolute control" over the construction of the Jewish subject (or the Christian subject, for that matter).

Homi Bhabha says that the stereotype is a "limited form of otherness." The stereotype is always partial and incomplete in its masking of ambivalence.[25] By reading "otherness" as "at once an object of desire and derision," Bhabha reveals the "boundaries of colonial discourses" and the possibilities for transgression "of these limits from the space of that otherness."[26] Future research into the relationship between discursive and material violence in late antiquity should take into account the possibilities for resistance and transgression that are enabled by stereotypical discourse. In relation to the present project, in particular, we might ask: What are the positions of resistance and subversion made possible by the sexualized representation of Jews in late antiquity? And how did late ancient Jews contest and transgress the limits of Christian stereotypical discourse from the space of otherness?

Abbreviations

Ancient Texts

Adv. Jud.	John Chrysostom, *Adversus Judaeos*
1 Apol.	Justin Martyr, *First Apology*
Cels.	Origen, *Contra Celsum*
Cod. Theod.	*Codex Theodosianus*
Comm. Cant.	Origen, *Commentarius in Canticum*
Comm. Dan.	Hippolytus, *Commentarium in Danielem*
Comm. Matt.	Origen, *Commentarium in evangelium Matthaei*
Comm. Rom.	Origen, *Commentarii in Romanos*
Contempl.	Philo, *De vita contemplativa*
Dial.	Justin Martyr, *Dialogue with Trypho*
Diogn.	*Epistle to Diognetus*
Ep. Afr.	Origen, *Epistula ad Africanum*
Ep. Barn.	*Epistle of Barnabas*
Hist.	Tacitus, *Historiae*
Hom. Col.	John Chrysostom, *Homiliae in epistulam ad Colossenses*
Hom. Exod.	Origen, *Homiliae in Exodum*
Hom. Gen.	Origen, *Homiliae in Genesim*
Hom. Jer.	Origen, *Homiliae in Jeremiam*
Hom. Lev.	Origen, *Homiliae in Leviticum*
Hom. Luc.	Origen, *Homiliae in Lucam*
Hom. Matt.	John Chrysostom, *Homiliae in Matthaeum*
Hom. Num.	Origen, *Homiliae in Numeros*
Hom. Rom.	John Chrysostom, *Homiliae in epistulam ad Romanos*
Ign. *Eph.*	Ignatius, *To the Ephesians*
Ign. *Mag.*	Ignatius, *To the Magnesians*
Ign. *Phld.*	Ignatius, *To the Philadelphians*

Ign. *Rom.*	Ignatius, *To the Romans*
LXX	Septuagint
Mem.	Xenophon, *Memorabilia*
Migr.	Philo, *De migratione Abrahami*
NRSV	New Revised Standard Version
Paed.	Clement of Alexandria, *Paedagogus*
Princ.	Origen, *De principiis*
Quis Dives	Clement of Alexandria, *Quis dives salvetur*
Spec. Laws	Philo, *De specialibus legibus*
Strom.	Clement of Alexandria, *Stromateis*
T. Levi	*Testament of Levi*
Θ	Theodotion

Scholarly Journals and Series

AB	Anchor Bible
AJA	*American Journal of Archaeology*
AJSR	*Association for Jewish Studies Review*
ANF	Ante-Nicene Fathers
ATR	*Anglican Theological Review*
Aug	*Augustinianum*
Bib	*Biblica*
BibInt	*Biblical Interpretation*
CH	*Church History*
CSEL	Corpus Scriptorum Ecclesiasticorum Latinorum
FC	Fathers of the Church
GCS	Griechischen Christlichen Schriftsteller
GOTR	*Greek Orthodox Theological Review*
HTR	*Harvard Theological Review*
Int	*Interpretation*
JAAR	*Journal of the American Academy of Religion*
JBL	*Journal of Biblical Literature*
JEA	*Journal of Egyptian Archaeology*
JECS	*Journal of Early Christian Studies*
JHS	*Journal of the History of Sexuality*
JJS	*Journal of Jewish Studies*
JMEMS	*Journal of Medieval and Early Modern Studies*

JOR	*Journal of Religion*
JQR	*Jewish Quarterly Review*
JRE	*Journal of Religious Ethics*
JRS	*Journal of Roman Studies*
JSNT	*Journal for the Study of the New Testament*
JTS	*Journal of Theological Studies*
LCL	Loeb Classical Library
NovT	*Novum Testamentum*
NPNF	Nicene and Post-Nicene Fathers
NTS	*New Testament Studies*
PG	Patrologia Graeca
RB	*Revue Biblique*
REJ	*Revue des Études Juives*
RevScRel	*Revue des Sciences Religieuses*
RSR	*Recherches de Science Religieuse*
SBL	Society of Biblical Literature
SC	Sources Chrétiennes
ScrHier	*Scripta Hierosolymitana*
SPhilo	*Studia Philonica*
StPatr	*Studia Patristica*
TS	*Theological Studies*
VC	*Vigiliae Christianae*
ZAC	*Zeitschrift für Antikes Christentum*
ZEE	*Zeitschrift für Evangelische Ethik*
ZKG	*Zeitschrift für Kirchengeschichte*

Notes

INTRODUCTION

1. John Chrysostom, *Adv. Jud.* 1.3.4 (PG 48, 817).

2. This term is Chrysostom's own: "And what excuse do you have, you who are only half a Christian? [καὶ ποίαν ἕξεις συγγνώμην, Χριστιανὸς ὢν ἐξ ἡμισείας]" (ibid., 1.4.7 [PG 48, 849]).

3. Charlotte Fonrobert's analysis of this passage also views Chrysostom's narrative as strongly insinuating the threat of sexual violence. See Fonrobert, "Jewish Christians, Judaizers, and Anti-Judaism," in *Late Ancient Christianity*, ed. Virginia Burrus (Minneapolis: Fortress, 2005), 234–254, esp. 238.

4. *Adv. Jud.* 4.1.2 (PG 48, 871). See also ibid., 3.1.1 (PG 48, 862) and 8.3.10 (PG 48, 932).

5. Aphrahat, *Demonstrations* 18.1, 18.4, 18.5. I have used the English translation of *Demonstration* 18 found in Jacob Neusner's *Aphrahat and Judaism: The Christian-Jewish Argument in Fourth-Century Iran* (Atlanta: Scholars Press, 1971), 76–83. In places, I have also consulted the translations of Naomi Koltun-Fromm in her "Sexuality and Holiness: Semitic-Christian and Jewish Conceptualizations of Sexual Behavior," *VC* 54 (2000): 375–395. See Koltun-Fromm, *Hermeneutics of Holiness: Ancient Jewish and Christian Notions of Sexuality and Religious Community* (New York: Oxford University Press, 2010).

6. Aphrahat, *Demonstration* 18.12: "I write you my beloved concerning virginity and holiness [*qaddishutha*] because I have heard from a Jewish man who insulted one of the brothers, members of our congregation, by saying to him: 'You are impure, you who do not marry women; but we are holy [*qaddishin*] and better, we who procreate and increase progeny in the world.' On this account have I written you this argument."

7. Augustine, *Tractates against the Jews*, 7.9, in *Sermon against the Jews*, ed. M. Ligouri, FC 27 (Washington, D.C.: Catholic University of America Press, 1955), 387–414.

8. Daniel Boyarin opens his *Carnal Israel* with the same quotation from Augustine's *Tractates against the Jews* that I have used in the discussion above. Remarking on these lines from Augustine, Boyarin suggests: "This accusation against the Jews, that they are indisputably carnal, was a topos of much Christian writing in late antiquity. I propose … to account for this practice of Augustine and the others who characterize the Jews as carnal, indeed to assert the essential descriptive accuracy of the recurring Patristic notion that what divides Christians from rabbinic Jews is the discourse of the body, and especially of sexuality, in the two cultural formations"; Boyarin, *Carnal Israel: Reading Sex in Talmudic Culture*

(Berkeley: University of California Press, 1993), 2. Boyarin's suggestion here served as the initial provocation for the present study.

9. In regard to the ancient world, see, e.g., Jennifer Wright Knust, *Abandoned to Lust: Sexual Slander and Ancient Christianity*, Gender, Theory, and Religion (New York: Columbia University Press, 2006); Catharine Edwards, *The Politics of Immorality in Ancient Rome* (New York: Cambridge University Press, 1993); and Edith Hall, *Inventing the Barbarian: Greek Self-Definition through Tragedy* (New York: Oxford University Press, 1989). For an analysis of a more recent example of the relationship between sexualized representation and state violence, see Judith Butler's essays on the scenes of torture of Iraqi prisoners at Abu Ghraib, "Torture and the Ethics of Photography: Thinking with Sontag" and "Sexual Politics, Torture, and Secular Time," in *Frames of War: When Is Life Grievable?* (London: Verso, 2009), 63–100 and 101–136.

10. For an analysis of the ways that charges of sexism and homophobia among Arabs are mobilized as rationale for the West's violent intervention, see Butler, "Sexual Politics, Torture, and Secular Time."

11. Daniel Boyarin makes this point in the introduction to *Border Lines*: "The self-definition by certain Christians of Christianity over and against Judaism and the self-definition of orthodoxy as opposed to heresy are closely linked, for much of what goes under the name of heresy in these early Christian centuries consists in one variety or another of Judaizing, or, sometimes the opposite, as in the case of Marcion, of denying any connection with the Bible and the 'Jewish' God. Heresy, then, is always defined with reference to *Judaism*"; Boyarin, *Border Lines: The Partition of Judaeo-Christianity* (Philadelphia: University of Pennsylvania Press, 2004), 12.

12. Hybridity is a key term in Homi Bhabha's theory of colonialism. For Bhabha, the hybrid threatens structures of colonial and cultural domination insofar as it exposes an ambivalence and uncertainty at the heart of colonial power. The hybrid "breaks down the symmetry and duality of self/other, inside/outside"; Bhabha, *The Location of Culture* (London: Routledge, 1994), 165. Bhabha writes: "Hybridity represents that ambivalent 'turn' of the discriminated subject into the terrifying, exorbitant object of paranoid classification—a disturbing questioning of the images and presences of authority" (ibid., 162).

13. Daniel Boyarin and Virginia Burrus, "Hybridity as Subversion of Orthodoxy? Jews and Christians in Late Antiquity," *Social Compass* 52 (2005): 431–441, at 432.

14. Michel Foucault, *The History of Sexuality*, trans. Robert Hurley. 3 vols. (New York: Vintage, 1980–1988), 1:103.

15. For a discussion of the use of the term "sexuality" in regard to the ancient world, see David Halperin, John Winkler, and Froma Zeitlin (eds.), *Before Sexuality: The Construction of Erotic Experience in the Ancient Greek World* (Princeton, N.J.: Princeton University Press, 1990), 5–7.

16. See Ross Kraemer's insightful analysis of gendered invective in John Chrysostom's sermons *Adversus Iudaeos* in her "The Other as Woman: An Aspect of Polemic among Pagans, Jews, and Christians in the Greco-Roman World," in *The Other in Jewish Thought and History: Constructions of Jewish Culture and Identity*, ed. Laurence J. Silberstein and

Robert L. Cohn, New Perspectives on Jewish Studies (New York: New York University Press, 1994), 121–144.

17. See discussion in Alan D. Schrift, *Nietzsche's French Legacy: A Genealogy of Post-structuralism* (New York: Routledge, 1995), 47.

18. Michel Foucault, "An Aesthetics of Existence," in *Michel Foucault: Politics, Philosophy, Culture: Interviews and Other Writings 1977–1984*, ed. Lawrence D. Kritzman (New York: Routledge, 1988), 50–51.

19. Michel Foucault, "Why Study Power? The Question of the Subject," in *Michel Foucault: Beyond Structuralism and Hermeneutics*, ed. Herbert L. Dreyfus and Paul Rabinow (Chicago: University of Chicago Press, 1982), 212.

20. Judith Butler provides a helpful summary of the term *assujettissement*: "The term 'subjectivation' carries the paradox in itself: *assujettissement* denotes both the becoming of the subject and the process of subjection—one inhabits the figure of autonomy only by becoming subjected to a power, a subjection which implies a radical dependency. For Foucault, this process of subjectivation takes place centrally through the body." See Butler, *The Psychic Life of Power: Theories in Subjection* (Stanford, Calif.: Stanford University Press, 1997), 83.

21. Ibid., 90–94.

22. On the burning of synagogues, see Ambrose, *Epistula* 74, in J. H. W. G. Liebeschuetz, ed. *Ambrose of Milan: Political Letters and Speeches*, Translated Texts for Historians 43 (Liverpool: Liverpool University Press, 2005), 95–111. On the forced conversion of Jews, see Scott Bradbury, *Severus of Minorca: Letter on the Conversion of the Jews*, Oxford Early Christian Texts (Oxford: Oxford University Press, 1996). For a helpful analysis of this letter, see Ross Kraemer, "Jewish Women's Resistance to Christianity in the Early Fifth Century: The Account of Severus, Bishop of Minorca," *JECS* 17 (2009): 635–665.

23. See Seth Schwartz, *Imperialism and Jewish Society, 200 B.C.E to 640 C.E.* (Princeton, N.J.: Princeton University Press, 2001). On the building of new synagogues in the fifth and sixth centuries, see, e.g., Jodi Magness, "The Date of the Sardis Synagogue in Light of the Numismatic Evidence," *AJA* 109 (2005): 443–476.

24. Bhabha, *The Location of Culture*; Robert J. C. Young, *Colonial Desire: Hybridity in Theory, Culture and Race* (London: Routledge, 1995); and Ann Laura Stoler, *Carnal Knowledge and Imperial Power: Race and the Intimate in Colonial Rule* (Berkeley: University of California Press, 2002).

25. For the usefulness of postcolonial theory to the study of late antiquity, see, e.g., Andrew Jacobs, *Remains of the Jews: The Holy Land and Christian Empire in Late Antiquity* (Stanford, Calif.: Stanford University Press, 2004); Elizabeth Clark, *History, Theory, Text: Historians and the Linguistic Turn* (Cambridge, Mass.: Harvard University Press, 2004), 181–185; and Stephen D. Moore, *Empire and Apocalypse: Postcolonialism and the New Testament* (Sheffield: Sheffield Phoenix, 2006), 8–11.

26. As Jacobs argues; see Jacobs, *Remains of the Jews*, 200–209.

27. Young, *Colonial Desire*, 26. For an analysis of the way that sexuality functions in relation to colonial encounters in the Dutch West Indies, see Stoler, *Carnal Knowledge and Imperial Power*.

28. Denise Kimber Buell has demonstrated the relevance of racial and ethnic reasoning to ancient understandings of Christianness and Jewishness. See Buell, *Why This New Race? Ethnic Reasoning in Early Christianity* (New York: Columbia University Press, 2005).

29. Bhabha, *The Location of Culture*, 101.

30. Ibid., 94.

31. Ibid., 95.

32. Ibid., 153.

33. See Hall, *Inventing the Barbarian*, 125. For more on *sōphrosynē*, see Helen North, *Sophrosyne: Self-Knowledge and Self-Restraint in Greek Literature* (Ithaca, N.Y.: Cornell University Press, 1966). For the difference between *sōphrosynē* and *enkrateia* (continence), see discussion in Kate Cooper, *The Virgin and the Bride: Idealized Womanhood in Late Antiquity* (Cambridge, Mass.: Harvard University Press, 1996), 56.

34. See discussion in Hall, *Inventing the Barbarian*, 121–133.

35. C. Edwards, *The Politics of Immorality in Ancient Rome*, 12.

36. Minucius Felix, *Octavius*, 9 (LCL 250, 336).

37. Justin Martyr, *First Apology*, 9, in *Iustini Martyris: Apologiae pro Christianis*, ed. Miroslav Marcovich, Patristische Texte und Studien 38 (New York: De Gruyter, 1994).

38. Justin Martyr, *1 Apol.* 9.

39. Knust, *Abandoned to Lust*, 112.

40. For the linkage of sexual immorality and apostasy in the Septuagint, see Kathy Gaca, *The Making of Fornication: Eros, Ethics, and Political Reform in Greek Philosophy and Early Christianity* (Berkeley: University of California Press, 2003), 122–123.

41. For more on the construction of Jews as sexually virtuous and Gentiles as sexually and morally impure, see Jonathan Klawans, *Impurity and Sin in Ancient Judaism* (New York: Oxford University Press, 2000); and Christine Hayes, *Gentile Impurities and Jewish Identities: Intermarriage and Conversion from the Bible to the Talmud* (New York: Oxford University Press, 2002).

42. Christine Hayes notes the proximity of idolatry and sexual sin when she writes that "idols and idolatry defile in the same way that other heinous sins defile—most analogous, the sin of adultery or fornication" (Hayes, *Gentile Impurities*, 42).

43. *Letter of Aristeas*, 151–152, in *Aristeas to Philocrates*, ed. Moses Hadas, Jewish Apocryphal Literature (New York: Harper, 1951), 161.

44. *Sibylline Oracles*, 3:594–600, in *The Apocrypha and Pseudepigrapha of the Old Testament*, ed. R. H. Charles, 2 vols. (Oxford: Clarendon, 1913), 2:389.

45. Jennifer Knust writes of these biblical texts: "'Idolatry'—itself a term of opprobrium meaning 'worships other gods'—was figured as *znh* or *porneia*; one usually implied the other" (Knust, *Abandoned to Lust*, 53). She cites several biblical texts that contain this figuration, including Lev 18:24–30, 20:1–9; Exod 23:32–33, 34:15–16; Deut 31:16; Judg 2:17, 8:27; 1 Chron 5:25; and 2 Kings 9:22 (ibid., 191 n. 14).

46. Philo, *Contempl.* 22, in F. H. Colson, *Philo*, vol. 9, LCL (Cambridge: Harvard University Press, 1960), 125.

47. Philo, *Contempl.* 50–53 (Colson, 143–145).

48. Philo, *Contempl.*, 60 (Colson, 149).

49. Philo, *Contempl.*, 2 (Colson, 113–115): "The vocation of these philosophers is at once made clear from their title of Therapeutae and Therapeutrides, a name derived from θεραπεύω, either in the sense of 'cure' because they profess an art of healing better than that current in the cities which cures only the bodies, while theirs treats also souls oppressed with grievous and nearly incurable diseases, inflicted by pleasure and desires and grief and fear, by acts of covetousness, folly and injustice and the countless host of the other passions and vices."

50. Philo, *Spec. Laws* 3.40 (Colson, 501).

51. Ibid., 3.37–38 (Colson, 499).

52. Josephus, *Contra Apionem* 2.199, in *Josephus: Against Apion*, trans. I I. St. J. Thackeray, LCL (Cambridge: Harvard University Press, 1961), 1:373.

53. Tacitus, *Histories* 5.5, in *Greek and Latin Authors on Jews and Judaism*, ed. Menahem Stern, 2 vols. (Jerusalem: Israel Academy of Sciences and Humanities, 1974), 2:26.

54. Tacitus, *Hist.* 5.4 (Stern, *Greek and Latin Authors*, 2:25).

55. Tacitus, *Hist.* 5.5 (Stern, *Greek and Latin Authors*, 2:26).

56. Judith Lieu, "'Impregnable Ramparts and Walls of Iron': Boundary and Identity in Early 'Judaism' and 'Christianity,'" *NTS* 48 (2002): 297–313, at 303–304.

57. Meleager, in Stern, *Greek and Latin Authors*, 1:138.

58. Stern, *Greek and Latin Authors*, 1:524–525.

59. Ancient Greek and Roman accusations of Jewish macrophallia and sexual potency, which often accompanied critiques of circumcision, also functioned in this context of sexualized invective. See the discussion of the poems of Martial and Rutilius Namatianus in Peter Schäfer, *Judeophobia: Attitudes toward the Jews in the Ancient World* (Cambridge, Mass.: Harvard University Press, 1997), 100–102. Greek vase painters typically depicted slaves and barbarians with large circumcised penises. See Frederick M. Hodges, "The Ideal Prepuce in Ancient Greece and Rome: Male Genital Aesthetics and Their Relation to *Lipodermos*, Circumcision, Foreskin Restoration, and the *Kynodesme*," *Bulletin of the History of Medicine* 75 (2001): 375–405, esp. 393.

60. *T. Levi*, 14.1. *The Testament of the Twelve Patriarchs*, in *The Apocrypha and Pseudepigrapha of the Old Testament*, ed. R. H. Charles, 2:312. Scholars debate the origination of the Testaments and the level to which they have been Christianized. For more discussion of this debate, see John J. Collins, *Between Athens and Jerusalem: Jewish Identity in the Hellenistic Diaspora* (Grand Rapids, Mich.: Eerdmans, 1999), 154–156.

61. *T. Levi*, 14.5–8 (Charles, 2:312–313).

62. See the comments of Collins: "It also seems likely that some of the material was composed in circles opposed to the Hasmoneans in the second century BCE, and that these circles were Hellenized in language and ethics. These circles could have been located in Palestine or may have been part of the Jewish emigration to Egypt during the period after the revolt. Ultimately the ethics of the Testaments cannot be pinpointed as the product of a specific situation. They are of interest for our purpose as material which seems to have accumulated and circulated in Hellenized Jewish circles over two

hundred years and was eventually taken over by Christianity" (Collins, *Between Athens and Jerusalem*, 156).

63. To use the phrase of Stoler, *Carnal Knowledge and Imperial Power*, 44.

64. See discussion of this strategy in Knust, *Abandoned to Lust*, 148–149; and Pier Cesare Bori, *The Golden Calf and the Origins of the Anti-Jewish Controversy*, trans. David Ward, South Florida Studies in the History of Judaism 16 (Atlanta: Scholars Press, 1990). Italian original: *Il vitello d'oro: Le radici della controversia antigiudaica* (Turin: Boringhieri, 1983).

65. Dale Martin, *Sex and the Single Savior: Gender and Sexuality in Biblical Interpretation* (Louisville, Ky.: Westminster John Knox, 2006), 32.

CHAPTER 1

1. Church fathers such as Tertullian, Ambrose, John Chrysostom, and Augustine recognized the multivalence of *skeuos* and translated it variously as body, penis, and wife, depending on their aims. See Augustine, *Marriage and Desire*, 1.8.9, and *City of God*, 14.16; Ambrose, *Epistle 15*; and John Chrysostom, *Homilies on 1 Thess*, 5. For *skeuos* as "flesh," see Tertullian, *Resurrection of the Flesh*, 16. For the modern scholarly debate, see George Carras, "Jewish Ethics and Gentile Converts: Remarks on 1 Thes 4:3–8," in *The Thessalonian Correspondence*, ed. Raymond F. Collins (Leuven: Leuven University Press, 1990), 306–315.

2. Denise Kimber Buell and Caroline Johnson Hodge, "The Politics of Interpretation: The Rhetoric of Race and Ethnicity in Paul," *JBL* 123 (2004): 244.

3. For more on the discourse of self-mastery in ancient Greek and Roman texts, see Michel Foucault, *The Use of Pleasure*, vol. 2 of *The History of Sexuality* (New York: Vintage, 1985), and idem, *The Care of the Self*, vol. 3 of *The History of Sexuality* (New York: Vintage, 1986). For an analysis of how this discourse is developed in Paul's writings, see Stanley Stowers, *A Rereading of Romans: Justice, Jews, and Gentiles* (New Haven, Conn.: Yale University Press, 1994).

4. Foucault, *The Use of Pleasure*, 63–93.

5. Philo, *Spec. Laws* 1.149, in F. H. Colson, *Philo*, vol. 7, LCL (Cambridge, Mass.: Harvard University Press, 1950), 184.

6. See discussion in Dale Martin, *The Corinthian Body* (New Haven, Conn.: Yale University Press, 1995), 214.

7. For more on the relation of sexual and religious sin, see Peter Zaas, "Catalogues and Context: 1 Corinthians 5 and 6," *NTS* 34 (1988): 622–629; and Dale Martin, *Sex and the Single Savior* (Louisville, Ky.: Westminster John Knox, 2006), 39–42.

8. For more on the authorship of Ephesians and Colossians, see F. F. Bruce, *The Epistle to the Colossians, to Philemon, and to the Ephesians* (Grand Rapids, Mich.: Eerdmans, 1984).

9. After explicating the nature of sexual sin, Paul lists other (nonsexual) vices in Rom 1:29–31: "They were filled with every kind of wickedness, evil, covetousness, malice. Full of envy, murder, strife, deceit, craftiness, they are gossips, slanderers, God-haters, insolent, haughty, boastful, inventors of evil, rebellious toward parents, foolish, faithless, heartless, ruthless."

10. Stowers, *A Rereading of Romans*, 94.

11. For a discussion of this passage, see ibid., 83–125; and Dale Martin, "Heterosexism and the Interpretation of Romans 1:18–32," *BibInt* 3 (1995): 332–355.

12. Dale Martin accentuates this point most forcefully: "For Jews, the [decline of civilization] stories served to highlight the fallenness not of Jewish culture or even of humanity in general, but of the Gentiles due to the corruption brought about by civilization. *Porneia*, as the sin of the Gentiles par excellence, is a polluted and polluting consequence of Gentile rebellion" (Martin, "Heterosexism," 336).

13. The most vivid expression of Paul's exhortation to sexual purity occurs in 1 Corinthians 7.

14. See Stowers, *A Rereading of Romans*, 108–109.

15. For the interchangeability of *sarx* and *sōma* in, e.g., 1 Cor 7:28, see Robert Jewett, *Paul's Anthropological Terms: A Study of Their Use in Conflict Settings* (Leiden: Brill, 1971), 454. For an alternative view, see Daniel Boyarin, *A Radical Jew: Paul and the Politics of Identity* (Berkeley: University of California Press, 1994): "Paul … distinguishes between the flesh and the body. The flesh, i.e., sexuality, has been dispensed with in the Christian dispensation, precisely in order to spiritualize the body" (172).

16. For a longer passage in which Paul opposes *sarx* and *pneuma*, see Romans 7–8.

17. Paul may have in mind here God's commandment to the first couple in Gen 1:28: "Be fruitful and multiply, and fill the earth, and subdue it."

18. Boyarin explains his understanding of Paul's use of "flesh" as a signifier of sexuality and ethnic particularity: "[F]or Paul the term flesh enters into a rich metaphorical and metonymic semantic field bounded on the one hand by the metaphorical usages already current in biblical parlance and on the other hand by the dualism of spirit and flesh current in the milieu of Hellenistic—that is, first-century—Judaism. It was the working out and through of these multiple semantic possibilities that generated Paul's major semantic innovations. Flesh is the penis and physical kinship; it is the site of sexuality, wherein lies the origin of sin; it is also the site of genealogy, wherein lies the ethnocentrism of Judaism as Paul encountered it" (*A Radical Jew*, 68).

19. For more on Paul and the extirpation of desire, see Martin, *Sex and the Single Savior.*

20. Boyarin, *A Radical Jew*, 68.

21. Jewett, *Paul's Anthropological Terms*, 454.

22. Ibid. Boyarin develops Jewett's view of 1 Cor 10:18 by suggesting that the phrase "*kata sarka* itself is morally neutral, although always subordinated to *kata pneuma*" (Boyarin, *A Radical Jew*, 72).

23. For more discussion of the relationship between Paul's understanding of hermeneutics and the body, see Boyarin, "Paul and the Genealogy of Gender," in *Feminist Companion to Paul*, ed. Amy-Jill Levine (London: T. & T. Clark, 2004), 19; and idem, *A Radical Jew*, 69–81.

24. See Augustine, *Tractate against the Jews*, 7.9: "Behold Israel according to the flesh (1 Cor 10:18). This we know to be the carnal Israel; but the Jews do not grasp this meaning and as a result they prove themselves indisputably carnal."

25. See discussion in Boyarin, *A Radical Jew*, 73.

26. It is, in fact, Paul's opponents (so-called Judaizers) about whom Paul complains when he writes, "Even the circumcised do not themselves obey the law, but they want you to be circumcised so that they may boast about your flesh" (Gal 6:13). The same goes for Phil 3:2–4. Thus the accusations about "boasting in the flesh" or "mutilating the flesh" are aimed not at all Jews, in general, but, rather, at those (Jews and Gentiles) who hold that circumcision is necessary for believers in Christ.

27. For discussions of the reception of Paul's letters in the second century, see Wilhelm Schneemelcher, "Paulus in der griechischen Kirche des zweiten Jahrhunderts," *ZKG* 75 (1964): 1–20; and Andreas Lindemann, *Paulus im ältesten Christentum: Das Bild des Apostels und die rezeption der paulinischen Theologie in der frühchristlichen Literatur bis Marcion* (Tübingen: Mohr Siebeck, 1979), esp. 71–91.

28. E.g., on Clement's use of *Barnabas* in relation to animals and Jewish dietary laws, see *Strom.* 2.67.1–3 and *Paed.* 2.84–88.

29. *Barnabas* uses a similar source as that found in the *Didache*. See Bart Ehrman, *The Apostolic Fathers*, vol. 2, LCL 25 (Cambridge, Mass.: Harvard University Press, 2003), introduction to the *Epistle of Barnabas*, 4–5.

30. The critical edition is Robert A. Kraft and Pierre Prigent, *Épître de Barnabé*, SC 172 (Paris: Cerf, 1971). For a summary of the scholarship on the date and provenance of *Barnabas*, see Reidar Hvalvik, *The Struggle for Scripture and Covenant: The Purpose of the Epistle of Barnabas and Jewish-Christian Competition in the Second Century* (Tübingen: Mohr Siebeck, 1996), 17–42.

31. The author occasionally refers to this community as "the children of love"; see *Ep. Barn.* 21.9.

32. It may be that some people in his own community are espousing the view that the covenant belongs to both Israel and the followers of Christ. See *Ep. Barn.* 9.6.

33. Most of these commandments are found in Leviticus 11 and Deuteronomy 14.

34. F. H. Colson, *Philo*, 8:68.

35. See Mary Pendergraft, "'Thou Shalt Not Eat the Hyena': A Note on 'Barnabas' Epistle 10.7," *VC* 46 (1992): 75–79, for an examination of the zoological speculation about the genitalia of hyenas in antiquity and today. See also Robert M. Grant, "Dietary Laws among Pythagoreans, Jews, and Christians," *HTR* 73 (1980): 299–310, esp. 307, for a description of Clement's reception of *Ep. Barn.* 10.6–8.

36. See also *Epistle to Diognetus* 5.8.

37. The phrase is from Judith Lieu, *Christian Identity in the Jewish and Graeco-Roman World* (Oxford: Oxford University Press, 2004), 291.

38. The critical edition is Philippe Bobichon, *Justin Martyr, Dialogue avec le Tryphon: Édition critique* (Fribourg: Academic Press Fribourg, 2003). For an English translation, see Thomas B. Falls, *Saint Justin Martyr: Dialogue with Trypho*, FC 6 (Washington, D.C.: Catholic University of America Press, 1965). For the most part, I follow the translation of Falls. See Falls, *Saint Justin Martyr*, xv, for discussion of date and provenance.

39. See the discussion in Daniel Boyarin, *Border Lines: The Partition of Judaeo-Christianity*

(Philadelphia: University of Pennsylvania Press, 2004), 4, 43–44. See also Boyarin's argument in "Justin Martyr Invents Judaism," *CH* 70:3 (2001), 427–461; and Alain le Boulluec, *La notion d'hérésie dans la littérature grecque II–III siècles* (Paris: Études Augustiniennes, 1985), 1:21–91.

40. *Dial.* 119.5, 135.3, 140.1.

41. Justin insidiously argues that the only use of circumcision after the advent of Christ is to "mark [the Jews] off for the suffering [they] now so deservedly endure" (19.2). For an analysis of this claim, see Jennifer Knust, "Roasting the Lamb: Sacrifice and Sacred Text in Justin's *Dialogue with Trypho*," in *Religion and Violence: The Biblical Heritage*, ed. David Bernat and Jonathan Klawans, Recent Research in Biblical Studies 2 (Sheffield: Sheffield Phoenix, 2007), 100–113.

42. *Dial.* 19.5, 132.1, 133.

43. See Origen, *On First Principles* 4.1.6: "And we must add that it was after the advent of Jesus that the inspiration of the prophetic words and the spiritual nature of Moses' law came to light. For before the advent of Christ it was not at all possible to bring forward clear proofs of the divine inspiration of the old scriptures."

44. Samuel Krauss contends that this is the only instance in which a church father accuses Jews of polygamy. See Krauss, "The Jews in the Works of the Church Fathers," *JQR* 5 (1892): 122–157, esp. 129–130.

45. For more on Justin and his knowledge of Paul, see Rodney Werline, "The Transformation of Pauline Arguments in Justin Martyr's 'Dialogue with Trypho,'" *HTR* 92 (1999): 79–93.

46. Bart Ehrman, "Letters of Ignatius," in *The Apostolic Fathers*, LCL 24 (Cambridge: Harvard University Press, 2003), 1:201–321. I follow this translation, except where indicated. The critical edition is P. T. Camelot, *Ignace d'Antioche: Lettres. Lettres et Martyre de Polycarpe de Smyrne*, SC 10 (Paris: Cerf, 1969).

47. See also Ign. *Phld.* 6.1: "But if anyone should interpret Judaism to you, do not hear him. For it is better to hear Christianity from a man who is circumcised than Judaism from one who is uncircumcised."

48. I follow the translation of Ehrman, "Epistle to Diognetus," in *The Apostolic Fathers*, LCL 25 (Cambridge, Mass.: Harvard University Press, 2003), 2:121–159. The critical edition is Henri Marrou, *A Diognète: Introduction, édition critique, traduction et commentaire*, SC 29 (Paris: Cerf, 1951).

49. For more on how church fathers invoked the "difference in times" between the Hebrew past and Christian present, see Elizabeth Clark, *Reading Renunciation: Asceticism and Scripture in Early Christianity* (Princeton, N.J.: Princeton University Press, 1999), 145–152.

50. Melito, *On Pascha*, 50; see also 49: "An inheritance was left by him to his children; for he left his children as inheritance not chastity but *porneia*." Greek text and English translation in *Melito of Sardis: On Pascha and Fragments*, ed. Stuart George Hall (Oxford: Clarendon, 1979). I have also consulted the more recent English translation by Alistair Stewart-Sykes, *On Pascha: With the Fragments of Melito and Other Material Related to the Quartodecimans* (Crestwood, N.Y.: St. Vladimir's Seminary Press, 2001).

51. For Melito's strident anti-Judaism, which includes the charge of deicide, see *On Pascha*, 72–80.

CHAPTER 2

1. See the discussion of Origen's life in Joseph Trigg, *Origen* (London: Routledge, 1998), 3–14.

2. For more on Rufinus's translations of Origen's works, see Caroline Hammond Bammel, *Origeniana et Rufiniana* (Freiburg: Herder, 1996); and, more recently, Catherine M. Chin, "Rufinus of Aquileia and Alexandrian Afterlives: Translation as Origenism," *JECS* 18 (2010): 617–647.

3. See Joseph Trigg, *Origen: The Bible and Philosophy in the Third-Century Church* (Atlanta: John Knox, 1983), 3–7. Trigg states that Origen also began commentaries on Genesis and John while in Alexandria, but he completed these while living in Caesarea (idem, *Origen,* 17).

4. See Lee I. Levine, *Caesarea under Roman Rule,* Studies in Judaism in Late Antiquity (Leiden: Brill, 1975). For more on Origen and Caesarea, see Hans Bietenhard, *Caesarea, Origenes und die Juden* (Stuttgart: Kohlhammer, 1974); and John McGuckin, "Caesarea Maritima as Origen Knew It," in *Origeniana Quinta,* ed. Robert J. Daly (Leuven: Leuven University Press, 1992), 3–25.

5. L. Levine, *Caesarea under Roman Rule,* 2.

6. Ibid., 63; and McGuckin, "Caesarea Maritima as Origen Knew It," 5.

7. See discussion in L. Levine, *Caesarea under Roman Rule,* 61.

8. By use of the phrase "cultural hybridity," I mean to invoke Homi Bhabha's terminology. Hybridity, for Bhabha, signals "the 'inter'—the cutting edge of translation and negotiation, the *in-between* space—that carries the burden of the meaning of culture." See Bhabha, *The Location of Culture* (New York: Routledge, 1994), 38.

9. Origen, *Hom. Lev.* 5.8.3 (GCS 6, 349).

10. Origen, *Hom. Jer.* 12.13.1. *Origène: Homélies sur Jérémie,* trans. Pierre Husson and Pierre Nautin, SC 238 (Paris: Cerf, 1977), 46. For another instance in which Origen chastises members of his congregation for participating in Jewish practices, see Origen's *Comm. Matt.* 15 (PG 13.1621a).

11. Origen, *Hom. Jer.* 12.13.2 (SC 238, 46–48). For more on accusations of this "blurring of the lines" between Jews and Christians in Origen's work, see John McGuckin, "Origen on the Jews," in *Christianity and Judaism: Papers Read at the 1991 Summer Meeting and the 1992 Winter Meeting of the Ecclesiastical History Society,* ed. Diana Wood (Oxford: Blackwell, 1992), 1–13, at 4; and Nicholas de Lange, *Origen and the Jews: Studies in Jewish-Christian Relations in Third-Century Palestine* (Cambridge: Cambridge University Press, 1976), 89–102.

12. See, e.g., Origen, *Cels.* 4.34. *Origène: Contre Celse, 3–4,* trans. Marcel Borret, SC 136 (Paris: Cerf, 1968), 270. For a discussion of Origen's reliance on Jewish informants, see

Andrew Jacobs, *Remains of the Jews: The Holy Land and Christian Empire in Late Antiquity* (Stanford, Calif.: Stanford University Press, 2004), 60–67.

13. See discussion in de Lange, *Origen and the Jews*, 30–31. My primary interest in this chapter lies in examining Origen's textual representations of Jewish identity and interpretation. My analysis differs from other helpful scholarly works that consider Origen's relationships with Jews and his knowledge of Jewish and rabbinic traditions of interpretation. Books and articles on this latter subject include: Gustave Bardy, "Les traditions juives dans l'oeuvre d'Origène," *RB* 34 (1925): 217–252; Bietenhard, *Caesarea, Origenes und die Juden*; Paul Blowers, "Origen, the Rabbis, and the Bible: Toward a Picture of Judaism and Christianity in Third-Century Caesarea," in *Origen of Alexandria: His World and Legacy*, ed. Charles Kannengiesser and William L. Petersen (Notre Dame, Ind.: University of Notre Dame Press, 1988), 96–116; and de Lange, *Origen and the Jews*.

14. For the dating of Origen's texts, see Pierre Nautin, *Origène: Sa vie et son oeuvre* (Paris: Beauchesne, 1977).

15. See, esp., Prologue 1–2 of Origen's *Commentary on the Song of Songs*. Origen, *Commentaire sur le Cantique des Cantiques*, trans. Luc Brésard and Henri Crouzel, SC 375, 2 vols. (Paris: Cerf, 1991), 81–125. For more on Origen's views on virginity, see Henri Crouzel, *Virginité et mariage selon Origène*, Museum Lessianum, section théologique 58 (Paris: Desclée de Brouwer, 1963).

16. Origen, *Hom. Exod.* 1.1. *Origenes Werke: Homilien zum Hexateuch in Rufins Übersetzung*, ed. W. A. Baehrens, GCS 6 (Berlin: Akademie, 1920), 145.

17. Origen most likely has in mind Paul's imagery in 1 Cor 3:6–9: "I planted, Apollos watered, but God gave the growth. So neither the one who plants nor the one who waters is anything, but only God who gives the growth. The one who plants and the one who waters have a common purpose, and each will receive wages according to the labor of each. For we are God's servants, working together; you are God's field, God's building." Paul returns to agricultural imagery in 1 Cor 9:10–11 and 1 Cor 15:37–38.

18. Thanks to one of my anonymous readers for pointing this out.

19. For a helpful description of how Origen uses the term ἀναγωγή and other Greek exegetical terms, such as ἀλληγορία and θεωρία, see Robert Grant, *The Letter and the Spirit* (London: SPCK, 1957), appendix 2, 120–142.

20. For more on the influence of Hellenistic rhetoric and philosophy on Origen, see Bernhard Neuschäfer, *Origenes als Philologe*, Schweizerische Beiträge zur Altertumswissenschaft 18, 2 vols. (Basel: Reinhardt, 1987); and R. P. C. Hanson, *Allegory and Event: A Study of the Sources and Significance of Origen's Interpretation of Scripture* (Richmond, Va.: John Knox, 1959).

21. For more on Origen's use of Philo, see Annewies van den Hoek, "Philo and Origen: A Descriptive Catalogue of Their Relationship," *SPhilo* 12 (2000): 44–121; and David Runia, *Philo and the Church Fathers: A Collection of Papers*, supplements to *VC* 32 (Leiden: Brill, 1995).

22. See, esp., Origen, *Hom. Gen.* 6.1 (GCS 6, 66); *Cels.* 4.44 (SC 136, 298); and *Hom. Num.* 11.1. *Origène: Homélies sur les Nombres*, trans. Louis Doutreleau, SC 442 (Paris: Cerf, 1999), 20–22.

23. Hanson notes that, before Origen, Clement of Alexandria associated literalistic hermeneutics with Jewishness: "Clement of Alexandria before [Origen] had used the word 'Jewishly' [Ιουδαικῶς] to mean 'literally'" (Hanson, *Allegory and Event*, 237). Hanson also notes that Clement "associates literalism" with the adverb "carnally" (σαρκίνως). See Clement, *Paed.* 1.6.34 (PG 8.292) and *Quis Dives* 18.

24. Origen, *Princ.* 4.2.2. *Origène: Traité des Principes*, trans. Henri Crouzel and Manlio Simonetti, SC 268 (Paris: Cerf, 1980), 300. For a study of Rufinus's translation of *On First Principles* and a comparison between Rufinus's translation and the extant Greek fragments, see Nicola Pace, *Ricerche sulla tradizione di Rufino del "De principiis" di Origene* (Florence: La Nuova Italia Editrice, 1990).

25. On the point of Origen's expropriation of Jewish scriptures and, in particular, the prophets, see Karen Jo Torjesen, "The Rhetoric of the Literal Sense: Changing Strategies of Persuasion from Origen to Jerome," in *Origeniana Septima* (Leuven: Leuven University Press, 1999), 633–644, esp. 639.

26. Cf. *Homilies on Joshua* 17.1.

27. For a similar point, see Origen, *Hom. Gen.* 6.1.1 (GCS 6, 66): "Although no one of us can by any means easily discover what kind of allegories these words should contain, nevertheless one ought to pray that 'the veil might be removed' from his heart, 'if there is anyone who tries to turn to the Lord'—'for the Lord is spirit'—that the Lord might remove the veil of the letter and uncover the light of the Spirit."

28. See Origen, *Princ.* 4.2.8 (SC 268, 334): "For the intention was to make even the outer covering of the spiritual truths, I mean the bodily part of the scriptures [τὸ σωματικὸν τῶν γραφῶν], in many respects not unprofitable but capable of improving the multitude in so far as they receive it"; and *Princ.* 4.2.4 (SC 268, 310): "One must therefore portray the meaning of the sacred writings in a threefold way upon one's soul, so that the simple man may be edified by what we may call the flesh of the scripture [σαρκὸς τῆς γραφῆς], this name being given to the interpretation at hand [τὴν πρόχειρον ἐκδοχήν]; while the man who has made some progress may be edified by its soul . . . and the man who is perfect, . . . this man may be edified by the spiritual law." For more on the comparison of the text of scripture to a body, see Annewies van den Hoek, "The Concept of σῶμα τῶν γραφῶν in Alexandrian Theology," *StPatr* 19 (1989): 250–254; and David Dawson, "Plato's Soul and the Body of the Text in Philo and Origen," in *Interpretation and Allegory: Antiquity to the Modern Period*, ed. Jon Whitman, Brill's Studies in Intellectual History (Leiden: Brill, 2000), 89–107.

29. See Torjesen, "The Rhetoric of the Literal Sense," 639–640.

30. Virginia Burrus, *Saving Shame: Martyrs, Saints, and Other Abject Subjects* (Philadelphia: University of Pennsylvania Press, 2008), 70.

31. Ruth Clements, "(Re)Constructing Paul: Origen's Readings of Romans in *Peri Archon*" (SBL Seminar Papers, 2001), 157.

32. For a discussion of how 1 Cor 10:18 functions for Origen as a "hermeneutical key to the reading of scripture," see ibid., 164–165.

33. After making a set of promises to Abraham, God requires Abraham and his

offspring to circumcise all males as a sign of the covenant: "This is my covenant, which you shall keep, between me and you and your offspring after you: Every male among you shall be circumcised. You shall circumcise the flesh of your foreskins, and it shall be a sign of the covenant between me and you.... So shall my covenant be in your flesh an everlasting covenant" (Gen 17:10–11, 13b).

34. "For a person is not a Jew who is one outwardly, nor is true circumcision something external and physical. Rather, a person is a Jew who is one inwardly, and real circumcision is a matter of the heart—it is spiritual and not literal."

35. Cf. what he says in his twelfth homily on Jeremiah: "The Jew does not hear the Law in a hidden way. Because of this he is circumcised outwardly, for he does not know that he is not a Jew who is one outwardly, nor is circumcision something outward in the flesh. But he who hears of circumcision in a hidden way will be circumcised in secret" (*Hom. Jer.* 12.13; SC 238, 44).

36. Origen, *Hom. Gen.* 3.5 (GCS 6, 45). See, e.g., Origen's interpretation of Jer 6:10 ("Their ears are uncircumcised, they cannot listen"): "For let your ears be circumcised according to the word of God that they may not receive the voice of the detractor, that they may not hear the words of the slanderer and blasphemer, that they may not be open to false accusations, to a lie, to an irritation. Let them be shut up and closed 'lest they hear the judgment of blood' or stand open to lewd songs and sounds of the theater. Let them receive nothing obscene, but let them be turned away from every corrupt scene."

37. For Paul's figuration·of circumcision as "mutilation" of the flesh, see Phil 3:2 and Gal 5:12. For comments on Origen's ascetic interpretation of circumcision, see Elizabeth Clark, *Reading Renunciation: Asceticism and Scripture in Early Christianity* (Princeton, N.J.: Princeton University Press, 1999), 133–134.

38. In his extensive discussion of circumcision in the *Commentary on the Epistle to the Romans*, Origen admits that he knows of previous allegorical interpretations of circumcision that view it as the "cutting away" of vices. He most likely has in mind the work of Philo (*Migr.* 92; *Spec. Laws* 1.1–11) and Clement of Alexandria (*Strom.* 3.5). See Origen, *Comm. Rom.* 2.13.19. Origen speaks approvingly of Philo's allegorical interpretation of the Bible in *Cels.* 4.51 and 6.21.

39. Philo, *Migr.* 92 (Colson, 4, 184).

40. Philo, *Spec. Laws* 1.8–9 (Colson 7, 104).

41. Italics mine.

42. In a homily on Numbers, Origen counsels his congregation on the proper interpretation of the observance of the new moon: "If these things are considered according to the letter, they will seem more superstitious than religious. However, the apostle Paul knew that the law does not speak of these things and did not ordain that rite which the Jews observe." Origen, *Hom. Num.* 23.5.1 (SC 126, 128).

43. I borrow the term "displacement" from Ruth Clements, "*Peri Pascha*: Passover and the Displacement of Jewish Interpretation within Origen's Exegesis" (Th.D. diss., Harvard University, 1997), 11–20.

44. Clements, "(Re)Constructing Paul," 165, maintains that in Origen's works,

oppositions such as Jewish/Christian and flesh/spirit come to stand for each other and for other Pauline dyadic pairs, including "outward" and "inward" Jews (Rom 2:28–29) and "letter" and "spirit" (2 Cor 3:6). In book 4 of *On First Principles*, phrases such as "Israel according to the flesh" (1 Cor 10:18) and the "the letter that kills" (2 Cor 3:6) thus function as signifiers for "the Jews" and their corresponding reading practices.

45. Here I am influenced by the thinking of Clements, who writes: "Because [Origen] brings together diverse texts which pose differently nuanced oppositions—flesh/spirit, letter/spirit, shadow/heavenly things, above/below, life/death, 'outward'/'inward' Jews, circumcision of the flesh/circumcision of the heart, within the law/without the law, slavery/ freedom—all these oppositions come to stand for one another. In Origen's reading, 'flesh' must always exist in opposition to 'spirit,' so that 'Israel according to the flesh,' by whom Paul means the biblical Israelites, must exist in opposition to 'Israel according to the Spirit,' a phrase Paul himself never uses"; Clements, "(Re)Constructing Paul," 165.

46. McGuckin, "Origen on the Jews," 12–13. Peter Gorday offers a similar analysis of Origen's use of Paul: "Origen constructed his understanding of Paul around key passages: Rom 9:6–24; Rom 8:18–39; 1 Cor 15:20–28, 35–58; Col 1:15–20; Phil 2:5–11 appear most often in Origen's works" and that "1 Corinthians and Romans often appear together" (Gorday, "Paulus Origenianus," in *Paul and the Legacies of Paul*, ed. William S. Babcock [Dallas: Southern Methodist University Press, 1990], 141).

47. McGuckin writes: "The personal reshaping by Origen of the Pauline Jewish apologetic suggests someone whose dialogue with the Jewish tradition in Caesarea had been neither successful nor particularly happy" (McGuckin, "Origen on the Jews," 13). This in contrast to de Lange, who argues that Origen "is excellently placed to give a sympathetic outsider's view of the Jews of his day and of their relations with their non-Jewish neighbors" (de Lange, *Origen and the Jews*, 1).

48. For issues related to Rufinus's translation of Origen's *Commentary on the Epistle to the Romans* and the manuscript tradition, see the introduction in Caroline P. Hammond Bammel, *Der Römerbriefkommentar des Origenes: Kritische Ausgabe der Übersetzung Rufins*, Vetus Latina 16 (Freiburg: Herder, 1990); and idem, "Notes on the Manuscripts and Editions of Origen's Commentary on the Epistle to the Romans in the Latin Translation by Rufinus," *JTS* 16 (1965): 338–357. For Hammond Bammel's analysis of Origen's view of Jews in his *Commentary on the Epistle to the Romans*, see her "Die Juden im Römerbriefkommentar des Origenes," in idem, *Tradition and Exegesis in Early Christian Writers* (Aldershot: Variorum, 1995), 145–151.

49. Origen, *Comm. Rom.* Prologue 4. Origen claims that when Paul discusses the war of flesh against spirit (Gal 5:17), he does not refer to his own experience but rather adopts a "persona of a weaker person"; *Comm. Rom.* 6.9.11 (FC 41).

50. I have been influenced here by the thinking of Karen Jo Torjesen, who has argued that Origen envisions a spiritual and pedagogical transformation of the interpreter within the exegetical process. Whereas Torjesen views this spiritual transformation as a rational, theological, and pedagogical progression, I argue that it also entails a transformation of the body. See Torjesen, *Hermeneutical Procedure and Theological Method in Origen's Exegesis*

(Berlin: De Gruyter, 1986), 147. For an examination of the ascetic aspects of Origen's biblical interpretive process, see Peter W. Martens, "Interpreting Attentively: The Ascetic Character of Biblical Exegesis according to Origen and Basil of Caesarea," in *Origeniana Octava* (Leuven: Leuven University Press, 2003), 2:1115–1121.

51. See Clark, *Reading Renunciation*, 194, for an analysis of this passage.

52. For more on Origen's accusations of Jewish textual interpolation, see Chapter 3 in this volume.

53. In his allegorical interpretation of this story, Origen argues that the regions in which the "law" [Lot] dwells represent the Jews: "A city is so named from the manner of life of the multitude, because it orders and holds together the lives of many in one place. These, therefore, who live by the law have a small and petty manner of life as long as they understand the law literally. For there is nothing great in observing Sabbaths and new moons and circumcision of the flesh and distinctions between foods in a fleshly manner. But if someone should begin to understand spiritually, these same observances, which in the literal sense were small and petty, in a spiritual sense are not small, but great" (*Hom. Gen.* 5.5; GCS 6, 63).

54. Burrus explores how manhood was reconceived as more closely aligned with spiritual practices during the Trinitarian controversies in the late fourth century: "The emergent corpus of 'patristic' writings, authored predominantly by ascetic bishops deeply involved in the Trinitarian controversies of their day, now stands on the near side of a chronological watershed that it initially helped to create: receding is the venerable figure of the civic leader and familial patriarch; approaching is a man marked as a spiritual father, by virtue of his place in the patrilineal chain of apostolic succession, and also as the leader of a new citizenry, fighting heroically in contest of truth in which (as Gregory of Nyssa puts it) the weapon of choice is the 'sword of the Word'"; Virginia Burrus, *"Begotten Not Made": Conceiving Manhood in Late Antiquity* (Stanford, Calif.: Stanford University Press, 2000), 4–5. Origen's work suggests that this alignment of practices of spiritual interpretation and "maleness" was already under way in the third century.

55. See Peter Brown's statement about how "Christian males [of the early Christian] period partook in the deeply ingrained tendency of all men in the ancient world, to use women 'to think with.' There is no doubt that women played an important role in the imaginative economy of the Church. Their presence condensed the deep preoccupation of male Christians with their own relations with the 'world.'" In Brown, *The Body and Society: Men, Women, and Sexual Renunciation in Early Christianity* (New York: Columbia University Press, 1988), 153. See also Elizabeth Clark, "Holy Women, Holy Words: Early Christian Women, Social History, and the 'Linguistic Turn,'" *JECS* 6 (1998): 413–430, esp. 426–427.

56. Cf. Ann Laura Stoler, *Carnal Knowledge and Imperial Power: Race and the Intimate in Colonial Rule* (Berkeley: University of California Press, 2002); and Robert J. C. Young, *Colonial Desire: Hybridity in Theory, Culture and Race* (London: Routledge, 1995).

57. Stoler, *Carnal Knowledge and Imperial Power*, 44.

58. See David Dawson, *Christian Figural Reading and the Fashioning of Identity* (Berkeley: University of California Press, 2001), 234 n. 14.

59. Origen, *Comm. Cant.* Prologue 1.6 (SC 375, 84).

60. Origen does speak approvingly about the "Hebrews" and their use of the Song of Songs. He writes, "For they say that with the Hebrews also care is taken to allow no one even to hold this book in his hands who has not reached a full and ripe age. And there is another practice too that we have received from them—namely, that all the Scriptures should be delivered to boys by teachers and wise men, while at the same time the four that they call *deuteroseis*—i.e., the beginning of Genesis, in which the creation of the world is described; the first chapters of Ezekiel, which tell about the cherubim; the end of that same book, which contains the building of the Temple; and this book of the Song of Songs—should be reserved for study till the last." See *Comm. Cant.* 1.7 (SC 375, 84–86).

61. Patricia Cox Miller argues for the "seduction of language" with regard to Origen's first homily on the Song of Songs: "[I]n both the *Commentary* and the *Homilies* on the Song of Songs Origen develops a picture of the Bridegroom as *Logos*—as language—who woos, entices, and seduces the Bride, a figure for a reader or interpreter of texts. In this case, Origen's lament about the disappearing Bridegroom, more present than when he is absent, can be read as hermeneutical comment. The word that slips away at the moment when one thinks that one has 'laid hold of it,' only to return with promise of renewed meaning, and so on *ad infinitum*, forms a precise picture of the deferral of final meaning characteristic of the interpreter's abyss" (Miller, "Poetic Words, Abysmal Words: Reflections on Origen's Hermeneutics," in *Origen of Alexandria*, ed. Charles Kannengiesser and William L. Petersen [Notre Dame, Ind.: University of Notre Dame Press, 1988], 164–178, at 174–175).

62. Here I mean to invoke the title of Jacobs's book *The Remains of the Jews*.

63. See discussion in Andrew Jacobs, "Dialogical Differences: (De)Judaizing Jesus' Circumcision," *JECS* (2007): 291–335, esp. 304.

64. Ibid., 310.

CHAPTER 3

My chapter title is borrowed from the title of a book by Toril Moi: *Sexual/Textual Politics: Feminist Literary Theory* (New York: Metheun, 1985).

1. The *cappella greca* is so named because of the presence of two Greek inscriptions in the tomb. See James Stevenson, *The Catacombs: Rediscovered Monuments of Early Christianity* (London: Thames and Hudson, 1978), 154, for a description of the inscriptions and chapel. For more on the Catacomb of Priscilla, see Leonard Rutgers, *Subterranean Rome: In Search of the Roots of Christianity in the Catacombs of the Eternal City* (Leuven: Peeters, 2000).

2. Other facts about Hippolytus's life, including dates and birthplace, are subject to debate. Most commentators think that Hippolytus lived from 170 to 236. For the debate on Hippolytus, his location, and his corpus, see Pierre Nautin, *Hippolyte et Josipe: Contribution à l'histoire de la littérature chrétienne du troisième siècle* (Paris: Cerf, 1947); and, more recently, J. A. Cerrato, *Hippolytus between East and West: The Commentaries and*

the Provenance of the Corpus (Oxford: Oxford University Press, 2002). The critical edition of his commentary on Daniel is G. Nathanael Bonwetsch and Marcel Richard, *Hippolyt Werke: Kommentar zu Daniel*, 2nd ed., GCS 7 (Berlin: Akademie Verlag, 2000).

3. See Hippolytus, *Comm. Dan.* 1.26 (GCS 7, 56). Commenting on this fresco (Fig. 1), Kathryn Smith suggests that the image does more than just illustrate an event in the story: "[T]his image carried other associations as well, and it sent a much more highly charged message to the early Christian viewer than it does to the modern one. The ramifications of sight, and particularly touch, and their relation to *porneia* were integral aspects of contemporary debates around sexuality and salvation" (6). See K. Smith, "Inventing Marital Chastity: The Iconography of Susanna and the Elders in Early Christian Art," *Oxford Art Journal* 16 (1993): 3–24.

4. The critical edition of the additions to Daniel is Joseph Ziegler, *Susanna, Daniel, Bel et Draco*, Septuaginta, Vetus Testamentum Graecum auctoritate Societatis Gottingensis editum (Göttingen: Vandenhoeck & Ruprecht, 1954). For more on the additions to Daniel, see Carey A. Moore (ed.), *Daniel, Esther, and Jeremiah: The Additions*, AB 44 (Garden City, N.Y.: Doubleday, 1977), 23–149. For more on Susanna, in particular, see Helmut Engel, *Die Susanna-Erzählung: Einleitung, Übersetzung und Kommentar zum Septuaginta-Text und zur Theodotion-Bearbeitung* (Göttingen: Vandenhoeck & Ruprecht, 1985).

5. See C. Moore, *Daniel, Esther, Jeremiah*, 6, 25, 81.

6. Ibid., 86–87.

7. Ibid., 17; Marti Steussy, *Gardens in Babylon: Narrative and Faith in the Greek Legends of Daniel* (Atlanta: Scholars Press, 1993), 31; see also 28 for a discussion of the limited manuscript tradition of the Old Greek version of Susanna.

8. For a list of these references, see Armin Schmitt, *Stammt der sogenannte "θ"-Text bei Daniel wirklich von Theodotion?*, Mitteilungen des Septuaginta-Unternehmens, vol. 9 (Göttingen: Vandenhoeck & Ruprecht, 1966), 12–14. Schmitt uses these references to argue that Theodotion could not have been the author of the Greek text of Susanna that Origen attributes to him. See, esp., Matt 28:3 (Dan-θ 7:9) and Heb 11:33 (Dan-θ 6:22).

9. Steussy, *Gardens in Babylon*, 35.

10. For a discussion of the Theodotion changes, see Engel, *Die Susanna-Erzählung*, 181–183.

11. Noting that the Theodotion text "displaced" the Old Greek version sometime in the third century CE, Betsy Halpern-Amaru observes of the latter version: "[I]t is noteworthy that the elevation of heroic and villainous characterization over communal, legal issues and the absence of explicit, positive Jewish associations (i.e., no reference to Susanna as 'Jewess' and the synagogue no longer the scene of justice)—are particularly significant when the story becomes intertwined with the development of Christian self-definition." See Halpern-Amaru, "The Journey of Susanna among the Church Fathers," in *The Judgment of Susanna: Authority and Witness*, ed. Ellen Spolsky (Atlanta: Scholars Press, 1996), 21–34, at 24.

12. Although the story of Susanna had a long and substantial afterlife in Christian imagery and text, no surviving Jewish writer referred to this story until the eleventh century.

For a discussion of the Jewish reception of the story, see Israel Lévi, "L'histoire de Suzanne et les deux vieillards dans la littérature juive," *REJ* 95 (1933): 157–171.

13. See also Hippolytus, *Comm. Dan.* 1.17 (GCS 7, 38–40).

14. Hippolytus explains the purpose behind this temporal inversion and implosion: "This was done by the *oikonomia* of the spirit, in order that the devil might not understand the things spoken in parables by the prophets and might not ensnare and destroy man a second time" (*Comm. Dan.* 1.5; GCS 7, 12). For more on exegetical and rhetorical strategies that church fathers employed in ascetic interpretation, see Elizabeth Clark, *Reading Renunciation: Asceticism and Scripture in Early Christianity* (Princeton, N.J.: Princeton University Press, 1999), 104–152. Clark registers "textual implosion" as one of these strategies (132–134).

15. See also Hippolytus, *Comm. Dan.* 1.23 (GCS 7, 52), where Susanna "prefigures the mysteries of the church."

16. Hippolytus uses the phrase "Jews of the circumcision," which may signal that he borrows from Paul in Rom 2:28–29 a distinction between true "inward" Jews (i.e., Christians) and false "outward" Jews, characterized by "external," "physical" circumcision.

17. See entries for φθείρω and μιαίνω in *Theological Dictionary of the New Testament*, ed. Gerhard Kittel (Grand Rapids, Mich.: Eerdmans, 1967), 4:644–647 and 9:93–106.

18. For more on this comparison, see Hippolytus, *Comm. Dan.* 1.25, where Susanna's trial is compared with that of a martyr.

19. See ibid., 1.21 (GCS 7, 48–50). For other references to chastity in Hippolytus's commentary on Susanna, see 1.20, 22.

20. See Maud Gleason, *Making Men: Sophists and Self-Presentation in Ancient Rome* (Princeton, N.J.: Princeton University Press, 1995), 160. For an examination of how metaphors of gender and sex operate in more modern configurations of power relationships, especially with relation to colonial contexts, see Robert J. C. Young, *Colonial Desire: Hybridity in Theory, Culture and Race* (London: Routledge, 1995); Ann Laura Stoler, *Race and the Education of Desire: Foucault's* History of Sexuality *and the Colonial Order of Things* (Durham, N.C.: Duke University Press, 1995); and idem, *Carnal Knowledge and Imperial Power: Race and the Intimate in Colonial Rule* (Berkeley: University of California Press, 2002).

21. See discussion in Amy-Jill Levine, "Hemmed in on Every Side: Jews and Women in the Book of Susanna," in *A Feminist Companion to Esther, Judith, and Susanna*, ed. Athalya Brenner (New York: T. & T. Clark, 1995), 303–323, esp. 309.

22. See Andrew Jacobs, "The Lion and the Lamb: Reconsidering Jewish-Christian Relations in Antiquity," in *The Ways That Never Parted: Jews and Christians in Late Antiquity and the Early Middle Ages*, ed. Adam H. Becker and Annette Yoshiko Reed (Tübingen: Mohr Siebeck, 2003), 95–118, esp. 109.

23. Kimberly Stratton has analyzed how this dynamic functions in early Christian representations of male magicians and their female victims:

Christian depictions of *female* victims and *male* magicians reflect an ego identification on the part of these male writers with vulnerable but chaste female bodies over against the invasive violence of Rome. . . . The victimized women thereby serve as a trope for early Christian writers to locate themselves and their communities in opposition to Rome's power and violence, imagined in terms of the sexualized masculinity and aggression of the "magician." Competing forms of Christianity—so-called "heresies"—are likewise demonized through identification with the violent danger of the male "other." Through these rhetorically crafted representations, competing forms of Christianity are collapsed into the same ideological opposition that Rome similarly occupies: between aggressive threatening masculinity and the vulnerable body of the "virgin" church. (Stratton, "The Rhetoric of 'Magic' in Early Christian Discourse: Gender, Power, and the Construction of 'Heresy,'" in *Mapping Gender in Ancient Religious Discourses*, ed. Todd Penner and Caroline Vander Stichele [Leiden: Brill, 2007], 89–114, at 114)

See also idem, *Naming the Witch: Magic, Ideology, and Stereotype in the Ancient World* (New York: Columbia University Press, 2007).

24. See Daniel Boyarin, *Dying for God: Martyrdom and the Making of Christianity and Judaism* (Stanford, Calif.: Stanford University Press, 1999), 67–92, for a description of how constructions of gender and power intersect in similar ways in early Christian martyrological discourse.

25. The critical edition of Origen's *Letter to Africanus* is in *Origène: Sur les Écritures: Philocalie, 1–20 et la Lettre à Africanus sur l'histoire de Suzanne*, ed. Marguerite Harl and Nicholas de Lange, SC 302 (Paris: Cerf, 1983), 522–573.

26. Daniel Boyarin, *Carnal Israel: Reading Sex in Talmudic Culture* (Berkeley: University of California Press, 1993), 8–9.

27. Pierre Nautin, *Origène: Sa vie et son oeuvre* (Paris: Beauchesne, 1977), 182.

28. For more recent debates about the original language of Susanna, see F. Zimmerman, "The Story of Susanna and Its Original Language," *JQR* 48 (1957): 236–241; and C. Moore, *Daniel, Esther, and Jeremiah*, 81–84, as well as the discussion above.

29. Jer 29:22 reads: "And on account of them this curse shall be used by all the exiles from Judah in Babylon: 'The Lord make you like Zedekiah and Ahab, whom the king of Babylon roasted in the fire,' because they have perpetrated outrage in Israel and have committed adultery with their neighbors' wives, and have spoken in my name lying words that I did not command them" (NRSV). Although there is no mention of Susanna in rabbinic literature, there is a legend about Zedekiah and Ahab recorded in the Babylonian Talmud (Sanhedrin 93a). See Nehemiah Brüll, "Das apokryphische Susanna-Buch," *Jahrbuch für jüdische Geschichte und Literatur* 3 (1877): 1–69; and Max Wurmbrand, "A Falasha Variant of the Story of Susanna," *Bib* 44 (1963): 29–37.

30. Note that in *Ep. Afr.* 13, Origen refers to Heb 11:37 and Matthew 23 for "confirmation" that the Jews killed their prophets. The charge of Jewish sexual immorality is often accompanied by charges of Christ-killing and prophet-killing. See Pier Cesare Bori, *The Golden Calf and the Origins of the Anti-Jewish Controversy*, trans. David Ward (Atlanta: Scholars Press, 1990).

31. Origen is quoting Isa 1:10. Isaiah 1 includes an indictment of Israel for religious infidelity; it is thus a fitting passage for Origen to cite in his condemnation of Jewish exegetes: "Hear the word of the Lord, you rulers of Sodom! Listen to the teaching of our God, you people of Gomorrah! What to me is the multitude of your sacrifices? says the Lord" (Isa 1:10–11a). Note that elsewhere, Origen does not understand Sodom as signifying a site of sexual sins; rather, for him, Sodom is destroyed on account of its lack of hospitality. See Origen, *Hom. Gen.* 5.1, in *Origène: Homélies sur la Gènese*, ed. L. Doutreleau, SC 7 (Paris: Cerf, 1976).

32. Andrew Jacobs helpfully suggests that Origen's repeated references to his Jewish informants not only shore up his claims to understand Jewish texts and Jewish biblical interpretation but also establish legitimacy for his own Christian interpretations of Jewish texts: "At the same time that Origen complained that Jewish understanding of the Bible was too 'fleshly'—that is, too focused on the literal, nonspiritual interpretation of the text—he relied on their philological and geographical expertise in his own interpretive efforts to produce a thoroughly spiritualized interpretation of the Old and New Testaments" (Jacobs, *Remains of the Jews: The Holy Land and Christian Empire in Late Antiquity* [Stanford, Calif.: Stanford University Press, 2004], 62).

33. For more on how Origen imagines sacred text as a body, see Patricia Cox Miller, "'Pleasure of the Text, Text of Pleasure': Eros and Language in Origen's *Commentary on the Song of Songs," JAAR* 54 (1986): 241–253.

34. Origen, *Hom. Lev.* 1.1, in *Origène: Homélies sur le Lévitique*, ed. Marcel Borret, SC 286 (Paris: Cerf, 1981), 66.

35. For an analysis of lion and lamb imagery in early Christian texts, see Jacobs, "The Lion and the Lamb."

36. For a discussion of the rhetorical usefulness of this discourse, see Jacobs, *Remains of the Jews*, 66 and 66 n. 41. See also idem, "The Lion and the Lamb," 109; Judith Perkins, *The Suffering Self: Pain and Narrative Representation in the Early Christian Era* (London: Routledge, 1995); and Averil Cameron, *Christianity and the Rhetoric of Empire: The Development of Christian Discourse* (Berkeley: University of California Press, 1991), 111–112.

37. Boyarin, *Dying for God*, 67–92; and Virginia Burrus, *"Begotten Not Made": Conceiving Manhood in Late Antiquity* (Stanford, Calif.: Stanford University Press, 2000), 7.

38. Boyarin, *Dying for God*, 69.

39. Burrus, *Begotten Not Made*, 5. See also Gleason, *Making Men*, for a description of the construction of manhood in the Second Sophistic.

40. For an analysis of how gender operates in the story of Perpetua and Felicitas, see Elizabeth Castelli, "'I Will Make Mary Male': Pieties of the Body and Gender Transformation of Early Christian Women in Late Antiquity," in *Bodyguards: The Cultural Contexts of Gender Ambiguity*, ed. Julia Epstein and Kristina Straub (New York: Routledge, 1991), 29–49.

41. Boyarin, *Dying for God*, 75.

42. Burrus, *Begotten Not Made*, 21.

43. Gillian Clark writes: "Christians inherited a discourse of sexuality as invasive and

violent." See her "Bodies and Blood: Late Antique Debate on Martyrdom, Virginity and Resurrection," in *Changing Bodies, Changing Meanings: Studies on the Human Body in Antiquity*, ed. Dominic Montserrat (London: Routledge, 1998), 107.

44. See also Irenaeus, *Adversus Haereses*, 4.26, who associated the wicked elders with heretics.

45. See Halpern-Amaru, "The Journey of Susanna among the Church Fathers"; and K. Smith, "Inventing Marital Chastity," who argues that among Latin writers, esp. Ambrose and Augustine, Susanna is presented as a model of chastity within marriage.

46. Clement, *Strom.* 4.19, in *Les Stromates: Stromate IV*, ed. Annewies van den Hoek and Claude Mondésert, SC 463 (Paris: Cerf, 2001), 254.

47. Methodius, *Symposium* 11.2, in *Méthode d'Olympe: Le Banquet*, ed. Herbert Musurillo and trans. Victor-Henry Debidour, SC 95 (Paris: Cerf, 1963), 316–318.

48. Asterius, *Homily 6*, in *Asterius of Amasea: Homilies I–XIV: Text, Introduction, and Notes*, ed. C. Datema (Leiden: Brill, 1970), 59–64. See Genesis 39 for the story of Joseph and Potiphar's wife.

49. Pseudo-Chrysostom, "On Susanna" (PG 56, 589–594). Like Asterius, Pseudo-Chrysostom compares Susanna's courage in the face of struggle to that of Joseph (591). On the identity of Pseudo-Chrysostom, see Sever J. Voicu, "Uno pseudocrisostomo (Cappadoce?) lettore di origene alla fine del sec. IV," *Aug* 26 (1986): 281–293; and idem, "Trentatré omelie pseudocrisostomiche e il loro autore," *Lexicum philosophicum. Quaderni di terminologia filosofica e storia dell'idée* 2 (1986): 73–141.

50. "On Susanna" (PG 56, 591). For an English translation and discussion of this passage, see Bruce Metzger, *An Introduction to the Apocrypha* (New York: Oxford University Press, 1957), 112.

CHAPTER 4

1. See John Chrysostom, *Adv. Jud.* 1.2.7; 1.3.1; 1.6.8; 2.3.4; 4.7.3; 6.7.6 (PG 48, 846, 847, 852–853, 860–861, 881).

2. Ibid., 4.1.2 (PG 48, 871): "Today the Jews, who are more dangerous than any wolves, are bent on surrounding my sheep; so I must spar with them and fight with them so that no sheep of mine may fall victim to those wolves." See also ibid., 8.3.10 (PG 48, 932).

3. In his fourth sermon against the Jews, Chrysostom states: "It is against [the Jews] that I wish to draw up my battle line" (. . . ἐπειδὴ δὲ καὶ πρὸς ἐκείνους ἀποτείνασθαι βούλομαι) (ibid., 4.4.2; PG 48, 876). See also ibid., 4.3.4 (PG 48, 875), for another use of battle imagery.

4. In the 2001 issue of *ZAC*, Wendy Pradels, Rudolf Brändle, and Martin Heimgartner published notes and a German translation of a rediscovered text of John Chrysostom's second sermon (Discourse 2) of *Adversus Iudaeos*. This discovery led the authors to propose a new order and dating of Chrysostom's sermons *Adversus Iudaeos*—an order and dating that differs from the one followed by Bernard de Montfaucon and J. P. Migne in

PG. This proposal, along with a fresh translation of the entire series of sermons, will be published by these authors in a forthcoming volume of SC. See Pradels, Brändle, and Heimgartner, "Das bisher vermisste Textstück in Johannes Chrysostomus, *Adversus Judaeos*, Oratio 2," *ZAC* 5 (2001): 22–49; and idem, "The Sequence and Dating of the Series of John Chrysostom's Eight Discourses *Adversus Iudaeos*," *ZAC* 6 (2002): 90–116. Their proposal includes the removal of Discourse 3 from the series, as it "is contained in only a handful or manuscripts, always in isolation, and was never published as part of the series until it was inserted by Bernard de Montfaucon" ("The Sequence and Dating of the Series," 91). The new order is as follows, with proposed dates of each discourse in parentheses: Discourse 1 (August or September 386), Discourse 4 (29 August 387), Discourse 2 (5 September 387), Discourse 5 (9 September 387), Discourse 6 (10 September 387), Discourse 7 (12 September 387), and Discourse 8 (19 September 387) ("The Sequence and Dating of the Series," 106). Given the authors' argument that Discourse 3 does not belong among the original set of sermons *Adversus Iudaeos*, I have refrained from using Discourse 3 as part of the current study.

5. See Marcel Simon, *Verus Israel: A Study in the Relations between Christians and Jews in the Roman Empire (135–425)*, trans. H. McKeating (Oxford: Oxford University Press, 1986); Wayne Meeks and Robert Wilken, *Jews and Christians in Antioch in the First Four Centuries of the Common Era*, SBL Sources for Biblical Study 13 (Missoula, Mont.: Scholars Press, 1978); and Robert Wilken, *John Chrysostom and the Jews: Rhetoric and Reality in the Late Fourth Century*, Transformation of the Classical Heritage 4 (Berkeley: University of California Press, 1983).

6. Isabella Sandwell, *Identity and Religious Interaction in Late Fourth-Century Antioch: Greeks, Jews and Christians in Antioch* (Cambridge: Cambridge University Press, 2007).

7. Homi Bhabha, *The Location of Culture* (London: Routledge, 1994), 100.

8. See also Chrysostom, *Adv. Jud.* 1.2.1; 1.5.1; 5.1.7 (PG 48, 845, 850, 884).

9. In his *Dialogue with Trypho*, Justin Martyr argues that the purpose of Jewish circumcision "was that you and only you might suffer the afflictions that are now justly yours; that only your land be desolate, and your cities ruined by fire; that the fruits of your land be eaten by strangers before your very eyes; that not one of you be permitted to enter your city of Jerusalem" (*Dial.* 16). See Jennifer Knust's analysis of Justin's claim that acts of violence toward the Jews are divinely ordained in Knust, "Roasting the Lamb: Sacrifice and Sacred Text in Justin's *Dialogue with Trypho*," in *Religion and Violence: The Biblical Heritage*, ed. David Bernat and Jonathan Klawans (Sheffield: Sheffield Phoenix, 2007), 100–113.

10. Dayna Kalleres argues that in "*Adversus Iudaeos*, Chrysostom identifies the synagogue as the principle locus of the daemonic in Antioch; in particular, it was a place which his congregants frequently visited to forge oaths"; Kalleres, "Exorcising the Devil to Silence Christ's Enemies: Ritualized Speech Practices in Late Antique Christianity" (Ph.D. diss., Brown University, 2002), 5.

11. Chrysostom continues: "If you fail to sign your forehead, you have immediately thrown away your weapon at the doors. Then the devil will lay hold of you, naked and unarmed as you are, and he will overwhelm you with ten thousand terrible wounds."

12. At the close of his seventh sermon, Chrysostom states: "We have an eager and vigilant concern for our brothers who have deserted over to the Jewish side. When the Jews find this out, it will be they, rather than we, who thrust out those of our number who frequent the synagogue. I should say, there will be no one hereafter who will dare flee to them, and the body of the church will be unsullied and pure" (7.6.10; PG 48, 928).

13. For an analysis of images of purity and contagion in Chrysostom's *Adversus Iudaeos* sermons, see Christine Shepardson, "Controlling Contested Places: John Chrysostom's *Adversus Iudaeos* Homilies and the Spatial Politics of Religious Controversy," *JECS* 15 (2007): 483–516, esp. 501–506.

14. For more on Chrysostom's view of gluttony and drunkenness, see Teresa Shaw, *The Burden of the Flesh: Fasting and Sexuality in Early Christianity* (Minneapolis: Fortress, 1998), 131–139.

15. See also Isa 48:4: "Because I know that you are obstinate, and your neck is an iron sinew" (NRSV).

16. The quotation here is from Deut 32:15. Note how Chrysostom turns the figure of Moses against the Jews. This is one of several places in his work where biblical heroes and prophets are transformed to serve anti-Jewish ends.

17. See Catharine Edwards, *The Politics of Immorality in Ancient Rome* (New York: Cambridge University Press, 1993), 195. Edwards critiques David Halperin and Michel Foucault for too easily separating discourses about sex from other discourses about luxury and excess: "Despite the concern of these studies with attitudes rather than real behavior in the ancient world, they have offered relatively little exploration of the relationship between discussions of sexual immorality and those concerning other vices, areas which are intimately connected in ancient literature" (*Politics of Immorality*, 9).

18. Pradels, Brändle, and Heimgartner comment on the unique nature of this first sermon when they remark: "Though all of the sermons are polemical in nature, Discourse 1 is more constantly excessive than the others in its language, and moreover, it never progresses beyond polemics into the realm of complex theological considerations." They suggest that the "reader is given the impression that the first sermon took up a very controversial subject, one about which the orator had already received sharp criticism on the part of certain individuals in his congregation, and that his rather superficial, polemical treatment of the issue must have reaped even more criticism and debate. Thus he decided to treat the matter more thoroughly and carefully the following year" (Pradels, Brändle, and Heimgartner, "The Sequence and Dating of the Series," 110).

19. In his second sermon, Chrysostom depicts Paul as the best "huntsman" for pursuing Jews and Judaizers: "Let us send to pursue them the best of huntsmen, the blessed Paul.... If they hear the shout of Paul, I am sure that they will easily fall into the nets of salvation and will put aside all the error of the Jews" (2.1.4–5; PG 48, 857). For more on Chrysostom's anti-Jewish transformations of Paul's texts, see Margaret Mitchell, *The Heavenly Trumpet: John Chrysostom and the Art of Pauline Interpretation* (Louisville, Ky.: Westminster John Knox, 2002), 233 n. 147; Peter Gorday, *Principles of Patristic Exegesis: Romans 9–11 in Origen, John Chrysostom, and Augustine* (New York: Edwin Mellen, 1983);

and Andrew Jacobs, "A Jew's Jew: Paul and the Early Christian Problem of Jewish Origins," *JOR* 86 (2006): 258–286, esp. 268–271.

20. For an analysis of this passage and a history of the image of the "Jewish dog" in early Christianity and the Middle Ages, see Kenneth Stow, *Jewish Dogs: An Image and Its Interpreters: Continuity in the Catholic-Jewish Encounter* (Stanford, Calif.: Stanford University Press, 2006), 4–9.

21. For another example of Chrysostom's argument for complete Christian supersession of God's promises to Israel, see *Hom. Rom.* 16.

22. Stow notes that the dog, in particular, is regarded as excessively sexual in ancient times. Stow points to a rabbinic teaching "which explains that almost alone of the creatures on Noah's Ark, the dog dared copulate, promiscuously at that, while waiting out the flood." He continues: "It was just such a portrait of promiscuity that John Chrysostom was recalling, when, commenting on Matthew, he said that the Christians, who have become true children, have shed their 'irrational [pagan, carnal, and, in context, doglike] nature.' And for Chrysostom, as we have seen, the dogs were now the Jews and their synagogues, kennels" (Stow, *Jewish Dogs*, 8–9).

23. Note that Chrysostom connects the prophetic images of brute beasts to his accusations of Jews as gluttons and drunkards. The passage, in its entirety, reads: "But what is the source of this hardness? It comes from gluttony and drunkenness. Who says so? Moses himself. 'Israel ate and was filled and the darling grew fat and frisky' (Deut 32:15). When brute animals feed from a full manger, they grow plump and become more obstinate and hard to hold in check; they endure neither the yoke, the reins, nor the hand of the charioteer. Just so the Jewish people were driven by drunkenness and plumpness to the ultimate evil; they kicked about, they failed to accept the yoke of Christ, nor did they pull the plow of his teaching. Another prophet hinted at this when he said, 'Israel is as obstinate as a stubborn heifer' (Hos 4:16). And still another called the Jews 'an untamed calf'" (Jer 31:18)" (*Adv. Jud.* 1.2.5; PG 48, 846).

24. In several places, Chrysostom emphasizes that his accusations against the Jews are in accordance with biblical texts—texts that Jews themselves hold to be authoritative: "If the words I speak are the words of the prophet, then accept his decision" (*Adv. Jud.* 1.2.7; PG 48, 847); and "It was not Paul who said this but the voice of the prophet speaking loud and clear" (*Adv. Jud.* 1.2.4; PG 48, 846).

25. For a repetition of these accusations, see *Adv. Jud.* 2.3.4 (PG 48, 860–861): "You let them be dragged off into licentious ways. For, as a rule, it is the prostitutes, the 'soft men', and the whole chorus from the theater who rush to that festival [of the Trumpets]."

26. Dale Martin, "*Arsenokoitês* and *Malakos*: Meanings and Consequences," in *Sex and the Single Savior: Gender and Sexuality in Biblical Interpretation* (Louisville, Ky.: Westminster John Knox, 2006), 44. See also John J. Winkler, *The Constraints of Desire: The Anthropology of Sex and Gender in Ancient Greece* (New York: Routledge, 1990), 50–52, who provides this anecdote from Xenophon's *Memorabilia*: " 'Tell me, Charmides, if a man is capable of winning a crown at contests and thus being honored in his own person and making his fatherland more renowned in Greece but does not wish to compete, what kind

of person do you think this man would be?' 'Obviously a soft [*malakos*] and cowardly one'" (*Mem.* 3.7.1, quoted in Winkler, 50). Winkler helpfully notes that "one axis along which masculinity could be measured was hardness/softness" (50).

27. The term "gendered invective" is borrowed from Maud Gleason's *Making Men: Sophists and Self-Presentation in Ancient Rome* (Princeton, N.J.: Princeton University Press, 1995), 166.

28. C. Edwards's analysis of Roman accusations of *mollitia* is helpful in this context. Edwards suggests that "accusations of *mollitia* were not so much responses to 'effeminate' sexual behavior as attempts to humiliate. The terms referring to *mollitia* and related notions have a much broader frame of reference than the specifically sexual" (*Politics of Immorality*, 68).

29. Blake Leyerle, *Theatrical Shows and Ascetic Lives: John Chrysostom's Attack on Spiritual Marriage* (Berkeley: University of California Press, 2001), 46. For more on Chrysostom's linkage of the theater with sexual immorality, see 43–44.

30. *Hom. Matt.* 37.6 (PG 57.426–427). Quoted in Leyerle, *Theatrical Shows*, 67–68.

31. See C. Edwards, *Politics of Immorality*, who notes that Roman moralists, in particular, "characterized the theater as a storehouse of obscenity, a place where lust, laughter and political subversion were incited in almost equal measures. Actors were viewed as base persons, of ambiguous and venal sexuality, whose words could not be trusted" (99).

32. The *Epistle of Barnabas* also understands the hyena as a sexually deviant animal (see discussion of this in Chapter 1 of this volume). For more on ancient understandings of the hyena, see Mary Pendergraft, "'Thou Shalt Not Eat the Hyena': A Note on 'Barnabas' Epistle 10.7," *VC* 46 (1992): 75–79; and Stephen E. Glickman, "The Spotted Hyena from Aristotle to the Lion King: Reputation Is Everything," *Social Research* 62 (1995): 501–537. See also the comments on the hyena in the *Physiologus*, a Greek text of unknown authorship dated between the second and fourth centuries: "The law says, 'You shall not eat the hyena and whatever resembles it' (cf. Deut 14:8). *Physiologus* says about the hyena that it is a hermaphrodite: at times it becomes male and at times female. The beast is unclean because of changing its nature. That is why Jeremiah says, 'Is my heritage a hyena's den?' (cf. Jer 12:9). Likewise every 'double-minded man is unstable in all his ways' (cf. James 1:8); he is also like the hyena. And now there are many that enter this church [ἐκκλησίαν] in the form of men, and when they come out of the assembly [συναγωγῆς], they have the habits of women. So *Physiologus* spoke well about the hyena"; *Physiologus* 27, trans. Gohar Muradyan, *Physiologus: The Greek and Armenian Versions with a Study of Translation Technique* (Leuven: Peeters, 2005), 131–132, 158–159.

33. Paul Harkins notes: "Chrysostom's citation is not accurate. It may be a conflation of Jer 7:11 (LXX), which reads: 'Is my house a den of thieves?' and Jer 12:9 (LXX), which reads: 'Is not my inheritance to me a hyena's cave?'" (Paul W. Harkins, trans. *St. John Chrysostom: Discourses against Judaizing Christians*, FC 68. [Washington, D.C.: Catholic University of America Press, 1979], 11 n. 40).

34. I am reminded here of Leyerle's suggestion in her book on Chrysostom: "In such a society, the accusation of sexual shamelessness is both metaphor and punishment for social misbehavior" (*Theatrical Shows*, 152).

35. On the problem of "mixing" Jewish and Christian practices, see *Adv. Jud.* 4.3.6. On the mutual exclusivity of Judaism and Christianity, see 1.6.5 (PG 48, 852): "If the ceremonies of the Jews move you to admiration, what do you have in common with us? If the Jewish ceremonies are venerable and great, ours are lies. But if ours are true, as they *are* true, theirs are filled with deceit."

36. See Leviticus 17 and Deuteronomy 16.

37. John Chrysostom, *Adv. Iud.* 2 (Pradels, Brändle, Heimgartner, "Das bisher vermisste Textstück in Johannes Chrysostomus," 123va–124ra).

38. Virginia Burrus notes that heretical women are typically portrayed as sexually promiscuous: "[T]he fourth-century figure of the heretical woman, who is almost invariably identified as sexually promiscuous, expresses the threatening image of a community with uncontrolled boundaries. Just as she allows herself to be penetrated sexually by strange men, so too she listens indiscriminately and babbles forth new theological formulations carelessly and without restraint: all the gateways of her body are unguarded"; Burrus, "The Heretical Woman as Symbol in Alexander, Athanasius, Epiphanius, and Jerome," *HTR* 84 (1991): 229–248, at 232.

39. Note that the "previous discourse" to which he refers is his first sermon (*Adv. Jud.* 1.4.2), which he may have repeated before starting the series of sermons in autumn 387. See Pradels, Brändle, and Heimgartner, "The Sequence and Dating of the Series," 108–109.

40. Note that this is another instance in the writings of the prophets in which female prostitution signifies the apostasy of Israel. Such passages were particularly useful for church fathers who wanted to provide prooftexts for their configuration of Jews as carnal and licentious.

41. Note that he mixes his prophetic metaphors here. The image of the dog is from Isa 56:10 and the image of the lustful horse from Jer 5:8.

42. Considered in this way, Chrysostom's discourses against the Jews function in a parallel fashion to modern European discourses about "Orientals." In *Orientalism*, Edward Said writes:

> The figures of speech associated with the Orient . . . are all declarative and self-evident; the tense they employ is the timeless eternal; they convey an impression of repetition and strength; they are always symmetrical to, and yet diametrically inferior to, a European equivalent, which is sometimes specified, sometimes not. For all these functions it is frequently enough to use the simple copula *is*. . . . Philosophically, then, the kind of language, thought, and vision that I have been calling orientalism very generally is a form of *radical realism*; anyone employing orientalism, which is the habit for dealing with questions, objects, qualities and regions deemed Oriental, will designate, name, point to, fix, what he is talking or thinking about with a word or phrase, which then is considered either to have acquired, or more simply to be, reality. (Said, *Orientalism* [New York: Vintage, 1978], 72)

43. For more on Chrysostom's comparison of carnal and spiritual bodies, see *Hom. Rom.* 13.8: "For as they that have the wings of the spirit make the body spiritual, so they

who turn away, and are the slaves of the belly and of pleasure, make the soul flesh. . . . And this mode of speaking is a trope in many parts of the Old Testament also, where flesh signifies the gross and earthly life, which is entangled in unnatural pleasures" (PG 60, 517).

44. Note that gladiatorial games were in decline in the fourth century CE because of imperial prohibitions and decreasing funds for games. Chrysostom may be forging a link between the spectacle of Christian martyrdom and that of the gladiatorial games.

45. For his recommendation of the use of force when dealing with Jews and Judaizers, see *Adv. Jud.* 1.8.3–4 (PG 48, 856) and 5.1.5–6 (PG 48, 883).

46. John Chrysostom, *Adv. Iud.* 2 (Pradels, Brändle, and Heimgartner, "Das bisher vermisste Textstück in Johannes Chrysostomus," 127rb–127va).

47. Chrysostom explains the mechanics of this spiritual transformation of the flesh in the following passage. After quoting Rom 8:9 ("But you are not in the flesh, but in the spirit"), he states, "What then? Were they not in the flesh, and did they go about without any bodies? What sense would this be? You see that it is the carnal life that [Paul] intimates. And why did he not say, 'But you are not in sin'? It is that you may come to know that Christ did not extinguish the tyranny of sin only, but made the flesh to weigh us down less, and to be more spiritual, not by changing its nature but, rather, by giving it wings. For as when fire comes into contact with iron, the iron also becomes fire, though it stays in its own nature still; thus with them that believe, and have the spirit, the flesh from then on goes over into that manner of working and becomes wholly spiritual, crucified in all parts, and flying with the same wings as the soul" (13.8). For an analysis of how Chrysostom draws upon Plato's image of the winged soul, see Constantine Bosinis, "Two Platonic Images in the Rhetoric of John Chrysostom: 'The Wings of Love' and 'The Charioteer of the Soul,'" *StPatr* 41 (2006): 433–438.

48. For more on Chrysostom's views on asceticism and monasticism, see Martin Illert, *Johannes Chrysostomus und das antiochenische-syrische Mönchtum: Studien zu Theologie, Rhetorik und Kirchenpolitik im antiochenischen Schrifttum des Johannes Chrysostomus* (Zurich: Pano, 2000).

49. Peter Brown notes that "it was through such themes that John wished to express a new view of the civic community. The body and its vulnerability, and especially its universal vulnerability to sexual shame and to sexual temptation, became, for Chrysostom, the one sure compass that would enable the Christians of Antioch to find their way in an urban landscape whose ancient, profane landmarks, he so dearly hoped, would disappear"; Brown, *Body and Society: Men, Women, and Sexual Renunciation in Early Christianity* (New York: Columbia University Press, 1988), 306.

50. Chrysostom goes on to state: "Therefore [Paul] scorned all luxuriousness and pleasure, and found his luxury in hunger and beatings and prisons, and he did not even feel pain in these things. And this he shows when he says, 'For this slight momentary affliction . . .' (2 Cor 4:17); so well had he trained the flesh to be in harmony with the spirit."

51. Recently, some scholars of early Christianity and Judaism have found Bhabha's analysis of colonial discourse helpful for examining the construction of identity in late ancient religious texts. See, e.g., Daniel Boyarin and Virginia Burrus, "Hybridity as Subversion

of Orthodoxy? Jews and Christians in Late Antiquity" *Social Compass* 52 (2005): 431–441; David Brakke, *Demons and the Making of the Monk: Spiritual Combat in Early Christianity* (Cambridge, Mass.: Harvard University Press, 2006), esp. 157–181; Jacobs, *Remains of the Jews*; and Daniel Joslyn-Siemiatkoski, *Christian Memories of the Maccabean Martyrs* (New York: Palgrave Macmillan, 2009).

52. Bhabha, *Location of Culture*, 94.

53. Ibid.

54. Ibid., 94–95.

55. "The construction of the colonial subject in discourse, and the exercise of colonial power through discourse, demands an articulation of forms of difference—racial and sexual. Such an articulation becomes crucial if it is held that the body is always simultaneously (if conflictually) inscribed in both the economy of pleasure and desire and the economy of discourse, domination and power" (ibid., 96).

56. Ibid.

57. In his first sermon against the Jews, Chrysostom uses "ethnic reasoning" when he associates Christianness with Roman identity and Jewishness with barbarians and Persians. Comparing the "Judaizer" to a defecting Roman soldier, he writes: "If any Roman soldier serving overseas is caught favoring the barbarians and the Persians, not only is he in danger but so also is everyone who was aware of how this man felt and failed to make this fact known to the general. Since you are the army of Christ, be overly careful in searching to see if anyone favoring an alien faith has mingled among you" (*Adv. Jud.* 1.4.9; PG 48, 849–850).

58. Charlotte Fonrobert comments on this passage:

Perhaps for John the problem is not that his people socialize with the Jews per se but that the very boundaries between Jewish and Christian practice remain blurred and porous, at least in the eyes of his flock. We may suspect that he has to convince even himself of the absolute difference between Jewish and Christian practice, if we recall the old principle that the person who screams the loudest is often guilty of (or insecure about) the very thing he or she does not like. Exclaims the orator, famously: "This is the reason I hate the Jews, because they have the law and the prophets: indeed I hate them more because of this than if they did not have them." A shared biblical heritage, in other words, blurs the boundaries between Christianity and Judaism, boundaries that Chrysostom attempts to strengthen by the very force of his hatred. (Fonrobert, "Jewish Christians, Judaizers, and Christian Anti-Judaism," in *Late Ancient Christianity*, ed. Virginia Burrus [Minneapolis: Fortress, 2005], 234–254, at 238–239)

59. Bhabha, *Location of Culture*, 95, emphasis in original. See also Brakke's use of this passage from Bhabha in *Demons and the Making of the Monk*, 158.

60. Bhabha, *Location of Culture*, 95.

CONCLUSION

1. Judith Butler, *Frames of War: When Is Life Grievable?* (London: Verso, 2009), 51.

2. See discussion in Pier Cesare Bori, *The Golden Calf and the Origins of the Anti-Jewish Controversy*, translated by David Ward, South Florida Studies in the History of Judaism 16 (Atlanta: Scholars Press, 1990), 28.

3. See Elizabeth Clark's analysis of the variety of ways that church fathers utilized Paul's distinction between "flesh" and "spirit" to slander opponents and promote programs of Christian asceticism: *Reading Renunciation: Asceticism and Scripture in Early Christianity* (Princeton, N.J.: Princeton University Press, 1999), 330–370.

4. Amnon Linder, *The Jews in Roman Imperial Legislation* (Detroit: Wayne State University Press, 1987), 60. For a similar observation, see Theodor Mommsen et al. (eds.), *Les lois religieuses des empereurs romains de Constantin à Theodose II, 312–438*, vol. 1, *Code théodosien, livre XVI*, SC 497 (Paris: Cerf, 2005), 95.

5. Linder, *Jews in Roman Imperial Legislation*, 54.

6. See ibid., 54, where Linder writes that the legislation's "official origin and character make it particularly useful for observing the interplay between individuals and institutions, between *ideologies* and *practical contingencies*" (italics mine).

7. Ibid., 74.

8. *Cod. Theod.* 16.8.12–13; 16.8.20; 16.8.25 (SC 387, 399–400, 409–410); and Linder, *Jews in Roman Imperial Legislation*, 25, 40, and 46–49, esp. 48.

9. *Cod. Theod.* 16.8.22, 27 (SC 403–404, 412–413); and Linder, *Jews in Roman Imperial Legislation*, 49.

10. Linder, *Jews in Roman Imperial Legislation*, 74.

11. Seth Schwartz, *Imperialism and Jewish Society, 200 B.C.E. to 640 C.E.* (Princeton, N.J.: Princeton University Press, 2001), 195. Schwartz remarks that "the prohibition of synagogue construction provides us with an important warning about the functioning of the law because, as is well known, the great age of synagogue construction in Palestine was in the fifth and sixth centuries, precisely the period when such construction was illegal" (195).

12. Ambrose, *Epistula* 74.14. I have consulted the translation of J. H. W. G. Liebeschuetz in *Ambrose of Milan: Political Letters and Speeches*, Translated Texts for Historians 43 (Liverpool: Liverpool University Press, 2005), 95–111, esp. 102. The critical edition is *Sancti Ambrosi Opera. Pars X, Epistulae et acta*, ed. Michaela Zelzer, CSEL 82 (Vienna: Verlag der Osterreichischen Akademie der Wissenschaften, 1990).

13. Ambrose, *Epistula* 74.8 (Liebeschuetz, 100).

14. Ambrose, *Epistula*, 74.15 (Liebeschuetz, 103).

15. Ambrose, *Epistula* 74.19 (Liebeschuetz, 105).

16. As Thomas Sizgorich observes: "Ambrose insists that in the case of Callinicum, it was Christian individuals and the Christian community that were imperiled, that they were always imperiled. If Jews were given the benefit of law . . . they would lie and turn the force of Roman law once again against the Christian church, as they had against Christ."

See Sizgorich, *Violence and Belief in Late Antiquity: Militant Devotion in Christianity and Islam* (Philadelphia: University of Pennsylvania Press, 2009), 84.

17. In "Sexual Politics, Torture, and Secular Time," an essay on the torture of prisoners at Abu Ghraib, Judith Butler writes that in addition to understanding the torture as a violation of cultural and human rights, we must view "these scenes of sexual debasement and physical torture [as] part of the civilizing mission and, in particular, of its efforts to seize absolute control over the construction of the subject of torture" (*Frames of War*, 127–128).

18. Michael Gaddis, *There Is No Crime for Those Who Have Christ: Religious Violence in the Christian Roman Empire*, The Transformation of the Classical Heritage 39 (Berkeley: University of California Press, 2005), 3.

19. Ibid., 155.

20. Ibid. For other scholarly explorations of the relationship of rhetoric and violence, especially as it pertains to Chrysostom's anti-Jewish rhetoric, see Robert Wilken, *John Chrysostom and the Jews: Rhetoric and Reality in the Late Fourth Century* (Berkeley: University of California Press, 1983), esp. chaps. 4–5; Christine Shepardson, "Controlling Contested Places: John Chrysostom's *Adversus Iudaeos* Homilies and the Spatial Politics of Religious Controversy," *JECS* 15 (2007): 483–516; and Dayna Kalleres, "Exorcising the Devil to Silence Christ's Enemies: Ritualized Speech Practices in Late Antique Christianity" (Ph.D. diss., Brown University, 2002), 125–132.

21. Judith Butler, *Excitable Speech: A Politics of the Performative* (New York: Routledge, 1997), 163.

22. Butler explains Foucault on this point: "For Foucault, the subject who is produced through subjection is not produced at an instant in its totality. Instead, it is in the process of being produced, it is repeatedly produced (which is not the same as being produced anew again and again). It is precisely the possibility of a repetition which does not consolidate that dissociated unity, the subject, but which proliferates effects which undermine the force of normalization." In Judith Butler, *The Psychic Life of Power: Theories in Subjection* (Stanford, Calif.: Stanford University Press, 1997), 93.

23. As Virginia Burrus, following Butler, states: "Although perhaps less obvious than its historicity, the futurity of hate speech—its 'unfixed and unfixable' end—is equally crucial not only to its injurious power, but also to its *subvertability*. Put simply, the future of hate speech remains open because success in injury is not assured." Burrus, "Hailing Zenobia: Anti-Judaism, Trinitarianism, and John Henry Newman," *Culture and Religion* 3 (2002): 163–177, at 164.

24. The hybrid, in Bhabha's words, "reverses the effects of the colonialist disavowal, so that other 'denied' knowledges enter upon the dominant discourse and estrange the basis of its authority—its rules of recognition"; Homi Bhabha, *The Location of Culture* (New York: Routledge, 1994), 160.

25. Ibid., 111.

26. Ibid., 96.

Bibliography

ANCIENT WORKS

Ambrose of Milan. *Political Letters and Speeches.* Translated by J. H. W. G. Liebeschuetz. Translated Texts for Historians 43. Liverpool: Liverpool University Press, 2005.

———. *Sancti Ambrosi Opera. Pars decima, Epistulae et acta.* Edited by Michaela Zelzer. CSEL 82 (pts. 1–4). Vienna: Verlag der Osterreichischen Akademie der Wissenschaften, 1990–1996.

Aphrahat. *Demonstrations.* In *Aphrahat and Judaism: The Christian-Jewish Argument in Fourth-Century Iran,* edited by Jacob Neusner. Atlanta: Scholars Press, 1971.

Augustine. *City of God.* Vols. 1–7. Translated by G. E. McCracken et al. LCL. Cambridge, Mass.: Harvard University Press, 1957–72.

———. *Marriage and Desire.* In *Answer to the Pelagians,* vol. 2. Translated by Roland J. Teske and edited by John Rotelle. Hyde Park, N.Y.: New City Press, 1998.

———. *Tractate against the Jews.* In *Sermon against the Jews,* edited by M. Ligouri. FC 27. Washington, D.C.: Catholic University of America Press, 1955.

Clement of Alexandria. *Protrepticus und Paedagogus.* Edited by Otto Stählin and Ursula Treu. GCS. Berlin: Akademie, 1972.

———. *Les Stromates: Stromate IV.* Edited by Annewies van den Hoek and Claude Mondésert. SC 463. Paris: Cerf, 2001.

———. *Stromata.* Edited by Otto Stählin, Ludwig Früchtel, and Ursula Treu. GCS. Berlin: Akademie, 1985.

Epistle of Barnabas. Épître de Barnabé. Edited by Robert A. Kraft and Pierre Prigent. SC 172. Paris: Cerf, 1971.

Epistle to Diognetus. A Diognète: Introduction, édition critique, traduction et commentaire. Edited by Henri Marrou. SC 29. Paris: Cerf, 1951.

Hippolytus. *Hippolyt Werke: Kommentar zu Daniel.* Edited by Georg Nathanael Bonwetsch and Marcel Richard. GCS 7. Berlin: Akademie, 2000.

Ignatius of Antioch. *Ignace d'Antioche: Lettres et Martyre de Polycarpe de Smyrne.* Edited by P. T. Camelot. SC 10. Paris: Cerf, 1969.

Irenaeus. *Adversus Haereses.* In *Irenäus von Lyon. Epideixis. Adversus Haereses,* edited by Norbert Brox. 3 vols. Fontes Christiani. Freiburg: Herder, 1993.

John Chrysostom. *Adversus Judaeos.* Edited by J. P. Migne. PG 48. Paris, 1857–1866.

———. *Discourses against Judaizing Christians.* Translated by Paul W. Harkins. FC 68. Washington, D.C.: Catholic University of America Press, 1979.

———. *Homilies on Matthew*. Edited by J. P. Migne. PG 57. Paris, 1857–1866.

———. *Homilies on Romans*. Edited by J. P. Migne. PG 60. Paris, 1857–1866.

———. *Homilies on First Thessalonians*. Edited by J. P. Migne. PG 62. Paris, 1857–1866.

Josephus. *Against Apion*. Edited by H. St. J. Thackeray. LCL. Cambridge, Mass.: Harvard University Press, 1961.

Justin Martyr. *Dialogue avec le Tryphon: Édition critique*. Edited by Philippe Bobichon. Fribourg: Academic Press Fribourg, 2003.

———. *Dialogue with Trypho*. Translated by Thomas B. Falls. FC 6. Washington, D.C.: Catholic University of America Press, 1965.

———. *First and Second Apologies*. In *Iustini Martyris: Apologiae pro Christianis*, edited by Miroslav Marcovich. Patristische Texte und Studien 38. New York: De Gruyter, 1994.

Letter of Aristeas. Aristeas to Philocrates. Edited by Moses Hadas. Jewish Apocryphal Literature. New York: Harper, 1951.

Melito of Sardis. *On Pascha and Fragments*. Edited by Stuart George Hall. Oxford: Clarendon, 1979.

———. *On Pascha: With the Fragments of Melito and Other Material Related to the Quartodecimans*. Edited by Alistair Stewart-Sykes. Crestwood, N.Y.: St. Vladimir's Seminary Press, 2001.

Methodius. *Le banquet*. Edited by Herbert Musurillo, with translation and notes by Victor-Henry Debidour. SC 95. Paris: Cerf, 1963.

Minucius Felix. *Octavius*. In *Tertullian and Minucius Felix*, edited by Gerald H. Rendall. LCL. Cambridge, Mass.: Harvard University Press, 1966.

Origen of Alexandria. *Commentaire sur le Cantique des Cantiques*. Edited by Luc Brésard and Henri Crouzel. SC 375. 2 vols. Paris: Cerf, 1991.

———. *Contra Celsum. Origène: Contre Celse, 3–4*. Edited by Marcel Borret. SC 136. Paris: Cerf, 1968.

———. *Homélies sur la Genèse*. Edited by L. Doutreleau. SC 7. Paris: Cerf, 1976.

———. *Homélies sur Jérémie*. Edited by Pierre Husson and Pierre Nautin. SC 238. Paris: Cerf, 1977.

———. *Homélies sur le Lévitique*. Edited by Marcel Borret. SC 286. Paris: Cerf, 1981.

———. *Homélies sur les Nombres*. Edited by Louis Doutreleau. SC 442. Paris: Cerf, 1999.

———. *Homilien zum Hexateuch in Rufins Übersetzung*. Edited by W. A. Baehrens. GCS 30 Berlin: Akademie, 1920.

———. *Letter to Africanus. Origène: Sur les Écritures: Philocalie, 1–20 et la Lettre à Africanus sur l'histoire de Suzanne*. Edited by Marguerite Harl and Nicholas de Lange. SC 302. Paris: Cerf, 1983.

———. *On First Principles. Origène: Traité des principes*. Edited by Henri Crouzel and Manlio Simonetti. SC 268. Paris: Cerf, 1980.

———. *Der Römerbriefkommentar des Origenes: Kritische Ausgabe der Übersetzung Rufins*. Edited by Caroline P. Hammond Bammel. Vetus Latina 16. Freiburg: Herder, 1990.

Paul. *The Greek New Testament*. Edited by Kurt Aland, Matthew Black, et al. New York: American Bible Society, 1983.

Philo. *Philo*. Vols. 1–10. Edited by F. H. Colson and G. H. Whitaker. LCL. Cambridge, Mass.: Harvard University Press, 1956–1962.

Pseudo-Phocylides. *Sentences of Pseudo-Phocylides*. Edited by Walter T. Wilson. Berlin: De Gruyter, 2005.

Sibylline Oracles. In *The Apocrypha and Pseudepigrapha of the Old Testament*, edited by R. H. Charles. Vol. 2. Oxford: Clarendon, 1913.

The Testament of the Twelve Patriarchs. In *The Apocrypha and Pseudepigrapha of the Old Testament*, edited by R. H. Charles. Vol. 2. Oxford: Clarendon, 1913.

Theodosian Code. Les lois religieuses des empereurs romains de Constantin à Theodose II, 312–438. Vol. 1, *Code théodosien, livre XVI*. Edited by Theodor Mommsen, Jean Rougé, Roland Delmaire, and François Richard. SC 497. Paris: Cerf, 2005.

MODERN WORKS

Aland, Kurt. "Methodische Bemerkungen zum Corpus Paulinum bei den Kirchenvätern des zweiten Jahrhunderts." In *Kerygma und Logos: Beiträge zu den geistesgeschichtlichen Beziehungen zwischen Antike und Christentum*, edited by Adolf Martin Ritter. Göttingen: Vandenhoeck & Ruprecht, 1979, 29–48.

Allert, Craig D. *Revelation, Truth, Canon, and Interpretation: Studies in Justin Martyr's Dialogue with Trypho*. Leiden: Brill, 2002.

Babcock, William S., ed. *Paul and the Legacies of Paul*. Dallas: Southern Methodist University Press, 1990.

Bachmann, Michael. *Anti-Judaism in Galatians?: Exegetical Studies on a Polemical Letter and on Paul's Theology*. Translated by Robert L. Brawley. Grand Rapids, Mich.: Eerdmans, 2010.

Baer, Itzhaq. "Israel, the Christian Church, and the Roman Empire." *ScrHier* 7 (1961): 79–149.

Bailey, John W. "The First and Second Epistles to the Thessalonians." In *The Interpreter's Bible*. New York: Abingdon, 1955, 11:294–295.

Balch, David L. "Backgrounds of 1 Corinthians 7: Sayings of the Lord in Q, Moses as an Ascetic *Theios Anēr* in 2 Corinthians 3." *NTS* 18 (1971–1972): 351–364.

Bammel, Caroline Hammond. "Notes on the Manuscripts and Editions of Origen's Commentary on the Epistle to the Romans in the Latin Translation by Rufinus." *JTS* 16 (1965): 338–357.

———. *Origeniana et Rufiniana*. Freiburg: Herder, 1996.

———. *Des Römerbrief des Rufin und seine Origenes-Übersetzung*. Freiburg: Herder, 1985.

———. *Der Römerbriefkommentar des Origenes: Kritische Ausgabe der Übersetzung Rufins*. 3 vols. Freiburg: Herder, 1990–1998.

———. *Tradition and Exegesis in Early Christian Writers*. Aldershot: Variorum, 1995.

Bammel, Ernst. "Origen *Contra Celsum* 1.41 and the Jewish Tradition." *JTS* 19 (1968): 211–213.

Bardy, Gustave. "Les traditions juives dans l'oeuvre d'Origène." *RB* 34 (1925): 217–252.

Barnard, Leslie W. "The Date of the Epistle of Barnabas: A Document of Early Egyptian Christianity." *JEA* 44 (1968): 101–107.

———. *Justin Martyr: His Life and Thought.* Cambridge: Cambridge University Press, 1967.

Barrett, Charles K. "Pauline Controversies in the Post-Pauline Period." *NTS* 20 (1974): 229–245.

Barton, Carlin. *The Sorrows of the Ancient Romans: The Gladiator and the Monster.* Princeton, N.J.: Princeton University Press, 1993.

Basser, Herbert W. *Studies in Exegesis: Christian Critiques of Jewish Law and Rabbinic Responses 70–300 CE.* Leiden: Brill, 2002.

Bassler, Jouette M. *Divine Impartiality: Paul and a Theological Axiom.* Atlanta: Scholars Press, 1982.

Bauer, Walter. *Orthodoxy and Heresy in Earliest Christianity.* Philadelphia: Fortress, 1971.

Baumeister, Theofried. "Zur Datierung der Schrift an Diognet." *VC* 42 (1988): 105–111.

Baur, Chrysostom. *John Chrysostom and His Time.* 5 vols. Translated by M. Gonzaga. Westminster, Md.: Newman, 1960–1961.

———. *S. Jean Chrysostome et ses oeuvres dans l'histoire littéraire.* Louvain: Bureaux du Recueil, 1907.

Becker, Adam H., and Annette Yoshiko Reed, eds. *The Ways That Never Parted: Jews and Christians in Late Antiquity and the Early Middle Ages.* Texts and Studies in Ancient Judaism. Tübingen: Mohr Siebeck, 2003.

Becker, Jürgen. *Untersuchungen zur Entstehungsgeschichte der Testamente der zwölfe Patriarchen.* Leiden: Brill, 1970.

Beker, Johan Christiaan. *Heirs of Paul: Paul's Legacy in the New Testament and the Church Today.* Edinburgh: T. & T. Clark, 1992.

———. *Paul the Apostle: The Triumph of God in Life and Thought.* Philadelphia: Fortress, 1980.

Bellis, Alice Ogden. *Helpmates, Harlots, and Heroes: Women's Stories in the Hebrew Bible.* Louisville, Ky.: Westminster John Knox, 1994.

Berchman, Robert M. *From Philo to Origen: Middle Platonism in Transition.* Brown Judaic Studies 69. Chico, Calif.: Scholars Press, 1984.

Bhabha, Homi. *The Location of Culture.* New York: Routledge, 1994.

Biale, David. *Eros and the Jews: From Biblical Israel to Contemporary America.* Berkeley: University of California Press, 1997.

Bietenhard, Hans. *Caesarea, Origenes und die Juden.* Stuttgart: Kohlhammer, 1974.

Blowers, Paul. "Origen, the Rabbis, and the Bible: Toward a Picture of Judaism and Christianity in Third-Century Caesarea." In *Origen of Alexandria: His World and Legacy,* edited by Charles Kannengiesser and William L. Petersen. Notre Dame, Ind.: University of Notre Dame Press, 1988, 96–116.

Boitani, Piero. "Susanna in Excelcis." In *The Judgment of Susanna: Authority and Witness,* edited by Ellen Spolsky. Atlanta: Scholars Press, 1996, 7–20.

Bori, Pier Cesare. *The Golden Calf and the Origins of the Anti-Jewish Controversy.* Translated by David Ward. South Florida Studies in the History of Judaism 16. Atlanta: Scholars Press, 1990. Italian original: *Il vitello d'oro: Le radici della controversia antigiudaica.* Turin: Boringhieri, 1983.

Bosinis, Constantine. "Two Platonic Images in the Rhetoric of John Chrysostom: 'The Wings of Love' and 'The Charioteer of the Soul.'" *StPatr* 41 (2006): 433–438.

Bostock, Gerald. "Allegory and the Interpretation of the Bible in Origen." *Journal of Literature and Theology* 1 (1987): 39–53.

Boulluec, Alain le. *La notion d'hérésie dans la littérature grecque II–III siècles.* 2 vols. Paris: Études Augustiniennes, 1985.

Bousset, Wilhelm. *Die Religion des Judentums in neutestamentlichen Zeitalter.* Berlin: Ruether and Reichard, 1903.

Boyarin, Daniel. "Apartheid Comparative Religion in the Second Century: Some Theory and a Case Study." *JMEMS* 36 (2006): 3–34.

———. *Border Lines: The Partition of Judaeo-Christianity.* Philadelphia: University of Pennsylvania Press, 2004.

———. *Carnal Israel: Reading Sex in Talmudic Culture.* Berkeley: University of California Press, 1993.

———. *Dying for God: Martyrdom and the Making of Christianity and Judaism.* Stanford, Calif.: Stanford University Press, 1999.

———. *Intertextuality and the Reading of Midrash.* Indiana Studies in Biblical Literature. Bloomington: Indiana University Press, 1990.

———. "Justin Martyr Invents Judaism." *CH* 70:3 (2001): 427–461.

———. "Paul and the Genealogy of Gender." In *A Feminist Companion to Paul*, edited by Amy-Jill Levine with Marianne Blinckenstaff. London: T. & T. Clark, 2004, 13–41.

———. "Philo, Origen, and the Rabbis." In *The World of Egyptian Christianity: Language, Literature, and Social Context: Essays in Honor of David W. Johnson*, edited by James Goehring and Janet Timbie. Washington, D.C.: Catholic University of America Press, 2007, 113–129.

———. *A Radical Jew: Paul and the Politics of Identity.* Berkeley: University of California Press, 1994.

———. "Semantic Differences; or, 'Judaism'/'Christianity.'" In *The Ways That Never Parted: Jews and Christians in Late Antiquity and the Early Middle Ages*, edited by Adam H. Becker and Annette Yoshiko Reed. Tübingen: Mohr Siebeck, 2003, 65–86.

———. "The Subversion of the Jews: Moses's Veil and the Hermeneutics of Supersession." *Diacritics* 23 (1993): 16–35.

———, and Virginia Burrus. "Hybridity as Subversion of Orthodoxy? Jews and Christians in Late Antiquity." *Social Compass* 52 (2005): 431–441.

Bradbury, Scott. *Severus of Minorca: Letter on the Conversion of the Jews.* Oxford Early Christian Texts. Oxford: Oxford University Press, 1996.

Brakke, David. *Demons and the Making of the Monk: Spiritual Combat in Early Christianity.* Cambridge, Mass.: Harvard University Press, 2006.

———. "Ethiopian Demons: Male Sexuality, the Black-Skinned Other, and the Monastic Self." *JHS* 10 (2001): 501–535.

———. "Jewish Flesh and Christian Spirit in Athanasius of Alexandria." *JECS* 9 (2001): 453–482.

Brändle, Rudolf. *Die Ethik den "Schrift an Diognet": Eine Wiederaufnahme paulinischer und johanneischer Theologie am Ausgang des zweiten Jahrhunderts.* Zurich: Theologischer Verlag, 1975.

———, and Martin Wallraff, eds. *Chrysostomosbilder in 1600 Jahren: Facetten der Wirkungsgeschichte eines Kirchenvaters.* New York: De Gruyter, 2008.

Brenner, Athalya. *A Feminist Companion to Esther, Judith, and Susanna.* Sheffield: Sheffield Academic Press, 1995.

Brown, Peter. *The Body and Society: Men, Women, and Sexual Renunciation in Early Christianity.* New York: Columbia University Press, 1988.

Bruce, Frederick F. *1 and 2 Thessalonians.* Word Biblical Commentary 45. Waco, Tex.: Word Books, 1982.

———. *The Epistle to the Colossians, to Philemon, and to the Ephesians.* Grand Rapids, Mich.: Eerdmans, 1984.

Brüll, Nehemiah. "Das apokryphische Susanna-Buch." *Jahrbuch für jüdische Geschichte und Literatur* 3 (1877): 1–69.

Buell, Denise Kimber. "Race and Universalism in Early Christianity." *JECS* 10 (2002): 429–468.

———. *Why This New Race? Ethnic Reasoning in Early Christianity.* New York: Columbia University Press, 2005.

———, and Caroline Johnson Hodge. "The Politics of Interpretation: The Rhetoric of Race and Ethnicity in Paul." *JBL* 123 (2004): 235–251.

Burrus, Virginia. *"Begotten Not Made": Conceiving Manhood in Late Antiquity.* Stanford, Calif.: Stanford University Press, 2000.

———. "Carnal Excess: Flesh at the Limits of Imagination." *JECS* 17 (2009): 247–265.

———. "Hailing Zenobia: Anti-Judaism, Trinitarianism, and John Henry Newman." *Culture and Religion* 3 (2002): 163–177.

———. "The Heretical Woman as Symbol in Alexander, Athanasius, Epiphanius, and Jerome." *HTR* 84 (1991): 229–248.

———. *Saving Shame: Martyrs, Saints, and Other Abject Subjects.* Philadelphia: University of Pennsylvania Press, 2008.

Butler, Judith. *Excitable Speech: A Politics of the Performative.* New York: Routledge, 1997.

———. *Frames of War: When Is Life Grievable?.* London: Verso, 2009.

———. *The Psychic Life of Power: Theories in Subjection.* Stanford, Calif.: Stanford University Press, 1997.

Cameron, Averil. *Christianity and the Rhetoric of Empire: The Development of Christian Discourse.* Sather Classical Lectures 55. Berkeley: University of California Press, 1991.

———. "Redrawing the Map: Early Christian Territory after Foucault." *JRS* 76 (1986): 266–271.

Carras, George. "Jewish Ethics and Gentile Converts: Remarks on 1 Thes 4:3–8." In *The Thessalonian Correspondence*, edited by Raymond F. Collins. Leuven: Leuven University Press, 1990, 306–315.

Caspary, Gerard. *Politics and Exegesis: Origen and the Two Swords*. Los Angeles: University of California Press, 1979.

Castelli, Elizabeth. "'I Will Make Mary Male': Pieties of the Body and Gender Transformation of Early Christian Women in Late Antiquity." In *Bodyguards: The Cultural Contexts of Gender Ambiguity*, edited by Julia Epstein and Kristina Straub. New York: Routledge, 1991, 29–49.

Cerrato, J. A. *Hippolytus Between East and West: The Commentaries and the Provenance of the Corpus*. Oxford: Oxford University Press, 2002.

Chadwick, Henry. *Origen: Contra Celsum*. Cambridge: Cambridge University Press, 1965.

———. "Rufinus and the Tura Papyrus of Origen's Commentary on Romans." *JTS* 10 (1959): 10–42.

Chau, Wai-Shing. *The Letter and the Spirit: A History of Interpretation from Origen to Luther*. American University Studies. Theology and Religion 167. New York: Peter Lang, 1995.

Childs, Brevard. "The Sensus Literalis of Scripture: An Ancient and Modern Problem." In *Beiträge zur alttestamentlichen Theologie: Festschrift für Walther Zimmerli zum 70. Geburtstag*, edited by Herbert Donner, Robert Hanhart, and Rudolf Smend. Göttingen: Vandenhoeck & Ruprecht, 1977, 80–93.

Chin, Catherine M. "Rufinus of Aquileia and Alexandrian Afterlives: Translation as Origenism." *JECS* 18 (2010): 617–647.

Clark, Elizabeth. "Foucault, the Fathers, and Sex." *JAAR* 56 (1988): 619–641.

———. *History, Theory, Text: Historians and the Linguistic Turn*. Cambridge, Mass.: Harvard University Press, 2004.

———. "Holy Women, Holy Words: Early Christian Women, Social History, and the 'Linguistic Turn.'" *JECS* 6 (1998): 413–430.

———. *Jerome, Chrysostom, and Friends: Essays and Translations*. New York: Edwin Mellen, 1979.

———. "On Not Retracting the Unconfessed." In *Augustine and Postmodernism: Confessions and Circumfession*, edited by John Caputo and Michael Scanlon. Bloomington: Indiana University Press, 2005, 222–243.

———. *The Origenist Controversy: The Cultural Construction of an Early Christian Debate*. Princeton, N.J.: Princeton University Press, 1992.

———. *Reading Renunciation: Asceticism and Scripture in Early Christianity*. Princeton, N.J.: Princeton University Press, 1999.

———. "Sex, Shame, and Rhetoric: En-Gendering Early Christian Ethics." *JAAR* 59 (1991): 221–245.

Clark, Gillian. "Bodies and Blood: Late Antique Debate on Martyrdom, Virginity and Resurrection." In *Changing Bodies, Changing Meanings: Studies on the Human Body in Antiquity*, edited by Dominic Montserrat. London: Routledge, 1998, 99–115.

Clarke, John. *Looking at Lovemaking: Constructions of Sexuality in Roman Art 100 B.C.–A.D. 250.* Berkeley: University of California Press, 1998.

Clements, Ruth. "*Peri Pascha*: Passover and the Displacement of Jewish Interpretation within Origen's Exegesis." Th.D. diss., Harvard University, 1997.

———. "(Re)Constructing Paul: Origen's Readings of Romans in *Peri Archon.*" *SBL Seminar Papers* 40 (2001): 151–174.

Cohen, Jeremy. *Be Fertile and Increase, Fill the Earth and Master It: The Ancient and Medieval Career of a Biblical Text.* Ithaca, N.Y.: Cornell University Press, 1989.

———. *Christ Killers: The Jews and the Passion from the Bible to the Big Screen.* Oxford: Oxford University Press, 2007.

———, ed. *Essential Papers on Judaism and Christianity in Conflict.* New York: New York University Press, 1991.

———. "Roman Imperial Policy toward the Jews from Constantine until the End of the Palestinian Patriarchate." *Byzantine Studies* 3 (1976): 1–29.

Cohen, Shaye. "Adolf Harnack's 'The Mission and Expansion of Judaism': Christianity Succeeds Where Judaism Fails." In *The Future of Early Christianity: Essays in Honor of Helmut Koester*, edited by Birger A. Pearson. Minneapolis: Fortress, 1991, 163–169.

———. "Ioudaios: 'Judean' and 'Jew' in Susanna, First Maccabees, and Second Maccabees." In *Geschichte-Tradition-Reflexion: Festschrift für Martin Hengel zum 70. Geburtstag*, edited by Peter Schäfer. Vol. 1, *Judentum.* Tübingen: Mohr, 1996, 211–220.

Collins, John J. *Between Athens and Jerusalem: Jewish Identity in the Hellenistic Diaspora.* Grand Rapids, Mich.: Eerdmans, 1999.

Collins, Raymond. *Studies on the First Letter to the Thessalonians.* Leuven: Leuven University Press, 1984.

Connolly, Richard H. "The Date and Authorship of the Epistle to Diognetus." *JTS* 36 (1935): 347–353.

Conzelmann, Hans. *1 Corinthians: A Commentary on the First Epistle to the Corinthians.* Translated by James W. Leitch. Philadelphia: Fortress, 1975.

Cooper, Kate. *The Virgin and the Bride: Idealized Womanhood in Late Antiquity.* Cambridge, Mass.: Harvard University Press, 1996.

Cranton, Dan W. *The Good, the Bold, and the Beautiful: The Story of Susanna and Its Renaissance Interpretation.* Library of Hebrew Bible / Old Testament Studies 430. London: T. & T. Clark, 2006.

Cribiore, Raffaella. *The School of Libanius in Late Antique Antioch.* Princeton, N.J.: Princeton University Press, 2007.

Crouzel, Henri. *Origen: The Life and Thought of the First Great Theologian.* Translated by A. S. Worrall. Edinburgh: T. & T. Clark, 1989.

———. *Virginité et mariage selon Origène.* Museum Lessianum, section théologique 58. Paris: Desclée de Brouwer, 1963.

Daniélou, Jean. *Origen.* New York: Sheed and Ward, 1955. Original publication: *Origène.* Paris: La Table Ronde, 1948.

Dassman, Ernst. *Der Stachel im Fleisch: Paulus in der frühchristlichen Literatur bis Irenäus.* Münster: Aschendorff, 1979.

Davies, W. D. "Paul and the People of Israel." *NTS* 24 (1977): 4–39.

Dawson, David. *Allegorical Readers and Cultural Revision in Ancient Alexandria.* New Haven, Conn.: Yale University Press, 1992.

———. *Christian Figural Reading and the Fashioning of Identity.* Berkeley: University of California Press, 2001.

———. "Plato's Soul and the Body of the Text in Philo and Origen." In *Interpretation and Allegory: Antiquity to the Modern Period,* edited by Jon Whitman. Brill's Studies in Intellectual History. Leiden: Brill, 2000, 89–107.

De Jonge, Marinus. *The Testaments of the Twelve Patriarchs: A Study of the Text, Composition, and Origin.* Assen: Van Gorcum, 1953.

De Lange, Nicholas R. M. "Origen and Jewish Bible Exegesis." *JJS* 22 (1971): 31–52.

———. *Origen and the Jews: Studies in Jewish-Christian Relations in Third-Century Palestine.* Cambridge: Cambridge University Press, 1976.

De Lubac, Henri. *History and Spirit: The Understanding of Scripture According to Origen.* Translated by Anne England Nash. San Francisco: Ignatius, 1950, 2007.

Donahue, Paul J. "Jewish-Christian Controversy in the Second Century: A Study in the Dialogue of Justin Martyr." Ph.D. diss., Yale University, 1973.

Donfried, Karl. *Paul, Thessalonica, and Early Christianity.* Grand Rapids, Mich.: Eerdmans, 2002.

Doran, Robert. "The Additions to Daniel." In *Harper's Bible Commentary,* edited by James Luther Mays. San Francisco: Harper and Row, 1988.

Dover, Kenneth. *Greek Popular Morality in the Time of Plato and Aristotle.* Berkeley: University of California Press, 1974.

Drake, Harold A., ed. *Violence in Late Antiquity.* Burlington, Vt.: Ashgate, 2006.

Edwards, Catharine. *The Politics of Immorality in Ancient Rome.* New York: Cambridge University Press, 1993.

Edwards, Douglas R. *Religion and Power: Pagans, Jews, and Christians in the Greek East.* New York: Oxford University Press, 1996.

Edwards, Mark. *Origen against Plato.* Burlington, Vt.: Ashgate, 2002.

Ehrman, Bart. *The Apostolic Fathers.* 2 vols. LCL. Cambridge, Mass.: Harvard University Press, 2003.

———. *Lost Christianities: The Battles for Scripture and the Faiths We Never Knew.* New York: Oxford University Press, 2003.

Engel, Helmut. *Die Susanna-Erzählung: Einleitung, Übersetzung und Kommentar zum Septuaginta-Text und zur Theodotion-Bearbeitung.* Göttingen: Vandenhoeck & Ruprecht, 1985.

Fausto-Sterling, Anne. *Sexing the Body: Gender Politics and the Construction of Sexuality.* New York: Basic Books, 2000.

Feldman, Louis H. *Jew and Gentile in the Ancient World: Attitudes and Interactions from Alexander to Justinian.* Princeton, N.J.: Princeton University Press, 1993.

———. "Origen's *Contra Celsum* and Josephus's *Contra Apionem*: The Issue of Jewish Origins." *VC* 44 (1990): 105–135.

Festugière, André J. *Antioche paienne et chrétienne: Libanius, Chrysostome et les moines de Syrie.* Paris: De Boccard, 1959.

Fitzmyer, John. *Romans.* New York: Doubleday, 1993.

Fonrobert, Charlotte Elisheva. "Jewish Christians, Judaizers, and Anti-Judaism." In *Late Ancient Christianity,* edited by Virginia Burrus. Minneapolis: Fortress, 2005, 234–254.

Ford, David Carleton. "Misogynist or Advocate? St. John Chrysostom and His Views on Women." Ph.D. diss., Drew University, 1989.

Foucault, Michel. "An Aesthetics of Existence." In *Michel Foucault: Politics, Philosophy, Culture: Interviews and Other Writings 1977–1984,* edited by Lawrence D. Kritzman. New York: Routledge, 1988, 47–53.

———. *The Archaeology of Knowledge.* Translated by A. M. Sheridan Smith. London: Tavistock, 1972.

———. *The History of Sexuality.* Translated by Robert Hurley. 3 vols. New York: Vintage, 1980–88.

———. "Why Study Power? The Question of the Subject." In *Michel Foucault: Beyond Structuralism and Hermeneutics,* edited by Herbert L. Dreyfus and Paul Rabinow. Chicago: University of Chicago Press, 1982, 208–226.

Frankel, Zacharias. *Über den Einfluss der palästinischen Exegese auf die alexandrinische Hermeneutik.* Leipzig, 1851.

Gaca, Kathy. *The Making of Fornication: Eros, Ethics, and Political Reform in Greek Philosophy and Early Christianity.* Berkeley: University of California Press, 2003.

Gaddis, Michael. *There Is No Crime for Those Who Have Christ: Religious Violence in the Christian Roman Empire.* Transformation of the Classical Heritage 39. Berkeley: University of California Press, 2005.

Gager, John. *The Origins of Anti-Semitism: Attitudes toward Judaism in Pagan and Christian Antiquity.* New York: Oxford University Press, 1995.

———. *Reinventing Paul.* New York: Oxford University Press, 2000.

Gleason, Maud. *Making Men: Sophists and Self-Presentation in Ancient Rome.* Princeton, N.J.: Princeton University Press, 1995.

Glickman, Stephen. "The Spotted Hyena from Aristotle to the Lion King: Reputation Is Everything." *Social Research* 62 (1995): 501–537.

Gögler, Rolf. *Zur Theologie des biblischen Wortes bei Origenes.* Düsseldorf: Patmos, 1963.

Goldenberg, Robert. *The Nations That Know Thee Not: Ancient Jewish Attitudes toward Other Religions.* New York: New York University Press, 1998.

Goodenough, Erwin R. *The Theology of Justin Martyr: An Investigation into the Conception of Early Christian Literature and Its Hellenistic and Judaistic Influences.* Amsterdam: Philo, 1968.

Goodspeed, Edgar J. *The Meaning of Ephesians.* Chicago: University of Chicago Press, 1933.

Gorday, Peter. "Paulus Origenianus." In *Paul and the Legacies of Paul,* edited by William S. Babcock. Dallas: Southern Methodist University Press, 1990, 141–164.

———. *Principles of Patristic Exegesis: Romans 9–11 in Origen, John Chrysostom, and Augustine.* Studies in the Bible and Early Christianity, vol. 4. New York: Edwin Mellen, 1983.

Grant, Robert. "Charges of 'Immorality' against Various Religious Groups in Antiquity." In *Studies in Gnosticism and Hellenistic Religions,* edited by R. Van den Broek and M. J. Vermaseren. Leiden: Brill, 1981, 161–170.

———. "Dietary Laws among Pythagoreans, Jews, and Christians." *HTR* 73 (1980): 299–310.

———. *The Letter and the Spirit.* London: SPCK, 1957.

Grissom, Fred A. "Chrysostom and the Jews: Studies in Jewish-Christian Relations in Fourth-Century Antioch." Ph.D. diss., Southern Baptist Theological Seminary, 1978.

Gruen, Erich. *Diaspora: Jews amidst Greeks and Romans.* Cambridge, Mass.: Harvard University Press, 2002.

———. "Jewish Perspectives on Greek Culture and Ethnicity." In *Ancient Perceptions of Greek Ethnicity,* edited by Irad Malkin. Cambridge, Mass.: Harvard University Press, 2001, 347–373.

Grypeou, Emmanouela, and Helen Spurling, eds. *The Exegetical Encounter between Jews and Christians in Late Antiquity.* Leiden: Brill, 2009.

Guillet, Jacques. "Les exégèses d'Alexandrie et d'Antioche: Conflit ou malentendu?." *RSR* 34 (1947): 256–302.

Hall, Edith. *Inventing the Barbarian: Greek Self-Definition through Tragedy.* New York: Oxford University Press, 1989.

Halperin, David, John Winkler, and Froma Zeitlin, eds. *Before Sexuality: The Construction of Erotic Experience in the Ancient Greek World.* Princeton, N.J.: Princeton University Press, 1990.

Halpern-Amaru, Betsy. "The Journey of Susanna among the Church Fathers." In *The Judgment of Susanna: Authority and Witness,* edited by Ellen Spolsky. Atlanta: Scholars Press, 1996, 21–34.

Hanson, Richard P. C. *Allegory and Event: A Study of the Sources and Significance of Origen's Interpretation of Scripture.* Richmond, Va.: John Knox, 1959.

Harnack, Adolf von. *Die Altercatio Simonis Iudaei et Theophilii Christiani nebst Untersuchungen über die antijüdische Polemik in der alten Kirche.* Leipzig: Hinrichs, 1883.

———. *Judentum und Judenchristentum in Justins Dialog mit Trypho.* Leipzig: Hinrichs, 1913.

———. *Lehrbuch der Dogmengeschichte.* Tübingen: Mohr Siebeck, 1909.

———. *Die Mission und Ausbreitung des Christentums in den ersten drei Jahrhunderten.* 2 vols. Leipzig: Hinrichs, 1915.

Hayes, Christine. *Gentile Impurities and Jewish Identities: Intermarriage and Conversion from the Bible to the Talmud.* New York: Oxford University Press, 2002.

Hays, Richard B. *The Moral Vision of the New Testament: A Contemporary Introduction to New Testament Ethics.* San Francisco: Harper, 1996.

———. "Relations Natural and Unnatural: A Response to John Boswell's Exegesis of Romans 1." *JRE* 14 (1986): 184–215.

Heine, Ronald E. *Origen: Scholarship in the Service of the Church.* Christian Theology in Context. Oxford: Oxford University Press, 2011.

Henrichs, Albert. "Pagan Ritual and the Alleged Crimes of the Early Christians: A Reconsideration." In *Kyriakon: Festschrift Johannes Quasten,* 2 vols., edited by Patrick Granfield and Josef A. Jungmann. Münster: Aschendorff, 1970, 1:18–35.

Hodges, Frederick M. "The Ideal Prepuce in Ancient Greece and Rome: Male Genital Aesthetics and Their Relation to *Lipodermos,* Circumcision, Foreskin Restoration, and the *Kynodesme.*" *Bulletin of the History of Medicine* 75 (2001): 375–405.

Horbury, William. "Jewish-Christian Relations in Barnabas and Justin Martyr." In *Jews and Christians: The Parting of the Ways A.D. 70 to 135,* edited by James Dunn. Tübingen: Mohr Siebeck, 1992, 315–345.

———. *Jews and Christians in Contact and Controversy.* Edinburgh: T. & T. Clark, 1998.

Horner, Timothy J. *"Listening to Trypho": Justin Martyr's Dialogue Reconsidered.* Leuven: Peeters, 2001.

Hruby, Kurt. "Exégèse rabbinique et exégèse patristique." *RevScRel* 47 (1973): 341–372.

Hunt, David. "Christianising the Roman Empire: The Evidence of the Code." In *The Theodosian Code: Studies in the Imperial Law of Late Antiquity,* edited by Jill Harries and Ian Wood. London: Duckworth, 1993, 143–158.

Hunter, David. *John Chrysostom, A Comparison between a King and a Monk / Against the Opponents of the Monastic Life: Two Treatises by John Chrysostom.* Lewiston, Maine: Edwin Mellen, 1988.

———. *Preaching and Propaganda in the Patristic Age.* New York: Paulist Press, 1989.

Hvalvik, Reidar. *The Struggle for Scripture and Covenant: The Purpose of the Epistle of Barnabas and Jewish-Christian Competition in the Second Century.* Tübingen: Mohr Siebeck, 1996.

Illert, Martin. *Johannes Chrysostomus und das antiochenische-syrische Mönchtum: Studien zu Theologie, Rhetorik und Kirchenpolitik im antiochenischen Schrifttum des Johannes Chrysostomus.* Zurich: Pano, 2000.

Ivarsson, Fredrik. "Vice Lists and Deviant Masculinity: The Rhetorical Function of 1 Corinthians 5:10–11 and 6:9–10." In *Mapping Gender in Ancient Religious Discourses,* edited by Todd Penner and Caroline Vander Stichele. Leiden: Brill, 2007, 163–184.

Jacobs, Andrew. "Dialogical Differences: (De)Judaizing Jesus' Circumcision." *JECS* (2007): 291–335.

———. "A Jew's Jew: Paul and the Early Christian Problem of Jewish Origins." *JOR* 86 (2006): 258–286.

———. "The Lion and the Lamb: Reconsidering Jewish-Christian Relations in Antiquity." In *The Ways That Never Parted: Jews and Christians in Late Antiquity and the Early Middle Ages,* edited by Adam H. Becker and Annette Yoshiko Reed. Tübingen: Mohr Siebeck, 2003, 95–118.

———. *Remains of the Jews: The Holy Land and Christian Empire in Late Antiquity.* Stanford, Calif.: Stanford University Press, 2004.

Jefford, Clayton N. *Reading the Apostolic Fathers: An Introduction.* Peabody, Mass.: Hendrickson, 1996.

Jewett, Robert. *Paul's Anthropological Terms: A Study of Their Use in Conflict Settings.* Leiden: Brill, 1971.

———. *Romans: A Commentary.* Minneapolis: Fortress, 2007.

Johnson, Luke Timothy. "The New Testament's Anti-Jewish Slander and the Conventions of Ancient Polemic." *JBL* 108 (1989): 419–441.

Joslyn-Siemiatkoski, Daniel. *Christian Memories of the Maccabean Martyrs.* New York: Palgrave Macmillan, 2009.

Juster, Jean. *Les juifs dans l'empire romain: Leur condition juridique, économique et sociale.* 2 vols. Paris: Paul Geuthner, 1914.

Kalleres, Dayna S. "Exorcising the Devil to Silence Christ's Enemies: Ritualized Speech Practices in Late Antique Christianity." Ph.D. diss., Brown University, 2002.

Kalmin, Richard. "Christians and Heretics in Rabbinic Literature of Late Antiquity." *HTR* 87 (1994): 155–169.

Kannengiesser, Charles. "The Bible as Read in the Early Church: Patristic Exegesis and Its Presuppositions." *Concilium* 1 (1991): 29–36.

———, and William L. Petersen, eds. *Origen of Alexandria: His World and Legacy.* Notre Dame, Ind.: University of Notre Dame Press, 1988.

Kelly, J. N. D. *Goldenmouth: The Story of John Chrysostom—Ascetic, Preacher, Bishop.* Ithaca, N.Y.: Cornell University Press, 1995.

Kiley, Mark Christopher. *Colossians as Pseudepigraphy.* Sheffield: JSOT, 1986.

Kimelman, Reuven. "*Birkat Ha-Minim* and the Lack of Evidence for an Anti-Christian Jewish Prayer in Late Antiquity." In *Jewish and Christian Self-Definition*, edited by E. P. Sanders et al. Philadelphia: Trinity, 1981, 226–244.

King, Karen. *What Is Gnosticism?* Cambridge, Mass.: Harvard University Press, 2003.

Kinzig, Wolfram. "'Non-Separation': Closeness and Co-operation between Jews and Christians in the Fourth Century." *VC* 45 (1991): 27–53.

Kittel, Gerhard, ed. *Theological Dictionary of the New Testament.* Grand Rapids, Mich.: Eerdmans, 1967.

Klawans, Jonathan. *Impurity and Sin in Ancient Judaism.* New York: Oxford University Press, 2000.

———. "Notions of Gentile Impurity in Ancient Judaism." *AJSR* 20 (1995): 285–312.

Knust, Jennifer. *Abandoned to Lust: Sexual Slander and Ancient Christianity.* Gender, Theory, and Religion. New York: Columbia University Press, 2006.

———. "The Politics of Virtue and Vice in the Pauline Epistles." *SBL Seminar Papers* 39 (2000): 436–451.

———. "Roasting the Lamb: Sacrifice and Sacred Text in Justin's *Dialogue with Trypho*." In *Religion and Violence: The Biblical Heritage*, edited by David Bernat and Jonathan Klawans. Recent Research in Biblical Studies 2. Sheffield: Sheffield Phoenix, 2007, 100–113.

Koester, Helmut. *History and Literature of Early Christianity.* 2 vols. Philadelphia: Fortress, 1982.

Koltun-Fromm, Naomi. *Hermeneutics of Holiness: Ancient Jewish and Christian Notions of Sexuality and Religious Community.* New York: Oxford University Press, 2010.
———. "Sexuality and Holiness: Semitic-Christian and Jewish Conceptualizations of Sexual Behavior." *VC* 54 (2000): 375–395.
Kraemer, Ross S. "Jewish Women's Resistance to Christianity in the Early Fifth Century: The Account of Severus, Bishop of Minorca." *JECS* 17 (2009): 635–665.
———. "The Other as Woman: An Aspect of Polemic among Pagans, Jews, and Christians in the Greco-Roman World." In *The Other in Jewish Thought and History: Constructions of Jewish Culture and Identity*, edited by Laurence J. Silberstein and Robert L. Cohn. New Perspectives on Jewish Studies. New York: New York University Press, 1994, 121–144.
———. *Unreliable Witnesses: Religion, Gender, and History in the Greco-Roman Mediterranean.* New York: Oxford, 2011.
Kraft, Robert A. *The Apostolic Fathers: A New Translation and Commentary.* Vol. 3, *Barnabas and the Didache.* Toronto: Thomas Nelson, 1965.
Krauss, Samuel. "The Jews in the Works of the Church Fathers." *JQR* 5 (1892): 122–157.
LaCocque, André. *The Feminine Unconventional: Four Subversive Figures in Israel's Tradition.* Overtures to Biblical Theology. Minneapolis: Fortress, 1990.
Lampe, G. W. H., and H. J. Witticombe. *Essays on Typology.* London: SCM, 1957.
Lévi, Israel. "L'histoire de Suzanne et les deux vieillards dans la littérature juive." *REJ* 95 (1933): 157–171.
Levine, Amy-Jill. "'Hemmed in on Every Side': Jews and Women in the Book of Susanna." In *A Feminist Companion to Esther, Judith, and Susanna*, edited by Athalya Brenner. Sheffield: Sheffield Academic Press, 1995, 303–323.
Levine, Lee I. *Caesarea under Roman Rule.* Studies in Judaism in Late Antiquity 7. Leiden: Brill, 1975.
Leyerle, Blake. *Theatrical Shows and Ascetic Lives: John Chrysostom's Attack on Spiritual Marriage.* Berkeley: University of California Press, 2001.
Lieu, Judith. *Christian Identity in the Jewish and Graeco-Roman World.* New York: Oxford University Press, 2004.
———. *Image and Reality: The Jews in the World of the Christians in the Second Century.* Edinburgh: T. & T. Clark, 1996.
———. "'Impregnable Ramparts and Walls of Iron': Boundary and Identity in Early 'Judaism' and 'Christianity.'" *NTS* 48 (2002): 297–313.
———, ed. *Neither Jew nor Greek? Constructing Early Christianity.* Edinburgh: T. & T. Clark, 2002.
———. "'The Parting of the Ways': Theological Construct or Historical Reality?" *JSNT* 56 (1994): 101–119.
Limor, Ora, and Guy G. Stroumsa, eds. *Contra Iudaeos: Ancient and Medieval Polemics between Christians and Jews.* Tübingen: Mohr Siebeck, 1996.
Lincoln, Andrew, and A. J. M. Wedderburn. *The Theology of the Later Pauline Letters.* Cambridge: Cambridge University Press, 1993.

Lindemann, Andreas. *Paulus im ältesten Christentum: Das Bild des Apostels und die Rezeption der paulinischen Theologie in der frühchristlichen Literatur bis Marcion.* Tübingen: Mohr Siebeck, 1979.

Linder, Amnon. *The Jews in Roman Imperial Legislation.* Detroit: Wayne State University Press, 1987.

Lowy, S. "The Confutation of Judaism in the Epistle of Barnabas." *JJS* 11 (1960): 1–33.

Lubac, Henri de. *Histoire et esprit: L'intelligence de l'écriture d'après Origène.* Paris: Aubier, 1950.

Lucas, Leopold. *Zur Geschichte der Juden im vierten Jahrhundert.* Berlin: Mayer and Müller, 1910.

MacDonald, Dennis R. *The Legend and the Apostle: The Battle for Paul in Story and Canon.* Philadelphia: Westminster, 1983.

Mach, Michael. "Justin Martyr's *Dialogus cum Tryphone Iudaeo* and the Development of Christian Anti-Judaism." In *Contra Iudaeos: Ancient and Medieval Polemics between Christians and Jews,* edited by Ora Limor and Guy G. Stroumsa. Tübingen: Mohr Siebeck, 1996, 27–47.

Magness, Jodi. "The Date of the Sardis Synagogue in Light of the Numismatic Evidence." *AJA* 109 (2005): 443–476.

Marcus, Joel. "Idolatry in the New Testament." *Int* (2006): 152–164.

Martens, Peter W. "Interpreting Attentively: The Ascetic Character of Biblical Exegesis according to Origen and Basil of Caesarea." In *Origeniana Octava,* edited by Lorenzo Perrone. Leuven: Leuven University Press, 2003, 2:1115–1121.

———. *Origen and Scripture: The Contours of the Exegetical Life.* Oxford Early Christian Studies. Oxford: Oxford University Press, 2012.

Martin, Dale. *The Corinthian Body.* New Haven, Conn.: Yale University Press, 1995.

———. "Heterosexism and the Interpretation of Romans 1:18–32." *BibInt* 3 (1995): 332–355.

———. *Sex and the Single Savior: Gender and Sexuality in Biblical Interpretation.* Louisville, Ky.: Westminster John Knox, 2006.

Mattingly, David J., ed. *Dialogues in Roman Imperialism: Power, Discourse, and Discrepant Experience in the Roman Empire.* Portsmouth, R.I.: Journal of Roman Archaeology supplementary series 23, 1997.

Maxwell, Jaclyn L. *Christianization and Communication in Late Antiquity: John Chrysostom and His Congregation in Antioch.* Cambridge: Cambridge University Press, 2006.

Mayer, Wendy. "Monasticism at Antioch and Constantinople in the Late Fourth Century: A Case of Exclusivity or Diversity?." In *Prayer and Spirituality in the Early Church,* edited by Pauline Allen, R. Canning, and L. Cross. Brisbane: Centre for Early Christian Studies, Australian Catholic University, 1998, 275–288.

———, and Pauline Allen. *John Chrysostom.* The Early Church Fathers. London: Routledge, 2000.

McGuckin, John. "Caesarea Maritima as Origen Knew It." In *Origeniana Quinta,* edited by Robert J. Daly. Leuven: Leuven University Press, 1992, 3–25.

———. "Origen on the Jews." In *Christianity and Judaism: Papers Read at the 1991 Summer Meeting and the 1992 Winter Meeting of the Ecclesiastical History Society*, edited by Diana Wood. Oxford: Blackwell, 1992, 1–13.

———. "Origen as Literary Critic in the Alexandrian Tradition." In *Origeniana Octava*, edited by Lorenzo Perrone. Leuven: Peeters, 2003, 121–135.

Meeks, Wayne, and Robert Wilken. *Jews and Christians in Antioch: In the First Four Centuries of the Common Era*. SBL Sources for Biblical Study 13. Missoula, Mont.: Scholars Press, 1978.

Metzger, Bruce. *An Introduction to the Apocrypha*. New York: Oxford University Press, 1957.

Miles, Margaret. "Santa Maria Maggiore's Fifth-Century Mosaics: Triumphal Christianity and the Jews." *HTR* 86 (1993): 155–175.

Millar, Fergus. "The Jews of the Graeco-Roman Diaspora between Paganism and Christianity, AD 312–438." In *Jews among Pagans and Christians*, edited by Judith Lieu, John North, and Tessa Rajak. London: Routledge, 1992, 97–123.

Miller, Patricia Cox. "Origen and the Witch of Endor: Towards an Iconoclastic Typology." *ATR* 66 (1984): 134–147.

———. "Pleasure of the Text, Text of Pleasure: Eros and Language in Origen's *Commentary on the Song of Songs*." *JAAR* (1986): 241–253.

———. "Poetic Words, Abysmal Words: Reflections on Origen's Hermeneutics." In *Origen of Alexandria*, edited by Charles Kannengiesser and William L. Petersen. Notre Dame, Ind.: University of Notre Dame Press, 1988, 164–178.

Mitchell, Margaret. *The Heavenly Trumpet: John Chrysostom and the Art of Pauline Interpretation*. Louisville, Ky.: Westminster John Knox, 2002.

———. *Paul, the Corinthians and the Birth of Christian Hermeneutics*. Cambridge: Cambridge University Press, 2010.

———, and Rowan Greer, eds. *The "Belly-Myther" of Endor: Interpretations of 1 Kingdoms 28 in the Early Church*. SBL Writings from the Greco-Roman World 16. Atlanta: SBL, 2007.

Mitton, C. Leslie. *The Epistle to the Ephesians: Its Authorship, Origin, and Purpose*. Oxford: Clarendon, 1951.

Mommsen, Theodor, Jean Rougé, Roland Delmaire, and François Richard, eds. *Les lois religieuses des empereurs romains de Constantin à Theodose II, 312–438*. Vol. 1, *Code théodosien, livre XVI*. SC 497. Paris: Cerf, 2005.

Montefiore, Claude. *Rabbinic Literature and Gospel Teachings*. New York: Macmillan, 1930.

Moore, Carey A., ed. *Daniel, Esther, and Jeremiah: The Additions*. AB 44. Garden City, N.Y.: Doubleday, 1977.

Moore, George Foot. *Judaism in the First Three Centuries of the Common Era: The Age of the Tannaim*. 3 vols. Cambridge, Mass.: Harvard University Press, 1927–1930.

Moore, Robert I. *Formation of a Persecuting Society: Power and Deviance in Western Europe, 950–1250*. New York: Basil Blackwell, 1987.

Moore, Stephen D. *Empire and Apocalypse: Postcolonialism and the New Testament*. Sheffield: Sheffield Phoenix, 2006.

Muradyan, Gohar. *Physiologus: The Greek and Armenian Versions with a Study of Translation Technique*. Leuven: Peeters, 2005.

Nautin, Pierre. *Hippolyte et Josipe: Contribution à l'histoire de la littérature chrétienne du troisième siècle*. Paris: Cerf, 1947.

———. *Origène: Sa vie et son oeuvre*. Paris: Beauchesne, 1977.

Neuschäfer, Bernhard. *Origenes als Philologe*. Schweizerische Beiträge zur Altertumswissenschaft 18. 2 vols. Basel: Reinhardt, 1987.

North, Helen. *Sophrosyne: Self-Knowledge and Self-Restraint in Greek Literature*. Ithaca, N.Y.: Cornell University Press, 1966.

Ó Fearghail, Fearghus. "Philo and the Fathers: The Letter and the Spirit." In *Scriptural Interpretation in the Fathers: Letter and Spirit*, edited by Thomas Finan and Vincent Twomey. Dublin: Four Courts, 1995, 39–60.

Osborn, Eric F. *Justin Martyr*. Beiträge zur historischen Theologie 47. Tübingen: Mohr, 1973.

Pace, Nicola. *Ricerche sulla tradizione di Rufino del "De principiis" di Origene*. Florence: La Nuova Italia Editrice, 1990.

Pagels, Elaine. *The Gnostic Paul: Gnostic Exegesis of the Pauline Letters*. Philadelphia: Fortress, 1975.

Paget, James Carleton. *The Epistle of Barnabas: Outlook and Background*. Tübingen: Mohr Siebeck, 1994.

———. "Paul and the Epistle of Barnabas." *NovT* 38 (1996): 359–381.

Parkes, James. *The Conflict of the Church and the Synagogue: A Study in the Origins of Anti-semitism*. New York: Meridian, 1961.

Paulsen, Henning. *Studien zur Theologie des Ignatius von Antiochien*. Forschungen zur Kirchen- und Dogmengeschichte 29. Göttingen: Vandenhoeck & Ruprecht, 1978.

Pearson, Birger. "1 Thessalonians 2:13–16: A Deutero-Pauline Interpolation." *HTR* 64 (1971): 79–94.

Pendergraft, Mary. "'Thou Shalt Not Eat the Hyena': A Note on 'Barnabas' Epistle 10.7." *VC* 46 (1992): 75–79.

Percy, Ernst. *Die Probleme der Kolosser- und Epheserbriefe*. Lund: C. W. K. Gleerup, 1946.

Perkins, Judith. *The Suffering Self: Pain and Narrative Representation in the Early Christian Era*. London: Routledge, 1995.

Petuchowski, Jakob J. "Halakah in the Church Fathers." In *Essays in Honor of Solomon B. Freehof*, edited by Walter Jacob, Frederick C. Schwartz, and Vigdor W. Kavaler. Pittsburgh: Rodef Shalom Congregation, 1964, 257–274.

Pfleiderer, Otto. *Paulinismus: Ein Beitrag zur Geschichte der urchristlichen Theologie*. Leipzig: Hinrichs, 1890.

Poliakov, Léon. *The History of Anti-Semitism*. Translated by Richard Howard. New York: Vanguard, 1965.

Pradels, Wendy. "Lesbos Cod. Gr. 27: The *Tale* of a *Discovery*." *ZAC* 6 (2002): 81–89.

———, Rudolf Brändle, and Martin Heimgartner. "Das bisher vermisste Textstück in Johannes Chrysostomus, *Adversus Judaeos*, Oratio 2." *ZAC* 5 (2001): 22–49.

———. "The Sequence and Dating of the Series of John Chrysostom's Eight Discourses *Adversus Judaeos.*" *ZAC* 6 (2002): 90–116.

Prigent, Pierre. *Justin et l'Ancien Testament: L'argumentation scripturaire du traité de Justin contre toutes les hérésies comme source principale du Dialogue avec Tryphon et de la première Apologie.* Paris: Librairie Lecoffre, 1964.

Raban, Avner, and Kenneth G. Holum, eds. *Caesarea Maritima: A Retrospective after Two Millennia.* Documenta et Monumenta Orientis Antiqui. Leiden: Brill, 1996.

Rabello, Alfredo M. "The Legal Condition of the Jews in the Roman Empire." *Aufstieg und Niedergang der Römischen Welt* 2 (1980): 662–762.

Rajak, Tessa. "Talking at Trypho: Christian Apologetic as Anti-Judaism in Justin's *Dialogue with Trypho the Jew.*" In *Apologetics in the Roman Empire: Pagans, Jews, and Christians,* edited by Mark Edwards, Martin Goodman, and Simon Price. Oxford: Oxford University Press, 1999, 59–80.

Rathke, Heinrich. *Ignatius von Antiochien und die Paulusbriefe.* Berlin: Akademie, 1967.

Rensberger, David. "As the Apostle Teaches: The Development of the Use of Paul's Letters in Second-Century Christianity." Ph.D. diss., Yale University, 1981.

Rhodes, James N. *The Epistle of Barnabas and the Deuteronomic Tradition: Polemics, Paraenesis, and the Legacy of the Golden-Calf Incident.* Tübingen: Mohr Siebeck, 2004.

Richardson, Peter. *Israel in the Apostolic Age.* SNTS Monograph Series 10. Cambridge: Cambridge University Press, 1969.

———, and Martin B. Shukster. "Barnabas, Nerva, and the Yavnean Rabbis." *JTS* 34 (1983): 31–55.

Rigaux, Béda. *Saint Paul: Les épîtres aux Thessaloniciens.* Études bibliques. Paris: Gabalda, 1956.

Ritter, Adolf M. "Erwägungen zum Antisemitismus in der alten Kirche: Acht Reden über die Juden." In *Bleibendes im Wandel der Kirchengeschichte,* edited by B. Moeller and G. Rubach. Tübingen, 1973, 71–91.

Robbins, Jill. *Prodigal Son / Elder Brother: Interpretation and Alterity in Augustine, Petrarch, Kafka, and Levinas.* Chicago: University of Chicago Press, 1991.

Robillard, Edmond. *Justin: L'itinéraire philosophique.* Paris: Cerf, 1989.

Rokéah, David. *Justin Martyr and the Jews.* Leiden: Brill, 2002.

Ruether, Rosemary Radford. *Faith and Fratricide: The Theological Roots of Anti-Semitism.* Eugene, Ore.: Wipf and Stock, 1995.

Runia, David. *Philo and the Church Fathers: A Collection of Papers.* Supplements to *VC* 32. Leiden: Brill, 1995.

———. *Philo in Early Christian Literature: A Survey.* Jewish Traditions in Early Christian Literature 3. Minneapolis: Fortress, 1993.

———, David M. Hay, and David Winston, eds. *Heirs of the Septuagint: Philo, Hellenistic Judaism, and Early Christianity: Festschrift for Earle Hilgert.* Atlanta: Scholars Press, 1991.

Runia, David, and Gregory Sterling, eds. *In the Spirit of Faith: Studies in Philo and Early Christianity in Honor of David Hay.* Brown Judaic Studies 13. Providence, R.I.: Brown Judaic Studies, 2001.

Rutgers, Leonard. *The Jews in Late Ancient Rome: Evidence of Cultural Interaction in the Roman Diaspora.* Leiden: Brill, 1995.

———. *Subterranean Rome: In Search of the Roots of Christianity in the Catacombs of the Eternal City.* Leuven: Peeters, 2000.

Said, Edward. *Orientalism.* New York: Vintage, 1978.

Sanchez, Sylvain Jean Gabriel. *Justin apologist chrétien: Travaux sur le* Dialogue avec Tryphon *de Justin Martyr.* Paris: Gabalda, 2000.

Sanders, Jack T. *Schismatics, Sectarians, Dissidents, Deviants: The First One Hundred Years of Jewish-Christian Relations.* Valley Forge, Pa.: Trinity Press International, 1993.

Sandmel, Samuel. *Philo of Alexandria: An Introduction.* New York: Oxford University Press, 1979.

Sandwell, Isabella. *Identity and Religious Interaction in Late Fourth-Century Antioch: Greeks, Jews and Christians in Antioch.* Cambridge: Cambridge University Press, 2007.

Satlow, Michael L. *Tasting the Dish: Rabbinic Rhetorics of Sexuality.* Brown Judaic Studies 303. Atlanta: Scholars Press, 1995.

Scalise, Charles J. "Allegorical Flights of Fancy: The Problem of Origen's Exegesis." *GOTR* 32 (1987): 69–88.

Schäfer, Peter. *The History of the Jews in Antiquity: The Jews of Palestine from Alexander the Great to the Arab Conquest.* Luxembourg: Harwood Academic, 1995.

———. *Judeophobia: Attitudes toward the Jews in the Ancient World.* Cambridge, Mass.: Harvard University Press, 1997.

Schäublin, Christoph. *Untersuchungen zu Methode und Herkunft der antiochenischen Exegese.* Theophania 23. Cologne: Hanstein, 1974.

Schlosser, Hanspeter. "Die Daniel-Susanna-Erzählung in Bild und Literatur der christlichen Frühzeit." *Tortulae: Studien zu altchristlichen und byzantinischen Monumenten.* Römische Quartalschrift für christlichen Altertumskunde und für Kirchengesichte 30 supplement (1965): 243–249.

———. "Susanna." In *Lexikon der christlichen Ikonographie.* Freiburg: Herder, 1972.

Schmidt, Daryl. "1 Thess 2:13–16: Linguistic Evidence for an Interpolation." *JBL* 102 (1983): 269–279.

Schmitt, Armin. *Stammt der sogenannte 'θ'-Text bei Daniel wirklich von Theodotion?*, Mitteilungen des Septuaginta-Unternehmens, vol. 9. Göttingen: Vandenhoeck & Ruprecht, 1966.

Schneemelcher, Wilhelm. "Paulus in der griechischen Kirche des zweiten Jahrhunderts." *ZKG* 75 (1964): 1–20.

Schneiders, Sandra. "Faith, Hermeneutics, and the Literal Sense of Scripture." *TS* 39 (1978): 719–736.

Schor, Adam M. "Theodoret on the 'School of Antioch': A Network Approach." *JECS* 15 (2007): 517–562.

Schremer, Adiel. *Brothers Estranged: Heresy, Christianity, and Jewish Identity in Late Antiquity.* Oxford: Oxford University Press, 2010.

Schrift, Alan D. *Nietzsche's French Legacy: A Genealogy of Poststructuralism.* New York: Routledge, 1995.

Schwartz, Seth. *Imperialism and Jewish Society, 200 B.C.E. to 640 C.E.* Princeton, N.J.: Princeton University Press, 2001.

Scott, James. "Paul's Use of Deuteronomic Tradition." *JBL* 112 (1993): 645–665.

Sgherri, Giuseppe. *Chiesa e Sinagoga nelle opere di Origene.* Studia Patristica Mediolanensia 13. Milan: Vita e Pensiero, 1982.

Shaw, Teresa. *The Burden of the Flesh: Fasting and Sexuality in Early Christianity.* Minneapolis: Fortress, 1998.

Shepardson, Christine. *Anti-Judaism and Christian Orthodoxy: Ephrem's Hymns in Fourth-Century Syria.* Washington, D.C.: Catholic University of America Press, 2008.

———. "Controlling Contested Places: John Chrysostom's *Adversus Iudaeos* Homilies and the Spatial Politics of Religious Controversy." *JECS* 15 (2007): 483–516.

Shotwell, Willis. *The Biblical Exegesis of Justin Martyr.* London: SPCK, 1965.

Siegfried, Carl. *Die hebräischen Worterklärungen des Philo und die Spuren ihrer Einwirkung auf die Kirchenväter.* Magdeburg: Baensch, 1863.

Simon, Marcel. "La polemique antijuive de saint Jean Chrysostome et le mouvement judaisant d'Antioche." *Annuaire de l'institute de philology et d'histoire orientales et slaves* 4 (1936): 140–153.

———. *Verus Israel: A Study of Relations between Christians and Jews in the Roman Empire.* Translated by H. McKeating. Oxford: Oxford University Press, 1986. French original: *Verus Israel: Étude sur les relations entre chrétiens et juifs dans l'empire romain, 135–425.* Paris: Boccard, 1948.

Sizgorich, Thomas. *Violence and Belief in Late Antiquity: Militant Devotion in Christianity and Islam.* Philadelphia: University of Pennsylvania Press, 2009.

Skarsaune, Oskar. *The Proof from Prophecy: A Study in Justin Martyr's Proof-Text Tradition: Text-Type, Provenance, Theological Profile.* Leiden: Brill, 1987.

Smallwood, E. Mary. *The Jews under Roman Rule: From Pompey to Diocletian.* Studies in Judaism in Late Antiquity 20. Leiden: Brill, 1976.

Smith, Jonathan Z. "What a Difference a Difference Makes." In *"To See Ourselves as Others See Us": Christians, Jews, "Others" in Late Antiquity,* edited by Jacob Neusner and Ernest Frerichs. Chico, Calif.: Scholars Press, 1985, 3–48.

Smith, Kathryn. "Inventing Martial Chastity: The Iconography of Susanna and the Elders in Early Christian Art." *Oxford Art Journal* 16 (1993): 3–24.

Sophocles, Evangelinus A. *Greek Lexicon of the Roman and Byzantine Periods.* Cambridge, Mass.: Harvard University Press, 1914.

Spolsky, Ellen, ed. *The Judgment of Susanna: Authority and Witness.* Atlanta: Scholars Press, 1996.

Stanton, Graham. "Aspects of Early Christian-Jewish Polemic and Apologetic." *NTS* 31 (1985): 377–392.

———, and Guy G. Stroumsa, eds. *Tolerance and Intolerance in Early Judaism and Christianity.* Cambridge: Cambridge University Press, 1998.

Stendahl, Krister. "The Apostle Paul and the Introspective Conscience of the West." *HTR* 56 (1963): 199–215.

————. *Paul among Jews and Gentiles*. Philadelphia: Fortress, 1976.

Sterk, Andrea. *Renouncing the World Yet Leading the Church: The Monk-Bishop in Late Antiquity*. Cambridge, Mass.: Harvard University Press, 2004.

Stern, Menahem, ed. *Greek and Latin Authors on Jews and Judaism*. 3 vols. Jerusalem: Israel Academy of Sciences and Humanities, 1974–1980.

Steussy, Marti. *Gardens in Babylon: Narrative and Faith in the Greek Legends of Daniel*. Atlanta: Scholars Press, 1993.

Stevenson, James. *The Catacombs: Rediscovered Monuments of Early Christianity*. London: Thames and Hudson, 1978.

Stoler, Ann Laura. *Carnal Knowledge and Imperial Power: Race and the Intimate in Colonial Rule*. Berkeley: University of California Press, 2002.

————. *Race and the Education of Desire: Foucault's* History of Sexuality *and the Colonial Order of Things*. Durham, N.C.: Duke University Press, 1995.

————. "Racial Histories and Their Regimes of Truth." *Political Power and Social Theory* 11 (1997): 183–206.

Stow, Kenneth. *Jewish Dogs: An Image and Its Interpreters: Continuity in the Catholic-Jewish Encounter*. Stanford, Calif.: Stanford University Press, 2006.

Stowers, Stanley. *A Rereading of Romans: Justice, Jews, and Gentiles*. New Haven, Conn.: Yale University Press, 1994.

Strack, Hermann, and Paul Billerbeck. *Kommentar zum Neuen Testament aus Talmud und Midrasch*. Munich: Beck, 1922.

Stratton, Kimberly. *Naming the Witch: Magic, Ideology, and Stereotype in the Ancient World*. New York: Columbia University Press, 2007.

————. "The Rhetoric of 'Magic' in Early Christian Discourse: Gender, Power, and the Construction of 'Heresy.'" In *Mapping Gender in Ancient Religious Discourses*, edited by Todd Penner and Caroline Vander Stichele. Leiden: Brill, 2007, 89–114.

Stylianopoulos, Theodore. *Justin Martyr and the Mosaic Law*. Missoula, Mont.: Scholars Press, 1975.

Swancutt, Diana. "Sexy Stoics and the Rereading of Romans 1:18–2:16." In *A Feminist Companion to Paul*, edited by Amy-Jill Levine with Marianne Blinckenstaff. London: T. & T. Clark, 2004, 42–73.

Taylor, Miriam. *Anti-Judaism and Early Christian Identity: A Critique of the Scholarly Consensus*. Studia Post-Biblica 46. Leiden: Brill, 1995.

Tkacz, Catherine Brown. "Susanna as a Type of Christ." *Studies in Iconography* 20 (1999): 101–153.

Torjesen, Karen Jo. "'Body,' 'Soul,' and 'Spirit' in Origen's Theory of Exegesis." *ATR* 67 (1985): 17–30.

————. *Hermeneutical Procedure and Theological Method in Origen's Exegesis*. Patristische Texte und Studien, vol. 28. Berlin: De Gruyter, 1986.

————. "The Rhetoric of the Literal Sense: Changing Strategies of Persuasion from Origen to Jerome." In *Origeniana Septima*, edited by Wolfgang Bienert and Uwe Kühneweg. Leuven: Leuven University Press, 1999, 633–644.

Trigg, Joseph. *Origen*. London: Routledge, 1998.

———. *Origen: The Bible and Philosophy in the Third-Century Church*. Atlanta: John Knox, 1983.

Urbach, Ephraim E. "The Homiletical Interpretations of the Sages and the Expositions of Origen on Canticles, and the Jewish-Christian Disputation." *ScrHier* 22 (1956): 272–289.

Valantasis, Richard. "Constructions of Power in Asceticism." *JAAR* 63 (1995): 775–821.

Van den Hoek, Annewies. "The Concept of σῶμα τῶν γραφῶν in Alexandrian Theology." *StPatr* 19 (1989): 250–254.

———. "Philo and Origen: A Descriptive Catalogue of Their Relationship." *SPhilo* 12 (2000): 44–121.

———. "Philo in the Alexandrian Tradition." *SPhilo* 6 (1994): 96–99.

Van der Horst, Pieter W. "Jews and Christians in Antioch at the End of the Fourth Century." In *Christian-Jewish Relations through the Centuries*, edited by Stanley E. Porter and Brook Pearson. Sheffield: Sheffield Academic Press, 2000, 228–238.

Visotzky, Burton. "Jots and Tittles: On Scriptural Interpretation in Rabbinic and Patristic Literatures." *Prooftexts* 8 (1988): 257–269.

Vögtle, Anton. *Die Tugend- und Lasterkataloge im Neuen Testament*. Münster: Aschendorff, 1936.

Voicu, Sever J. "Trentatré omelie pseudocrisostomiche e il loro autore." *Lexicum philosophicum: Quaderni di terminologia filosofica e storia delle idée* 2 (1986): 73–141.

———. "Uno pseudocrisostomo (Cappadoce?) lettore di origene alla fine del sec. IV." *Aug* 26 (1986): 281–293.

Wengst, Klaus. "Paulus und die Homosexualität: Überlegungen zu Röm, 1, 26f." *ZEE* 31 (1987): 72–81.

———. *Tradition und Theologie des Barnabasbriefes*. Arbeiten zur Kirchengeschichte 42. Berlin: De Gruyter, 1971.

Werline, Rodney. "The Transformation of Pauline Arguments in Justin Martyr's 'Dialogue with Trypho.'" *HTR* 92 (1999): 79–93.

Wharton, Annabel. "Erasure: Eliminating the Space of Late Ancient Judaism." In *From Dura to Sepphoris: Studies in Jewish Art and Society in Late Antiquity*, edited by Lee Levine and Zeev Weiss. Portsmouth, R.I.: Journal of Roman Archaeology supplementary series 40, 2000, 195–214.

White, Carolinne. *The Correspondence (394–419) between Jerome and Augustine of Hippo*. Studies in Bible and Early Christianity 23. Lewiston, Maine: Edwin Mellen, 1990.

Whitton, J. "A Neglected Meaning for *Skeuos* in 1 Thessalonians 4:4." *NTS* 28 (1982): 142–143.

Wiles, Maurice. *The Divine Apostle: The Interpretation of St. Paul's Epistles in the Early Church*. Cambridge: Cambridge University Press, 1967.

Wilken, Robert L. *John Chrysostom and the Jews: Rhetoric and Reality in the Late Fourth Century*. Transformation of the Classical Heritage 4. Berkeley: University of California Press, 1983.

Williams, A. Lukyn. *Justin Martyr: The Dialogue with Trypho*. London: SPCK, 1930.

Williams, Patrick, and Laura Chrisman, eds. *Colonial Discourse and Postcolonial Theory: A Reader*. New York: Columbia University Press, 1994.

Williamson, Ronald. *Jews in the Hellenistic World: Philo*. Cambridge Commentaries on Writings of the Jewish and Christian World, 200 BCE to 200 CE. Cambridge: Cambridge University Press, 1989.

Wilson, Stephen. *Related Strangers: Jews and Christians, 70–170 C.E.* Minneapolis: Fortress, 1995.

Wimbush, Vincent. *Paul, the Worldly Ascetic: Response to the World and Self-Understanding According to 1 Corinthians 7*. Macon, Ga.: Mercer University Press, 1987.

Winkler, John J. *The Constraints of Desire: The Anthropology of Sex and Gender in Ancient Greece*. New York: Routledge, 1990.

Winter, Bruce. "Carnal Conduct and Sanctification in 1 Corinthians: Simul Sanctus et Peccator?." In *Holiness and Ecclesiology in the New Testament*, edited by Kent E. Brower and Andy Johnson. Grand Rapids, Mich.: Eerdmans, 2007, 184–200.

Wisse, Frederik. "The Epistle of Jude in the History of Heresiology." In *Essays on the Nag Hammadi Texts in Honour of Alexander Böhlig*, edited by Martin Krause. Nag Hammadi Studies 3. Leiden: Brill, 1972, 133–143.

Wolfson, Harry A. *Philo: Foundations of Religious Philosophy in Judaism, Christianity, and Islam*. Cambridge, Mass.: Harvard University Press, 1948.

Wurmbrand, Max. "A Falasha Variant of the Story of Susanna." *Bib* 44 (1963): 29–37.

Young, Frances. "The Rhetorical Schools and Their Influence on Patristic Exegesis." In *The Making of Orthodoxy: Essays in Honour of Henry Chadwick*, edited by Rowan Williams. Cambridge: Cambridge University Press, 1989, 182–199.

Young, Robert J. C. *Colonial Desire: Hybridity in Theory, Culture and Race*. London: Routledge, 1995.

———. *Postcolonialism: A Very Short Introduction*. Oxford: Oxford University Press, 2003.

Zaas, Peter. "Catalogues and Context: 1 Corinthians 5 and 6." *NTS* 34 (1988): 622–629.

Zeller, Dieter. *Juden und Heiden in der Mission bei Paulus*. Stuttgart: Katholisches Bibelwerk, 1976.

Ziegler, Joseph. *Susanna, Daniel, Bel et Draco*, Septuaginta, Vetus Testamentum Graecum auctoritate Societatis Gottingensis editum. Göttingen: Vandenhoeck & Ruprecht, 1954.

Zimmerman, Frank. "The Story of Susanna and Its Original Language." *JQR* 48 (1957): 236–241.

Index

Abraham, circumcision of, 45–46, 122n33
adultery: Chrysostom on Judaizers and, 89–
90; David's affair with Bathsheba, 34; Jeremiah's wicked elders (Zedekiah and Ahab),
68, 129n29; Justin Martyr on Jewish, 34;
Origen on, 52–53, 68; Paul on Jewish, 24;
prophets' charges against Israel, 15
Against the Jews. See John Chrysostom, *Adversus Iudaeos*
Alexandria, 38, 120n3. *See also* Clement of
Alexandria; Philo of Alexandria
allegorical interpretations: Chrysostom's,
91–92; of circumcision, 46–48, 123n38;
Ezekiel's story of the prostituting daughters, 53, 91–92; Hippolytus's, 59–60,
62–66, 76; of Levitical sacrifices, 51–52,
71; Lot and his daughters, 53–54, 125n53;
Origen's, 46–48, 51–58, 70–71, 122n27,
125n53; Philo's discussions of, 42; Song
of Songs (linking chastity and allegory),
55–58; Susanna and the elders, 59–60,
62–66, 70–71, 76
Ambrose of Milan, 102, 103, 116n1
animals (sexual stereotypes): the amorous
stallion of Jeremiah, 84–85, 92; Chrysostom's caricatures of Jews, 1, 75–76, 78–79,
84–85, 87, 92, 131n2, 134n22; and
Chrysostom's justifications for violence
against Jews, 93–94, 100, 133n19; dogs,
84, 92, 134n22; *Epistle of Barnabas*, 29–
31, 135n32; hyenas, 31, 87, 135nn32–33;
stubborn heifers, 84, 93; wolves in pursuit of Christian sheep/lambs, 1, 75–76,
78–79, 131n2
Antioch, late fourth-century, 1–2, 79. *See also*
John Chrysostom, *Adversus Iudaeos*
Aphrahat, 2, 111n6
Arcadius, 101
asceticism (*askēsis*), 4–5; and circumcision,
46–48; Origen on, 46–48, 50–51, 100;

and Paul, 21, 50–51; and purity, 4; and
rhetoric of dehumanization, 4; Therapeutae community, 12, 115n49
Asterius of Amasea, 75
Augustine: on Jewish carnality, 2, 111n4,
117n24; and *skeuos* ("vessel"), 116n1

Basilides, 38
"Bel and the Dragon," 60
bestial stereotypes. *See* animals (sexual stereotypes)
Bhabha, Homi: and cultural hybridity,
112n12, 120n8, 140n24; on difference
articulated in terms of race and sexuality,
97, 138n55; *The Location of Culture*, 96;
on the stereotype in colonial discourse, 8,
79–80, 96–97, 98, 105; theory of colonialism, 7, 112n12
biblical interpretation, literal: and carnality, 33, 40–45, 48–58, 66–67, 69–72,
99–100, 105, 130n32; Clement of Alexandria on, 122n23; and dietary laws, 29–31;
Epistle of Barnabas on, 29–31, 99; and failure to use Christ as interpretive lens, 43,
119n43; and Jewish circumcision, 48–49;
Justin Martyr on, 33, 99; misreading the
Levitical laws, 71–72; Origen on, 40–45,
48–58, 66–67, 69–72, 100, 105, 130n32;
Origen's analogy between Jewish sexual
practices and, 52–53; Origen's differentiation of Jews/Christians based on, 66–67,
69–72, 73, 77, 130n32; and seduction of
the literal (Song of Songs), 55–58
biblical interpretation, spiritual: Origen on,
40–41, 50–54, 56–58, 70–72, 100, 104,
124n50, 130n32; Paul and, 50–54, 100,
124n49; Song of Songs, 40–41, 55–58,
126nn60–61; and Susanna's perilous
bind, 71–72. *See also* allegorical interpretations

body: Chrysostom on the Jewish body as sacrificial animal, 93–94; Chrysostom on the
spiritual Christian body, 94–96, 137n47,
137nn49–50; Origen on circumcision and
the Jewish body, 45–49; Origen on the
"veil of the flesh," 70–71; Paul's flesh/spirit
dichotomy, 25–28, 44–45, 49–50, 99–
100, 117n15, 117n18, 123n44, 124n45,
124n49; and sexual chastity/purity, 95,
137nn49–50; *skeuos* ("vessel"), 19, 116n1.
See also flesh

Boyarin, Daniel, 66; on Augustine's accusations against Jews, 111n8; *Border Lines*,
78, 112n11; on borders between Christianity and Judaism, 78; on heresy and
self-definition of orthodoxy, 112n11; on
hybridity and purity, 4; on Paul's understanding of the flesh/spirit, 26, 117n15,
117n18; on shifting definitions of gender/
masculinity, 72

brothels, 76, 86–87, 91. *See also* prostitution

Buell, Denise Kimber, 20, 114n28

Burrus, Virginia, 44; on hate speech and the
subject, 140n23; on hybridity and purity,
4; on manhood and spiritual practice in
late fourth century, 125n54; on portrayals
of heretical women, 136n38; on shifting
definitions of gender/masculinity, 72–73

Butler, Judith: on critique of violence and
representability of life, 99; *Excitable Speech:
A Politics of the Performative*, 104; on Foucauldian understanding of the subject produced through subjection, 140n22; *Frames
of War*, 99; on slander (hate speech), 104;
on subjectivation (*assujettissement*), 6,
113n20; on violence (torture) and control
over the subject, 140n17

Caesarea Maritima, 38–39, 67

Callinicum, synagogue at, 102, 139n16

carnality, Jewish: Augustine on, 2, 111n4,
117n24; Chrysostom on the carnal Jewish
sacrifice, 95; and Origen's view of Jewish
literalism, 40–45, 48–58, 66–67, 69–72,
99–100, 105, 130n32; Paul's understanding of *sarx*, 25–28, 117n15, 117n18;
as topos of early Christian literature, 2,
111n8

Catacomb of Praetextatus, 75–76

Catacomb of Priscilla, 59–60, 61, 127n3

celibacy, 21

chastity: Chrysostom's idealized Christian
body and, 95; Origen's comparison of
spiritual circumcision to, 47; Origen's
interpretation of Song of Songs linking
allegory and, 56–57; Susanna as model of,
74–77. *See also enkrateia* (self-mastery);
sōphrosynē (bodily self-control)

Chrysostom. *See* John Chrysostom, *Adversus
Iudaeos*

circumcision: of Abraham, 45–46, 122n33;
and asceticism, 46–48, 123n38; of the
ears, 46, 123n36; Greek/Latin poets linking to Jewish lust and lechery, 14, 115n59;
of the heart, 46; Ignatius on, 119n47; Justin Martyr on, 119n41, 132n9; of the lips,
46; Origen on, 45–49, 123n35, 123n38;
Paul on, 26, 46, 118n26, 123n34; Philo
on, 46–47, 123n38; spiritual, 46–48,
123n38; uncircumcision, 47–48

Clark, Elizabeth, 113n25, 119n49, 123n37,
125n55, 128n14, 139n3

Clement of Alexandria, 28, 38, 74, 122n23

Clements, Ruth, 44, 123n44, 124n45

Codex Sinaiticus, 28

colonialism/post-colonial theory, 7–8, 54–55;
Bhabha's theory of, 7, 112n12; critique of
violence, 99; discourses of sexuality and
power, 54–55; and hybridity, 7, 112n12,
140n24; and orientalism, 136n42; and the
stereotype, 7–88, 79–80, 96–97, 98, 105

Colossians, 22–23

1 Corinthians, 2, 16, 20–23, 24–27, 90,
117n13; Paul on "Israel according the
flesh," 26, 27, 44, 100, 123n44; Paul's vice
catalogs, 22–23

2 Corinthians, 43, 44, 49, 51, 100, 123n44,
137n50

Daniel, book of: Hippolytus's *Commentary
on Daniel*, 62–65; story of Susanna and
the Elders, 60–62. *See also* Susanna and
the Elders

Daphne, synagogue in, 79

De Lange, Nicholas, 39, 124n47

demons: Chrysostom on, 81, 83–84, 90–91,
132nn10–11; Matthew's image of the
tormented Canaanite woman, 83–84;
the synagogue as dwelling place of, 81,
132nn10–11

Deuteronomy, 11, 30, 88

dietary laws, 29–31

difference (sexual/racial): Bhabha on articulation of, 97, 138n55; stereotypes, 7, 97, 138n55. *See also* sexual slander (and sexual stereotypes)

difference, Jewish-Christian: ancient Jewish texts that produced difference based on sexual practice, 10–13; and appropriation of Susanna by Christian writers, 62, 127n11; Chrysostom and, 1–2, 78–98, 104–5, 131n3, 138n58; defining boundaries of orthodoxy and heresy, 3, 32, 112n11; Justin Martyr on, 32–34; Origen's differentiation based on interpretative methods, 66–67, 69–72, 73, 77, 130n32; Origen's gender categories and construction of, 40, 54–55, 72–73, 102; Origen's interpretation of Susanna and the elders, 59–60, 66–73, 76; use of stereotypes to "fix," 8, 22, 79–80, 96–98, 104–5

disease (pollution, illness): Chrysostom's images of Jews, 81–82, 83, 100; imperial laws associating Jewishness with, 100–101

drunkenness, Chrysostom on, 82–83

effeminacy: Chrysostom's charges of, 78, 85–88, 96, 100; *malakoi*, 5, 12–13, 78, 85–86, 96; *mollitia*, 9, 12, 135n28

enkrateia (self-mastery), 20, 21, 24, 30, 35

Ephesians, 22–23

Epistle of Barnabas, 19, 28–32, 99

Epistle to Diognetus, 35–36

exegesis. *See* biblical interpretation, literal; biblical interpretation, spiritual

Exodus, 11, 40, 41–42

Ezekiel: allegory of the two prostituting daughters, 53, 91–92; Chrysostom on, 89, 91–92; and Israel's sexual immorality, 15, 53, 91–92; Origen on, 53

Fanon, Frantz, 97

fasting, 39, 82, 87

femininity: Chrysostom on Jewish men and, 78, 85–86, 96; Hippolytus's gendered imagery, 65–66; Jewish men as *malakoi*, 5, 12–13, 78, 85–86, 96; Origen on Jews, 54; Origen's feminization of Christians, 72–73, 102; shifting definitions between second and fourth centuries, 72–73. *See also* gender

figurative reading. *See* allegorical interpretations; biblical interpretation, spiritual

fixity: Bhabha on, 8, 96; and stereotypes to "fix" Jewish-Christian identities, 8, 22, 79–80, 96–98, 104–5

flesh: Origen on the "veil of the flesh," 70–71; Paul and flesh/spirit dichotomy, 25–28, 44–45, 49–50, 99–100, 117n15, 117n18, 123n44, 124n45, 124n49; Paul and "Israel according to the flesh," 25–28, 44–45, 100, 117n22, 117n24, 124n45; Paul's understanding of *sarx*, 25–28, 117n15, 117n18. *See also* asceticism (askēsis); body

Foucault, Michel, 133n17; on formation of the subject (and power), 6, 104, 140n22; on sexuality and power, 4–5

Gaddis, Michael, 103

Galatians: Paul's negative evaluation of *sarx*, 25; Paul's vice catalogs, 22–23

gender: and Chrysostom's sexualized invective against Jews, 78–79, 85–86, 91–92, 96–97; Hippolytus's imagery, 65–66; Jewish men as *malakoi*, 5, 12–13, 78, 85–86, 96; Jewish women as prostitutes (*pornai*), 78, 85–86, 91–92, 96; Origen's discourse of sexuality (and production of Jewish-Christian difference), 40, 54–55, 72–73, 102; Philo on, 12–13; and power relations, 5, 65–66, 85–86, 128n23, 135n28; Roman rhetorical tradition, 65–66, 135n28; shifting definitions between second and fourth centuries, 72–73; Susanna and the elders, 65–66, 72–73, 102. *See also* femininity; masculinity

Genesis: circumcision of Abraham, 45–46, 122n33; Origen's allegorical interpretation of Lot and his daughters, 53–54, 125n53; Origen's homily on, 40, 45–49, 53, 55, 125n53

Gentiles: idolatry and *porneia*/sexual vice, 12, 19, 22–25, 114n42, 114n45; Jewish writers' on *porneia*/sexual immorality of, 10–13, 19, 20–28, 117n12; Josephus on, 13; Paul on nonsexual vices of, 116n9; Paul on *porneia* and, 12, 19, 20–28, 99; Philo on, 12–13. *See also* difference, Jewish-Christian

Gleason, Maud, 65, 72

gluttony, 82–83, 93

Hagar, 49

Hebrew Bible. *See* biblical interpretation, literal; biblical interpretation, spiritual

Hebrews (*Hebraioi*), 39

heresiology, 3

heresy/heretics: Boyarin on, 112n11; defining boundaries of orthodoxy, 3, 32, 112n11; heretical women portrayed as sexually promiscuous, 136n38; Origen on shameful sexuality and, 48; and sexualized/gendered representations of power relations, 128–29n23

hermeneutics. *See* biblical interpretation, literal; biblical interpretation, spiritual

Hippolytus's allegorical interpretation of Susanna, 59–60, 62–66, 76, 128n14; *Commentary on Daniel*, 62–65; gendered imagery (feminine metaphors), 65–66; Susanna as the church/the elders as the church's opponents, 62–65; temporal inversion of the story, 63, 128n14; violent verbs/vocabulary, 64–65

Hodge, Caroline Johnson, 20

Honorius, 100–101

Hosea, 15, 84, 89

hybridity, cultural: Bhabha on, 112n12, 120n8, 140n24; and post-colonial theory, 7, 112n12; and purity, 4; and sexual slander, 4, 7, 105. *See also* difference, Jewish-Christian

hyenas, 31, 87, 135nn32–33

idolatry: Jewish portrayals of Gentile sexual immorality and, 11–12, 114n42, 114n45; Paul on Gentile *porneia* and, 12, 19, 22–25; and prostitution, 11, 15

Ignatius of Antioch, 35, 119n47

interpretation. *See* biblical interpretation, literal; biblical interpretation, spiritual

Ioudaioi (vs. *Hebraioi*), 39–40

Isaac, 57

Isaiah's story of Sodom and Gomorrah, 70, 92, 130n31

Jacobs, Andrew, 57, 130n32

Jeremiah: and Chrysostom on the amorous stallion, 84–85, 92; and Chrysostom's association of Jewish impiety and *porneia*, 89; and Chrysostom's depiction of the synagogue, 86–87, 135n33; and circumcision of the heart/ears, 46, 123n36; story of the wicked elders of (Zedekiah and Ahab), 68–70, 129n29

Jerusalem, destruction of, 80–81, 94

Jewett, Robert, 26

Jewish elders. *See* rabbis/Jewish elders

Jewish practices, 4; and anti-Jewish rhetoric in the century after Paul, 35–36; Chrysostom against Christian participation in, 79, 81–82, 87–88, 89–91, 136n35; and *Epistle to Diognetus*, 35–36; fasting, 39, 82; festival of Sukkot, 92; Ignatius on, 35; Justin Martyr on, 32, 119n41; Origen on, 39. *See also* circumcision; Sabbath observance

John Chrysostom, *Adversus Iudaeos* (*Sermons Against the Jews*), 1–2, 78–98, 100; accusations against the Jews, 80–83; on adultery, 89–90; animal caricatures, 1, 75–76, 78–79, 84–85, 92, 131n2, 134n22; appropriation of the prophets, 84–85, 86–87, 89, 91–92, 93, 134n24; associating Jewish impiety/licentiousness and *porneia*, 78, 82–83, 89, 91–92; associating present Jewish sins and past (biblical) sins, 92; on Christian participation of Jewish practices, 79, 81–82, 87–88, 89–91, 136n35; on demon possession, 81, 83–84, 90–91, 132nn10–11; depiction of the idealized, spiritual Christian body, 94–96, 137n47; "ethnic reasoning," 138n57; final sermons, 82, 91–92, 133n12; first sermon, 1–2, 79, 81, 83–88, 93, 133n18, 138n57; fourth sermon, 80, 91, 92, 131n3; gendered invective and sexual stereotypes, 78–79, 85–86, 91–92, 96–97; images of Jewish disease and pollution, 81–82, 83, 100; and Jewish-Christian differences, 1–2, 78–98, 104–5, 131n3, 138n58; on Jewish drunkenness and gluttony, 82–83; on Judaizers as sexual aggressors, 1, 79, 87–88, 89–91, 96, 102–3, 111n3; on Judaizers' jeopardized purity, 81, 87, 133n12; on Judaizers' shamelessness, 87, 135n34; justified violence against Jews, 80–81, 93–94, 98, 100, 103, 133n19; and late fourth-century Antioch, 1–2, 79; and Paul, 28, 83, 84, 95, 133n19, 137n50; on sacrifice, 88, 93–94, 95, 100; second sermon, 88–91, 133n19; sequence and dating of the sermons, 131n4; sexual stereotypes, 1–2, 5, 78–80, 83–92, 96–98, 100; and *skeuos* ("vessel"), 116n1; and *sōphrosynē*, 89; story of Christian woman abducted by the Judaizer, 1–2, 78–79, 87–88, 111n3; on synagogues,

78, 81, 85–89, 91, 132n10; warnings to
Christian husbands, 90–91
Josephus, *Against Apion*, 13
Judah/Judaeans, 53
Judaizers: Chrysostom on, 1, 79, 81, 87–88,
89–91, 96, 102–3, 111n3, 133n12,
135n34; jeopardized purity, 81, 87,
133n12; Paul on, 118n26; as sexual aggressors, 1, 79, 87–88, 89–91, 96, 102–3,
111n3; sexual shamelessness, 87, 135n34
Julius Africanus, 67
Justin Martyr: on circumcision, 119n41,
132n9; *Dialogue with Trypho*, 19, 32–34,
132n9; and divinely ordained acts of violence against the Jews, 80–81, 132n9; *First
Apology*, 9; on Jacob's multiple marriages,
33–34; and Jewish-Christian difference,
32–34; on Jewish interpretive practices,
33, 99; on Jewish men as lustful and polygamous, 34, 119n44

Knust, Jennifer Wright, 10, 114n45

Lacan, Jacques, 97
law: dietary, 29–31; imperial legislation,
100–102, 103; Jewish obedience to, 32;
Levitical, 71–72, 88; Mosaic, 29–32
Letter of Aristeas, 10–11
Levine, Lee, 38
Leviticus, 51–52, 71, 88
Leyerle, Blake, 86, 135n34
Lieu, Judith, 14
Linder, Amnon, 101
literalism/literal interpretations. *See* biblical
interpretation, literal
Lot and his daughters, 53–54, 125n53
Lot's wife, 53–54
Luke, Gospel of, 52

malakos/malakoi: Chrysostom on, 78, 85–86,
96; Jewish men as, 5, 12–13, 78, 85–86,
96; as term, 85, 134n26
Marcion, 3, 112n11
marriage: Chrysostom's depiction of syna-
gogue/theater as disruptive of, 86–87;
Chrysostom's warnings to Christian husbands, 90–91; Jacob's multiple marriages,
33–34; Justin on spiritual, 33–34; Origen's
comparison of spiritual circumcision to
chastity in, 47; Paul on, 21; and purity, 2,
111n6

Martial, 14
Martin, Dale, 15, 85, 117n12
martyrdom: and gladiatorial games, 93,
137n44; Hippolytus's comparison of Susanna's fate to, 65; the masculine female
martyr in second and third centuries, 73
masculinity: alignment of spiritual practices
with, 54, 125n54; Chrysostom's challenge
to Jewish, 78–79, 85–86, 96–97, 103; and
the female martyr, 73; hyper-masculinization of Jews, 72–73, 102; and *malakoi*, 5,
12–13, 78, 85–86, 96, 134n26; masculine
sōphrosynē, 54; Origen on, 54, 73, 102;
Philo on, 12–13; shifting definitions between second and fourth centuries, 72–73,
125n54; during Trinitarian controversies,
125n54. *See also* gender
Matthew, Gospel of, 83–84, 86, 129n30
McGuckin, John, 50, 124n47
Meeks, Wayne, 79
Meleager, 14
Melito of Sardis, 35, 36; Paschal homily (*On
Pascha*), 35, 36, 119n50
Methodius of Olympus, 74–75; *Symposium*,
74–75
Minucius Felix, 9
mollitia (effeminacy), 9, 12, 135n28
Moses: Chrysostom on (turning against
Jews), 82, 133n16; commandments given
to, 10, 11, 29–30; and dietary laws/sexual
regulations, 31; *Epistle of Barnabas*, 29–32;
Mosaic law, 29–32; veil of, 43

Oholah and Oholibah, 53, 91–92
On First Principles (Origen), 38, 40, 42–45,
53, 119n43
orientalism, 136n42
Origen, 38–58, 66–73, 99–100, 104; accusations against his Jewish contemporaries,
69–70, 130n32; on asceticism, 46–48,
50–51, 100; in Caesarea, 38–39, 67,
124n47; on circumcision, 46–48, 123n35,
123n38; *Commentary on Romans*, 40, 44,
50–54, 123n38, 124n49; denigration of
Jewish practices, 39, 52, 125n53; first
Homily on Leviticus, 70–72; *On First Principles*, 38, 40, 42–45, 53, 119n43; gender
categories and "discourse of sexuality," 40,
54–55, 72–73, 102; *Homilies on Exodus*,
40, 41–42; and "Israel according to the
flesh," 44–45, 100, 124n45; *Letter to*

Origen (*cont.*)
  Africanus, 66–70, 72, 73; life of, 38;
    misappropriation of Paul, 28, 40, 41–45,
    46, 49–54, 99–100, 123n42, 123n44,
    124nn45–47, 124n49; and Paul's flesh/
    spirit dichotomy, 44–45, 49–50, 99–100,
    123n44, 124n45, 124n49; and Susanna
    and the elders, 59–60, 66–73, 76; term
    for Jews (*Ioudaioi*), 39–40; third *Homily
    on Genesis*, 40, 45–49, 53, 55, 125n53. *See
    also* Origen on biblical interpretation
Origen on biblical interpretation: comparison
    of the text of scripture to flesh/body, 43–
    44, 122n28; Jewish-Christian difference
    based on interpretative methods, 66–67,
    69–72, 73, 77, 130n32; on Jewish literal-
    ism and carnality, 40–45, 48–58, 66–67,
    69–72, 100, 105, 119n43, 122nn27–28,
    130n32; and Paul's spiritual understand-
    ing of scripture, 50–54, 100, 124n49; on
    seduction of the literal, 55–58; Song of
    Songs, 40–41, 55–58, 126n61; "spiritual"
    interpretation, 40–41, 50–54, 56–58, 70–
    72, 100, 104, 124n50, 126n61, 130n32;
    and Susanna's perilous bind, 71–72
orthodoxy: defining boundaries of, 3–4, 32,
    112n11; and heresy, 3, 32, 112n11

Paul, 20–28; and asceticism, 21, 50–51;
    Chrysostom and, 28, 83, 84, 95, 133n19,
    137n50; on circumcision, 26, 46, 118n26,
    123n34; flesh/spirit dichotomy, 25–28,
    44–45, 49–50, 99–100, 117n15, 117n18,
    123n44, 124n45, 124n49; and "Israel
    according to the flesh" (*kata sarka*), 26–28,
    44–45, 100, 117n22, 117n24, 124n45;
    misrepresented as supersessionist, 49–50,
    83; Origen on Paul's spiritual interpreta-
    tion of scripture, 50–54, 124n49; Origen's
    misappropriation of, 28, 40, 41–45,
    46, 49–54, 99–100, 123n42, 123n44,
    124nn45–47, 124n49; on *porneia* as Gen-
    tile problem, 12, 19, 20–28, 99, 116n9;
    suffering of, 95, 137n50; vice catalogs,
    22–23
Perpetua, 72
Philippians: Chrysostom and the image of
    dogs, 84; Paul on Jewish practice of cir-
    cumcision, 26, 46
Philo of Alexandria, 20, 38; on allegory, 42;
    on circumcision and Christian asceticism,

46–47, 123n38; *On the Contemplative Life*,
    12, 115n49; on gender categories, 12–13;
    on Jewish interpretations of dietary laws,
    29; *On the Migration of Abraham*, 46–47;
    On the Special Laws, 12–13, 47
Physiologus, 135n32
polygamy, 34, 119n44
porneia (sexual immorality): Chrysostom on
    Jewish impiety and, 78, 82–83, 89, 91–92;
    and Gentiles, 10–13, 19, 20–28, 99,
    114n42, 114n45, 117n12; and idolatry, 12,
    19, 22–25; Paul on, 12, 19, 20–28, 99; rhe-
    torical project of ancient Greek and Roman
    moralists, 9, 20, 82–83, 135n31; Susanna
    and the elders (interplay of touch and
    porneia), 59–60, 127n3; and synagogues as
    brothels (*porneion*), 78, 86–87, 91
Pradels, Wendy, 131n4, 133n18
"The Prayer of Azariah and the Song of the
    Three Jews," 60
prophets/prophetic writings: Christian writ-
    ers' appropriation as "prooftexts," 15, 84–
    85, 86–87, 91–92, 134n24; Chrysostom
    and, 84–85, 86–87, 89, 91–92, 134n24;
    Chrysostom's depiction of synagogue as
    theater/brothel, 86–87, 135n33; Ezekiel's
    allegory of the two prostituting sisters,
    53, 91–92; and female prostitution, 15,
    91–92, 136n40; Isaiah's story of Sodom
    and Gomorrah, 70, 92, 130n31; Jeremiah's
    story of the wicked elders, 68–70, 129n29
prostitution: Chrysostom's accusations
    against Jewish women, 78, 85–86,
    91–92, 96; Chrysostom's depiction of the
    synagogue as brothel, 78, 86–87, 91; and
    idolatry, 11, 15; and prophetic writings,
    15, 53, 91–92, 136n40; stories of Oholah
    and Oholibah, 53, 91–92
Pseudo-Chrysostom, 75
purity: asceticism (*askēsis*), 4; Chrysostom on
    Judaizers', 81, 87, 133n12; Chrysostom's
    depiction of the spiritual Christian body,
    95, 137nn49–50; and hybridity, 4; and
    marriage, 2, 111n6; Origen's spiritual in-
    terpretation of Song of Songs, 56–57. *See
    also* asceticism (*askēsis*)

rabbis/Jewish elders: Origen's accusations
    against his Jewish contemporaries, 68–70,
    130n32; Origen's paradoxical images of,
    70; rabbinic teaching on promiscuity of

dogs, 134n22. *See also* Susanna and the elders

rhetoric, anti-Jewish: in the century after Paul, 34–37; and civic life in the Roman Empire, 100–101; *Epistle to Diognetus*, 35–36; Ignatius's letters, 35, 119n47; Melito of Sardis's Paschal homily, 35, 119n50. *See also* sexual slander (and sexual stereotypes)

rhetoric, Greco-Roman: anti-Jewish stereotypes and civic life, 100–101; gendered imagery and power relations, 65–66; sexual slander/accusations of carnality and *porneia*, 9, 20, 82–83, 135n31

rhetoric of dehumanization, 4

Roman Empire: anti-Jewish stereotypes and civic life, 100–101; Chrysostom's justifications for imperial violence against Jews, 80–81, 94; Hippolytus's depiction of Christians as victims of imperial violence, 66; imperial legislation and anti-Jewish violence, 100–102, 103; imperial protection of synagogues, 101–2; rhetorical tradition of gendered imagery, 65–66, 135n28; shifting gender definitions, 72–73, 125n54

Romans, Paul's Letter to: ambiguous associations of *sarx* and sexuality, 26–27; and Chrysostom on spiritual transformation of the flesh, 95, 137n47; image of the olive tree, 83; Origen's *Commentary* on, 40, 44, 50–54, 123n38, 124n49; polemic against Gentile idolatry and sexual immorality, 12, 23–25, 116n9; spiritual circumcision, 46, 123n34

Rufinus of Aquileia, 38

Sabbath observance, 14, 39

sacrifices: Chrysostom on Jews as sacrificial animals, 93–94, 100; Chrysostom on temple sacrifices and spatial violations, 88; Chrysostom's contrast between "living sacrifice" and carnal Jewish sacrifice, 95; Origen's interpretation of Levitical sacrifices, 51–52, 71

Said, Edward, 136n42

Samaria/Samaritans, 53

Sandwell, Isabella, 79

Sarah, 49

sarx (flesh), 25–28, 117n15, 117n18; Israel *kata sarka* ("Israel according to the flesh"), 26–28, 44–45, 100, 117n22, 117n24,

124n45; Paul's association of circumcision with, 26, 118n26; and *pneuma* (spirit), 25. *See also* flesh

Schwartz, Seth, 101, 139n11

self-mastery (*enkrateia*), discourse of, 20, 21, 24, 30, 35

sexual immorality. See *porneia* (sexual immorality)

sexuality and post-colonial theory, 4–5, 7–8, 54–55

sexual renunciation: Origen on spiritual circumcision, 47–48; Paul on, 21. *See also* asceticism (*askēsis*); chastity

sexual slander (and sexual stereotypes), 3–15, 19–37, 104–5; accusations of carnality and *porneia*, 9–10, 99; ancient portrayals of Jewish lust and hypersexuality, 13–15, 115n59; and cultural hybridity, 4, 7, 105; defining boundaries of orthodoxy, 3, 32, 112n11; early Christian apologists' responses to, 9–10; in first and second centuries, 19–37; to "fix" Jewish/Christian identities, 8, 22, 79–80, 96–98, 104–5; Jewish portrayals of Gentile lust, 10–13, 19, 20–28; Jewish writers' invective against other Jews, 14–15, 115n62; as justifications for violence, 3–4, 99–105; possibilities for resistance and transgression enabled by, 104–5; rhetorical project of Greek and Roman moralists, 9, 20, 82–83, 135n31; and the subject, 104–5, 140n22. *See also* John Chrysostom, *Adversus Iudaeos;* Origen; Susanna and the elders

Sibylline Oracle, third, 11

Simon, Marcel, 79

skeuos ("vessel"), 19, 116n1

slavery and Chrysostom's sexualized representation of the synagogue, 88–89

Sodom and Gomorrah, 70, 92, 130n31

Song of Songs: Origen's spiritual interpretation of, 40–41, 55–58, 126n61; and seduction of the literal, 40–41, 55–58, 126nn60–61

sōphrosynē (bodily self-control): Chrysostom and, 88–89; as Greek/Roman virtue, 9, 20; Hippolytus's allegorical interpretation of Susanna as the church, 65; Origen's masculine *sōphrosynē*, 54; and spiritual interpretation (Origen), 51–52; Susanna's co-optation as model for Christian women, 74–77 stereotypes: Bhabha on, 8, 79–80, 96–97, 98, 105; in colonial discourse, 7–8, 79–80, 96–97, 98, 105; to "fix" identities of the Other, 8, 22, 79–80, 96–98, 104–5; possibilities for resistance and transgression enabled by, 98, 104–5, 140n23; and "processes of subjectification," 8, 98, 103, 140n17; racial and sexual, 7, 97, 138n55. *See also* animals (sexual stereotypes); sexual slander (and sexual stereotypes)

Stoler, Ann Laura, 7, 55

Stowers, Stanley, 24

Stratton, Kimberly, 128n23

subjectification, processes of, 8, 98, 103, 140n17

subjectivation (*assujettissement*), 6, 113n20

Susanna and the elders, 59–77; appropriation by Christian writers, 62, 127n11; and book of Daniel, 60–62; and feminine vulnerability, 65–66; frescos, 59–60, 61, 75–76, 127n3; gendered imagery, 65–66, 72–73, 102; Hippolytus's allegorical interpretation, 59–60, 62–66, 76, 128n14; interplay of touch and *porneia*, 59–60, 127n3; and Jeremiah's story of wicked elders, 68–70, 129n29; Old Greek version, 62, 127n11; Origen on Jewish-Christian difference and, 59–60, 66–73, 76; Origen's claim that Jewish sages hid the story, 68–70, 129n29; and Origen's differentiation of Jews/Christians based on scriptural interpretations, 66–67, 69–72, 73, 77, 130n32; Origen's first *Homily on Leviticus*, 70–72; Origen's gender discourse, 72–73, 102; Origen's *Letter to Africanus*, 66–70, 72, 73; Susanna as the church, 62–65; Susanna's co-optation as model of chastity and *sōphrosynē*, 74–77; Susanna's perilous bind, 71–72; Theodotion version, 62, 127n11; versions and provenance, 60–62, 67

synagogues: as brothels (*porneion*), 78, 86–87, 91; Callinicum, 102, 139n16; Chrysostom on, 78, 81, 85–89, 91, 132n10; destruction of, 101–2; as dwelling places of demons/the devil, 81, 132nn10–11; imperial protection of, 101–2; late fourth-century Antioch, 79; as "lodging place" of hyenas, 87, 135n33; prohibitions on construction, 101, 139n11; as theaters, 85, 86–87, 91

Tacitus, *Histories*, 13–14

Temple, Jerusalem: biblical law regarding sacrifices in, 88; Chrysostom's sexualized depiction of, 88, 91; Roman destruction of, 80–81, 94

Tertullian, 116n1

The Testament of the Twelve Patriarchs, 14–15, 115n62

theater: Chrysostom on synagogues as, 85, 86–87, 91; Roman moralists' characterizations of, 135n31

Thecla, 73, 74

Theodosius, 101, 102, 103

Theodosius II, 100–101

Theodotion version of Susanna, 62, 127n11

Therapeutae community, 12, 115n49

1 Thessalonians, 16, 19, 20–21, 23–24

Torjesen, Karen Jo, 124n50

Trigg, Joseph, 120n3

Trinitarian controversies (late fourth century), 125n54

Valentinus, 38

veil of Moses, 43

"veil of the flesh" and "veil of the letter," 70–71, 122n27

vice catalogs, Paul's, 22–23

violence, anti-Jewish, 3–4, 6–7, 99–105; Ambrose's justifications for, 102, 103, 139n16; Chrysostom's justifications for, 80–81, 93–94, 98, 100, 103, 133n19; destruction of synagogues, 101–2; as effort to seize control over the subject, 103, 140n17; images of imperiled Christians used to justify, 102–3; and imperial ideology/rhetoric of anti-Jewish stereotypes, 100–101; imperial legislation of late Roman era, 100–102, 103; Justin Martyr's justifications for, 80–81, 132n9; rhetoric of dehumanization, 4. *See also* sexual slander (and sexual stereotypes)

violence against Christian women: Chrysostom on Judaizers as sexual aggressors, 1, 79, 87–88, 89–91, 96, 102–3, 111n3; patristic interpretations of Susanna and the elders, 59–77

Wilken, Robert, 79

Wisdom of Solomon, 10, 11–12

women: Chrysostom on vulnerability to predatory Judaizers, 1, 79, 87–88, 89–91,

90–91, 96, 102–3, 111n3; Chrysostom's claims about Jewish *porneia* and prostitution, 78, 85–86, 91–92, 96; heretical, 136n38; Origen on Sabbath observance by, 39; role in imaginative economy of the early Christian world, 125n55; Susanna as model of chastity and *sōphrosynē* for, 74–77. *See also* femininity

Xenophon's *Memorabilia*, 134n26

Young, Robert J. C., 7

Zechariah, 48

Acknowledgments

It is a pleasure to acknowledge the many people who helped make this book possible. My deepest thanks go to Elizabeth Clark, my teacher and mentor. Liz's cheerful and thoughtful guidance has made the years that I wrote and conducted research for this book all the brighter. Bart Ehrman, Kalman Bland, Sheila Dillon, and Warren Smith also gave generously of their time to read and comment on this project. I thank each of them for their insight and support. Other friends, colleagues, and conversation partners offered suggestions and encouragement at various stages in the writing process. These include Lori Baron, Catherine Chin, Maria Doerfler, Anne Foley, William Garriott, Andrew Jacobs, Dayna Kalleres, Jennifer Wright Knust, Ariel Bybee Laughton, Christie and Tim Luckritz Marquis, Michael Penn, Tina Shepardson, Kyle Smith, Sarah Strickler, SherAli Tareen, and Kristi Upson-Saia. Special thanks to two of my friends, Bart Scott and Ben Dunning, who read chapters, offered invaluable feedback, and encouraged me at crucial stages in the revision process.

I am lucky to have wonderful colleagues and students at Macalester College who supported this project in various ways. Special thanks to Jim Laine, Paula Cooey, Erik Davis, Brett Wilson, Barry Cytron, Toni Schrantz, Amy Damon, Amanda Ciafone, and Ellen Arnold. I am grateful for the questions and suggestions I received from those who attended presentations of this research in Chicago; Durham, North Carolina; Grinnell, Iowa; Oxford, England; Saint Paul, Minnesota; and San Diego. I thank the members of the Divinations editorial board—Virginia Burrus, Daniel Boyarin, and Derek Krueger—for their interest in this project and their wise recommendations for improvement. Derek Krueger deserves special thanks for his willingness to guide me through the final revision process and help this project travel the distance from manuscript to book. Jerry Singerman, Caroline Winschel, Erica Ginsburg, Janice Meyerson, and the staff at the University of Pennsylvania Press have been a delight to work with throughout the publishing process. Wendy Mayer and Shira Lander read and commented on the entire manuscript and offered insightful feedback. I have incorporated many of their suggestions; any errors that remain are my own.

Part of Chapter 3 appeared in an earlier form as "Images of Jewishness in Origen's *Letter to Africanus*," *Studia Patristica* 46 (2010): 253–266. I thank Peeters Publishers for permitting me to reprint some of that work here.

My parents, John and Frances Drake, deserve special mention. I thank them for their encouragement and love, and I am especially grateful for their friendship and conversation during the years when this book took shape. Emma, Hilary, Inga, Paul, and Lenore Drake continue to enrich my life. Every day, I am grateful for the supportive love of my husband, Michael Butler, and the joy of our sons, Alston and Inman. Thanks also to the Drake family, the Strickler family, the Butler family, and the Sunset Beach family. This book is dedicated to my grandparents, who pursued their academic and artistic passions with gusto, discipline, wonder, and generosity. They continue to inspire me.